BLACKS

Justice in

Justice in Error

Edited by

Clive Walker
Director of the Centre for Criminal Justice Studies and
Reader in Law, University of Leeds

and

Keir Starmer
Barrister and Secretary of the Haldane Society of
Socialist Lawyers

BLACKSTONE
PRESS LIMITED

First published in Great Britain 1993 by Blackstone Press Limited,
9-15 Aldine Street, London W12 8AW. Telephone 081-740 1173

© Blackstone Press Limited, 1993
The contributors hold the copyright for their respective chapters.

ISBN: 1 85431 234 0

British Library Cataloguing in Publication Data
A CIP catalogue record for this book is available from the British Library

Typeset by Style Photosetting Limited, Mayfield, East Sussex
Printed by BPCC Wheatons Limited, Exeter

Contents

List of Contributors

John Bell is Professor at the Faculty of Law, University of Leeds. He previously lectured at Oxford University.

Keith Bottomley is Professor and Director of the Centre for Criminology and Criminal Justice, University of Hull.

Lee Bridges is Research and Policy Officer for the Public Law Project. He previously lectured at Birmingham University and has acted as consultant to many bodies, including the Legal Aid Board. He is a member of the Management Committee of the Legal Action Group.

Clive Coleman is a Lecturer in the Centre for Criminology and Criminal Justice, University of Hull.

Brice Dickson is Professor of Law at the University of Ulster. He formerly lectured at the University of Leicester and Queen's University, Belfast.

David Dixon is Senior Lecturer in the Faculty of Law at the University of New South Wales. Until 1989, he was a Lecturer in Law, University of Hull.

John Jackson is a Reader in Law, University of Sheffield. He previously lectured at Queen's University, Belfast.

Fiona McElree is Campaigns Officer at Liberty.

Michael Mansfield is a Barrister practising at 14 Tooks Court. He has acted in many of the recent miscarriage of justice cases.

Patrick O'Connor is a Barrister practising at 14 Tooks Court. He has acted in many of the recent miscarriage of justice cases.

Andrew Sanders is a Lecturer in Criminal Justice at the University of Oxford and a Fellow of Pembroke College. He formerly lectured at Birmingham University. He is a member of the Parole Board.

Keir Starmer is a Barrister practising in the Doughty Street chambers and is the Secretary of the Haldane Society of Socialist Lawyers.

Russell Stockdale is a partner of Forensic Access, a group of independent scientific consultants to the legal profession. He was previously a Principal Scientist in the Home Office Forensic Science Service.

Nicholas Taylor is a researcher at the Centre for Criminal Justice Studies, University of Leeds.

Clive Walker is a Reader in Public Law and Director of the Centre for Criminal Justice Studies, University of Leeds. He previously lectured at Manchester University and practised as a solicitor.

Dermot Walsh is a Barrister and a Senior Lecturer in Law at the University of Ulster. He was formerly a Lecturer in Law at University College, Cork and the holder of the Cobden Trust Studentship at Queen's University, Belfast.

James Wood is a Barrister practising in the Doughty Street chambers and an executive member of Liberty. He has acted in several of the recent miscarriage of justice cases.

Table of Cases

1

Introduction

Clive Walker

Prefatory Remarks

The Royal Commission on Criminal Justice was established in 1991 under the chairmanship of Lord Runciman with the following terms of reference:

> To examine the effectiveness of the criminal justice system in England and Wales in securing the conviction of those guilty of criminal offences and the acquittal of those who are innocent, having regard to the efficient use of resources, and in particular to consider whether changes are needed in
> i   the conduct of police investigations . . .
> ii   the role of the prosecutor . . .
> iii the role of experts . . .
> iv   the arrangements for the defence . . .
> v   the opportunities available for an accused person to state his position . . .
> vi   the powers of the courts in directing proceedings . . .
> vii the role of the Court of Appeal . . .
> viii the arrangements for considering and investigating miscarriages of justice. . .

The fact that this was the first Royal Commission for 10 years underlines its importance and the depth of the concerns which gave rise to it. Therefore, it seems timely to produce a commentary on miscarriages of justice, and we hope to contribute to the great debate on the future shape of the criminal justice system in two ways. The first is by explicating those steps in the system which are capable of giving rise to miscarriages. Secondly, we offer suggestions as to how errors can be avoided in the future.

The genesis of this book lies in a conference held in York in April 1990. The speakers included academics, campaigners and practitioners, many of whom have been involved in the well-publicised cases (described below) at the centre of the crisis. A similar mixture is reflected in the panel of contributors to this book, who also encompass a number of writers not present at the conference. As well as changes in line-up, events have certainly gathered pace since our conference. Thus, many of the papers have been substantially rewritten, and the editors have endeavoured to take account of events up to 18 December 1992. It should be noted that the views of individual chapter authors or of the editors are not necessarily shared by other contributors. Readers who find our views unpalatable at least have the consolation of knowing that royalties from the sale of this book are being donated to the Prison Reform Trust.

The Nature of Miscarriages of Justice

A 'miscarriage' means literally a failure to reach an intended destination or goal. A miscarriage of justice is therefore, *mutatis mutandis*, a failure to attain the desired end result of 'justice'. The meaning of justice and the ways in which it may be denied need to be dissected further.

Justice is about distributions — according persons fair shares and treatment. As far as the impact of the criminal justice system is concerned, one could argue that just treatment in a liberal, democratic society means that the State should treat individuals with equal respect for their rights and for the rights of others.[1] Conversely, theories of justice which elevate in priority general, collective interest (such as utility),[2] or which define rights in terms of class rather than individual interests (Marxism-Leninism) must be discarded,[3] though this does not entail the

---

1 See Dworkin, R., *Taking Rights Seriously* (Duckworth, London, 1977) chs. 7 and 12.
2 See Smart, J. J. C. and Williams, B., *Utilitarianism: For and Against* (Cambridge University Press, Cambridge 1973); Lyons, D., 'Human rights and the general welfare' (1976–77) 6 *Philosphy & Public Affairs* 113.
3 See Markovits, I., 'Socialist vs. bourgois rights' (1978) 45 U Chi L Rev 612; Osakwe, C., 'The Soviet view of human rights law' (1981) 56 Tulane L Rev 299.

rejection of rights to basic welfare provision for individuals.[4] It does not follow that individual, liberal rights must always be treated as absolute. It is rational to accept limitations for the sake of preserving the rights of others or competing rights. More controversially, it has been argued that an exercise of a right might be disallowed if its social costs (such as the downfall of a liberal society by inciting disaffection in wartime) are greater than the cost paid to grant the original right.[5] One would hope that a sceptical attitude will be taken to claims of catastrophic damage in a stable, well-established polity such as the United Kingdom. However, recent evidence of panic repression may be found in the case of *Secretary of State for the Home Department, ex parte Cheblak*,[6] in which the courts refused to reverse a deportation order against a Palestinian, who had fallen into disfavour because of xenophobia and hysteria at the time of the Gulf War rather than because of any security risk. One looks in vain for an echo of the sentiments expressed two centuries earlier by Lord Mansfield in *R* v *Wilkes* to the effect that:[7]

> We must not regard political consequences; however formidable soever they may be; if rebellion was the certain consequence, we are bound to say '*fiat justitia, ruat caelum*'.

As for rights potentially affected by the operation of the criminal justice system, several are at risk, including liberty, privacy and family life, and even the very right to existence in those jurisdictions which operate capital punishment. These costs to the individual will be substantial. Nevertheless, criminal and anti-social behaviour also have a real, adverse effect on the enjoyment of rights by others. Hence, it is justifiable and necessary for the criminal justice system to take steps against the rights of suspects — by way of loss of liberty, property or other proportionate means — in order to protect the rights of others.

At the same time, it is wise to recognise that the responsibility of the State to treat its citizens justly is awesome, and that if their treatment is disproportionate to the need to protect the rights of others or is wholly unwarranted, then serious damage will be inflicted not only on the individual but on society as a whole. The ever-present dangers of mistakes in the criminal justice system are reflected in the oft-repeated sentiment that 'It is better that ten guilty persons escape than that one

---

4 Scheffler, S., 'Natural rights, equality and the minimal state' (1976) 6 Can J of Phil 59.
5 Dworkin, R., *op. cit.*, p. 200. This idea is also reflected in the European Convention on Human Rights (1950), Art. 17.
6 [1991] 2 All ER 319.
7 (1770) 98 ER 327, at p. 347 ('Though the heavens fall, let justice be done').

innocent suffer.'[8] It may also be reflected in features such as the burden
of proof and the privilege against self-incrimination, though the rational
connection between these features and the ethos of the system has become
controversial.[9]

Leaving aside issues of evidence and proof, it is now possible to offer a
definition of 'miscarriage' in the context of criminal justice. A miscarriage
occurs as follows: whenever individuals are treated by the State in breach
of their rights; whenever individuals are treated adversely by the State to
a disproportionate extent in comparison with the need to protect the
rights of others; or whenever the rights of others are not properly
protected or vindicated by State action against wrongdoers. Each of these
three categories may be illustrated by several examples.

The treatment of individuals in breach of their rights will occur when
individuals are subjected to arrest or detention without due cause. For
example, there is evidence that young black males are subjected to an
unsupportable degree of police attention because of the colour of their
skins.[10] The conviction of a person known to be innocent, or who is in
fact innocent, would obviously fall into this category of breach of rights,
and indeed might be said to be a core case.[11] However, the conviction of
anyone, even one who has committed a crime, on the basis of inadequate
legal proof could equally be said to be a breach of rights. Some observers
attempt to distinguish between those who are really 'innocent' and those
who are acquitted 'on a technicality'. However, a conviction arising from
deceit or illegalities is corrosive of the State's claims to legitimacy on the
basis of due process and respect for rights,[12] and there may be practical
deleterious effects in terms of diminished confidence in the forces of law
and order, leading to fewer active citizens aiding the police and fewer
jurors willing to convict even the blatantly guilty. Accordingly, even a
person who has in fact and with intent committed a crime could be said
to have suffered a miscarriage if convicted on evidence which is legally
inadmissible or which is not proven beyond reasonable doubt.

---

8   Blackstone, *Commentaries on the Law of England* (1765–9), vol. iv, p. 27. See also
    Stephen, Sir J., *History of the Criminal Law of England* (1883, Burt Franklin, New
    York, 1973 ed.), vol. I, p. 438; Fletcher, G. P., 'Two kinds of legal rules' (1968) 77 Yale
    LJ 880; Shavario, D., 'Statistical probability evidence and the appearance of justice'
    (1989–90) 103 Harv LR 530.
9   See ch. 4.
10 See Jefferson, T., and Walker, M. A., 'Ethnic minorities in the criminal justice system'
    [1992] Crim LR 83.
11 Compare Brandon, R., and Davies, C., *Wrongful Imprisonment* (Allen, London, 1973),
    p. 19.
12 See Beetham, D., *The Legitimation of Power* (MacMillan, London, 1991).

Another conceivable category of persons suffering a miscarriage because of a denial of their rights comprises those who fall foul of laws which are inherently unjust rather than unjustly applied. In a responsive, liberal democracy, such failures of the system should be few and far between. Nevertheless, claims along these lines have been made in recent years by persons convicted of failure to pay the poll tax or taxes to finance nuclear weapons, or by women provoked (in fact but not so defined in law) into retaliation by the violence of male relatives.[13] This book will mainly reflect upon dysfunctions in application of the law, but some space is given to laws which some people view as inherently unfair, especially (in chapter 9) the Prevention of Terrorism (Temporary Provisions) Acts 1974–89. A more blatant example may be South African apartheid, which involved many denials of rights and thereby miscarriages. That system was often rational and predictable according to its own lights, but to sanction it with the term 'justice' because it observed regular patterns and solemn procedures would be blinkered.[14]

Illustrations of miscarriages resulting from disproportionate treatment in terms of rights might include the granting of arrest or extensive search powers, or excessively harsh sentences in respect of trivial anti-social conduct.[15] Similarly, the imposition of conditions during punishment which serve little purpose other than degradation, and which therefore do not ultimately bolster respect for rights, should be treated as a miscarriage of justice. It should be noted that sentencing and penal regimes are not covered in the remainder of this book.

The third type of miscarriage, a failure to protect and vindicate the rights of potential or actual victims, can arise in various ways. For example, a lack of security forces to guard against violent attackers could be a breach of rights.[16] A refusal to prosecute particular types of suspects, especially members of the security forces, may also be viewed as a miscarriage. Such a situation arose in 1988, when the Attorney-General blocked proceedings against RUC officers accused by the Stalker/Sampson inquiry of perverting the course of justice and obstruction of

---

13 See *Cheney* v *Conn* [1968] 1 All ER 779; Dignan, J., 'A right not to render unto Caesar' (1983) 34 NILQ 20; Finnis, J., et al., *Nuclear Deterrence, Morality and Realism* (Oxford University Press, 1987); *R* v *Thornton* [1992] 1 All ER 306; *R* v *Ahluwalia* [1992] 4 All ER 889.
14 See Mathews, A. S., *Freedom, State Security and the Rule of Law* (Sweet & Maxwell, London, 1988); Dyzenhaus, D., *Hard Cases and Wicked Legal Systems* (Clarendon Press, Oxford, 1991).
15 Some of the powers of arrest in PACE, s. 25 may serve as an example.
16 See *X* v *UK and Ireland*, Appl no. 9825/82, (1985) 8 EHRR 49.

the police investigation.[17] Similarly, the prosecutions of several police officers accused of assaults during demonstrations by print workers at Wapping were stopped as an abuse of process because of delay. The decision may have been fair to the accused, but it did result in a failure to protect the rights of others because of State mismanagement of the process.[18] A failure to vindicate rights may equally occur when a jury perversely refuses to convict an individual. Disregard for the right of a black suspect not to be beaten up by white policemen sparked riots in Los Angeles in May 1992,[19] and criticisms in some quarters were also expressed in response to the acquittals of Ponting in 1985[20] and Randle and Pottle in 1991.[21] However, decisions by jurors are not treated here as miscarriages of justice.[22] The State is not responsible for their decisions and, in the case of an unfair acquittal, has no further responsibility for the treatment of the accused.[23]

In summary, there are three points to infer from the definition of 'miscarriages' adopted herein. First, the meaning is not confined to miscarriages in court or in the penal system. Miscarriages can happen on the street when the police unjustly exercise their coercive powers. Secondly, miscarriages can be institutionalised within laws as well as failures in the application of laws. Thirdly, a miscarriage of justice must involve a shortcoming by some form of State agency and therefore a degree of State responsibility. Deceit, negligence or violence by private persons or bodies may result in gross hardship and unfairness but are not necessarily attributable to any deficiency in the criminal justice system.

The Crisis in Criminal Justice — a Chronology of *Causes Célèbres*

Since justice is applied by fallible, prejudiced human beings, miscarriages of justice are inevitable. However, it is not intended in this

---

17   See HC Debs, vol. 126, col. 21, 25 January 1988. See also, in Australia, Carrington, K., et al, *Travesty!* (Pluto Press, NSW, 1991), chs. 11 and 12.
18   CPS, Annual Report 1990–91, p. 28.
19   (1992) *The Times*, 1 May, p. 1.
20   [1985] Crim LR 318, [1986] Crim LR 491.
21   (1991) *The Times*, 27 June, p. 24.
22   See also Devlin, P., 'The conscience of the jury' (1991) 107 LQR 398.
23   The State has responsibility for the design of the jury system. Concerns include its ethnic representativeness (see *R* v *Ford* [1989] 3 WLR 762, and Commission for Racial Equality, *Submission* (1991)), the abolition of the defence's rights to peremptory challenge (Criminal Justice Act 1988, s. 118) and the rules about jury vetting (*Practice Direction* [1988] 3 All ER 1086).

commentary to go further back than those cases which will provide the meat to be chewed upon by the Runciman Commission. The deadline may be taken to be around 1981, when the last major inquiry into the subject, the Royal Commission on Criminal Procedure (the 'Philips Report'), was published.[24] That Commission had in turn been mainly prompted by a miscarriage of justice in the *Confait* case (see below), and its report promoted sweeping changes in terms of police powers (the Police and Criminal Evidence Act 1984: PACE) and a new Crown Prosecution Service (the Prosecution of Offences Act 1985).[25] Accordingly, this book will tend to focus upon later cases which have not been previously digested and which are likely to be most compelling in the minds of the present Commissioners, and therefore most influential in future policy-making. Another point is that many earlier miscarriages are already the subject of voluminous documentation to which little can usefully be added here. Cases in this category include those of *Rowland* (1947),[26] *Evans* (1950),[27] *Bentley* (1952),[28] *Hanratty* (1962),[29] *Stafford and Luvaglio* (1967),[30] *Murphy, McMahon and Cooper* ('the Luton Post Office murder' in 1970),[31] *Lattimore, Salih and Leighton* (the *Confait* case in 1972),[32] *Dougherty* (1973),[33] and *Maynard and Dudley* ('the Legal and

---

24 Cmnd 8092.
25 But note that the Philips Commission accepted without argument that an adversarial form of justice should be maintained and that its focus should be on pre-court issues: ibid. paras 1.6–1.8.
26 See Report of an Inquiry by J. C. Jolly (Cmd 7049, 1947); Cecil, H., *The Trial of Walter Rowland* (David & Charles, Newton Abbot, 1975); Cotton, P., 'The Deansgate mistake' (1990) 98 *Police Rev* 1104.
27 See Report of an Inquiry by Scott Henderson (Cmd 8896 and 8946, 1953); Paget, R. T. and Silverman, S., *Hanged and Innocent?* (Gollancz, London, 1953); Eddowes, M., *The Man on Your Conscience* (Cassell, London, 1955); Grigg, J., and Gilmour, I., *The Case of Timothy Evans* (Spectator, London, 1956); Tennyson, F. J., *The Trials of Timothy John Evans and John Reginald Christie* (Hodge, London, 1957); Hale, L., *Hanged in Error* (Penguin, London, 1961); L. Kennedy, *Ten Rillington Place* (Gollancz, London, 1961); Report of an Inquiry by Mr Justice Brabin (Cmnd 3101, 1966).
28 See Yallop, D., *To Encourage the Others* (W. H. Allen, London, 1972). 'The Home Secretary has refused a pardon' (1992) *The Times*, 2 October, p. 1.
29 See Blom Cooper, L., *The A6 Murder* (Penguin, London, 1963); Russell, E. F. L., *Deadman's Hill* (Secker & Warburg, London, 1965); Foot, P., *Who Killed Hanratty?* (Cape, London, 1971); Report of Mr C. Hawser QC (Cmnd 5021, 1975).
30 See [1968] 3 All ER 752, [1972] 1 WLR 1649, [1974] AC 878; Lewis, D., and Hughman, P., *Most Unnatural* (Penguin, London, 1971).
31 (1975) 65 Cr App R 215; (1978) 68 Cr App R 18.
32 See (1975) 62 Cr App R 53; Report of an Inquiry by the Hon. Sir Henry Fisher (1977–78 HC 90).
33 See Report of the Departmental Committee on evidence of identification in criminal cases (the 'Devlin Report') (1975–76 HC 338).

General Gang' in 1977).[34] Although no detailed description will be given
of the foregoing, one should not assume that all (or even any) of the
problems illustrated by them have been solved by previous inquiries or
legislation. Indeed, most of the present concerns were equally current
during the previous two decades, despite the intercession of several
inquiries and a Royal Commission. Accordingly, many of the aforemen-
tioned cases will be discussed in the following chapters.

As for the most recent cases, which will figure more prominently both
in this book and in the deliberations of the Royal Commission, the list
may begin with the *Guildford Four* and the *Maguire Seven*. The *Guildford
Four* (Hill, Richardson, Conlon and Armstrong)[35] were convicted of pub
bombings on behalf of the IRA in Guildford and Woolwich. An appeal
against conviction failed in 1977 despite the fact that other IRA
defendants awaiting trial had by then claimed responsibility. However,
other new evidence was eventually amassed which convinced the Home
Secretary to order further investigations and a referral back to the Court
of Appeal. Once it was discovered that detectives in the Surrey Police
involved in the case had fabricated evidence and suppressed possible
exculpatory evidence, the DPP decided not to contest the convictions,
which were quashed in 1989. This outcome immediately prompted
reconsideration of the *Maguire Seven* case.[36] Suspicion first fell on the
Maguire household when Gerard Conlon (one of the *Guildford Four*)
made statements to the police that his aunt, Anne Maguire, had taught
him to manufacture bombs. The police raided the house, and convictions
were obtained mainly on the basis of forensic tests which were said to
show traces of nitroglycerine. The Court of Appeal, on a reference back
in 1990,[37] grudgingly overturned the convictions because of the possibility that third parties had left the traces in the house and so caused

---

34   See (1979) 69 Cr App R 309; Hilliard, B., 'Criminal complicity' (1992) 100 *Police Rev*
      1226; Wickstead, A., 'Truth and the torsos' (1992) 100 *Police Rev* 1370; Goldberg, J,
      'Brief's nightmare' (1992) 100 *Police Rev* 1506.
35   See *R v Hill and others, R v Richardson and others* (1975) *The Times*, 23 October, p. 1,
      (1977) *The Times*, 28 February, p. 2, (1989) *The Times*, 20 October; Kee, R., *Trial and
      Error* (Hamish Hamilton, London, 1986); McKee, G., and Franey, R., *Time Bombs*
      (Bloomsbury, London, 1988); Lords Devlin and Scarman, '*Justice and the Guildford
      Four*' (1988) *The Times*, 30 November, p. 16; Scrivener, A., 'The Guildford Four'
      (1989) *Counsel*, November, p. 15; Hilliard, B., 'The time bomb goes off' (1989) 97
      Police Rev 2174; Hill, P., and Burnett, R., *Stolen Years* (Doubleday, London, 1990);
      Conlon, G., *Proved Innocent* (Hamilton, London, 1990).
36   See (1976) *The Times*, 5 March, p. 1; Kee, R., *op. cit.*
37   *The Times*, 28 June, [1992] 2 All ER 433. The accused had all by then served their
      sentences, but one, Guiseppe Conlon (father of Gerard) had died in prison in 1980.
      Four police officers are being prosecuted for malpractices: *R v Bow Street Stipendiary
      Magistrates, ex parte DPP* (1992) 95 Cr App R 9.

innocent contamination (the non-disclosure of evidence was also a material irregularity in the case). However, the May Inquiry's Interim and Second Reports on the *Maguire* case more realistically cast doubt on whether the tests used and circumstantial evidence could in any event be taken to be conclusive proof of the knowing handling of explosives.[38]

The next blow to confidence in the criminal justice system was the *Birmingham Six* case in 1991.[39] The six (Hill, Hunter, McIlkenny, Power, Walker and Callaghan) had been convicted along with three others of bombings in two Birmingham pubs in 1974. The attacks had caused more deaths than any other IRA incident in Britain and were the signal for the passage of the Prevention of Terrorism Acts.[40] The prosecution evidence rested upon three legs: confessions, which the accused claimed had been beaten out of them; forensic tests, which the accused claimed were inherently unreliable and had been performed unsatisfactorily by Dr Skuse; and highly circumstantial evidence, such as links to known Republicans, their movements and demeanour. After being refused leave to appeal in 1976, the six ploughed a furrow in the civil courts by way of a claim for damages for assault against the police and prison warders. However, their path was eventually blocked by the House of Lords as an abuse of process, since any civil victory would undermine the finality of their criminal conviction. Their focus then switched back to the criminal courts, and their new evidence was referred back to the Court of Appeal in 1988. The Court was then unpersuaded, but further revelations about the police fabrication of statements and new uncertainties about the quality of the forensic tests eventually resulted in their release in 1991. That outcome was swiftly followed by the establishment of the Royal Commission.[41]

The next Irish-related case of relevance is that of Judith Ward, who was convicted in 1974 for delivering the bombs which resulted in 12

---

38   1989–90 HC 556; 1992–93 HC 296. This argument was expressly rejected by the Court of Appeal (*loc. cit.* at p. 444), which judgment the Second Report in turn criticises (*loc. cit.* paras 1.6–1.8).

39   See (1975) *The Times*, 16 August, p. 1, (1976) *The Times*, 31 March, p. 9, [1980] 2 All ER 227, [1981] 3 WLR 906, [1988] 1 WLR 1, (1988) *The Times*, 29 January, p. 5, (1988) *The Times*, 22 March, p. 1, (1988) 88 Cr App R 40, (1991) *The Times*, 1 April, [1992] 2 All ER 417. Commentaries include: Gibson, B., *The Birmingham Bombs* (Rose, Chichester, 1976); Yahuda, J., 'The Birmingham bombers' (1988) 152 JP 230; Hilliard, B., 'Soldiers of nothing' (1990) 140 NLJ 160; Dunne, D., *The Birmingham Six*, 2nd ed. (The Birmingham Six Committee, 1989); Mullin, C., *Error of Judgment*, 2nd ed. (Chatto & Windus, London, 1990).

40   See ch. 9; Walker, C., *The Prevention of Terrorism in British Law*, 2nd ed. (Manchester University Press, Manchester, 1992), ch. 4.

41   Another outcome is that three police officers have been committed for trial: (1992) *The Times*, 30 May, p. 2.

deaths on an Army coach travelling along the M62 in Yorkshire.[42] The
conviction was once again undermined by the unreliability of the forensic
evidence (Skuse's name appears once more) and of the confessions she
made (though this time more because of her mental instability than
because of police mistreatment of her). In the background were
allegations of non-disclosure. Ward's case was referred to the Court of
Appeal unilaterally by the Home Office, and she was released in 1992
after the prosecution declined to contest the matter. The Court's
judgment was particularly censorious of the non-disclosure of evidence
by named forensic scientists and prosecution counsel.

The final case arising from Irish terrorism concerns the '*Armagh Four*'
— Latimer, Allen, Bell and Hegan.[43] The four co-accused were members
of the UDR who were convicted of the murder in Armagh city of Adrian
Carroll, whom they believed to be active in the IRA.[44] Their allegation
of injustice arose from three main concerns. First, Latimer pointed to
conflicting identification evidence and to oppressive treatment during his
police interrogation. Further, it was shown that the police had tampered
with the confessions by rewriting some notes, deleting references to
requests to see solicitors and attaching false authentications. After
referral back to the Court of Appeal in 1992, Allen, Bell and Hegan were
all freed on the basis that the police had indeed tampered with the
evidence, but Latimer's conviction was not overturned in the light of the
identification evidence against him, his confirmation of his admission at
the original trial in 1985 and the finding that he had lied to the court.[45]

There are lastly various recently recognised miscarriages which do not
relate to Irish terrorism. Most of these cases arise out of the business of
the West Midlands Police Serious Crime Squad, whose activities have
given rise to 91 complaints about beatings, the fabrication of evidence
and denial of access to lawyers.[46] Some of those affected have been
released. An investigation into the conduct of the police resulted in the

---

42   See (1974) *The Times*, 5 November, p. 4, (1992) *The Times*, 12 May, p. 1, (1992) 96 Cr
     App R 1.
43   See [1986] 9 NIJB 1 (trial); [1988] 11 NIJB 1 (appeal).
44   His brother, Roddy, was shot by an RUC squad in 1982: Stalker, J., *Stalker* (Penguin,
     London, 1988).
45   (1992) *The Times*, 30 July, pp. 1, 2. See also (1992) 3 BNIL n. 73.
46   See *R v Khan* (1990) *Independent,* 2 March; *R v Edwards* [1991] 1 WLR 207; *R v
     Binham* (1991) NLJ 189; *R v Wellington* (1991) *The Times*, 26 March, p. 7; *R v Lynch*
     (1991) *The Times*, 22 October, p. 3; *Ex parte Coventry Newspapers Ltd* [1992] 3 WLR
     916; Kirby, T., 'The force of corruption' (1989) *Independent Magazine*, 14 October, p.
     14; Kaye, T., *Unsafe and Unsatisfactory* (Civil Liberties Trust, 1991); Maloney, J.,
     'The squad that lost its way' (1991) *Police Rev* 2234.

disbandment of the Squad in 1989 but no convictions.[47] Another relevant case is that of the *Tottenham Three* (Silcott, Raghip and Braithwaite), who were convicted of the murder of PC Blakelock during the Broadwater Farm riot in 1985.[48] On a referral back to the Court of Appeal in 1991, it was accepted that notes of the interview had been altered in the case of Silcott,[49] that Raghip's confession was negated by his mental state and that Braithwaite had been unfairly denied a lawyer. Release after an even longer period of imprisonment was also ordered in the case of Kiszko.[50] His conviction for murder was accepted as unsustainable in the light of the medical evidence that he was unable to produce the sperm found on the victim. The handling of this evidence by prosecution counsel also gave rise to concern. The next entry in the catalogue concerns the Darvell brothers,[51] who had been convicted in Swansea Crown Court in June 1986 of murdering the manageress of a sex shop. Their convictions were overturned after an uncontested appeal in 1992. Evidence was then presented that police notes about the investigation and a confession had been redrafted at a later date, that police witnesses who had identified the brothers as being in the area of the murder at the crucial time were in fact nine miles away, and that fingerprint evidence at the scene of the crime which pointed elsewhere was not disclosed to the defence, was not fully investigated and was even destroyed before the trial. Finally, the convictions in 1990 of the *Cardiff Three* for the murder of a prostitute were overturned in December 1992 on referral to the Court of Appeal.[52] The Court expressed itself as horrified by evidence of oppression from the police interview tapes.

Aside from these notorious cases, it is difficult to obtain a complete picture of the number of miscarriages produced overall. In a report in 1989, the organisation JUSTICE estimated that up to 15 defendants per year sentenced to four years or more on indictment have been wrongly convicted.[53] Just over 1 per cent of those convicted on indictment fall into

47　See *R* v *Mills* (1991) *The Times*, 21 June, p. 3; (1992) *The Times*, 20 May, pp. 1, 3; (1992) 89/20 LS Gaz 10.

48　(1991) *The Times*, 9 December.

49　Three police officers have been charged with perversion of the course of justice: (1992) *The Times*, 18 June, p. 2.

50　See (1978) 68 Cr App R 62; (1992) *The Times*, 18 February, p. 5; 19 February, p. 3.

51　See (1992) *The Times*, 15 July, pp. 1, 3. An earlier appeal had been rejected in 1987, but a further investigation had been oredered after a *Rough Justice* TV programme on the case.

52　*R* v *Paris, Miller, Abdullahi* (1992) *The Times*, 24 December.

53　*Miscarriages of Justice*, p. 1 and see also app. 1. One of the most famous which has not resulted in acquittals concerns the Bridgewater murder: Foot, P., *Murder at the Farm* (Penguin, London, 1988). Following a reinvestigation, the Home Secretary concluded that the convictions are sound: (1992) *The Times*, 19 September, p. 6.

this sentencing band, so the total number of miscarriages in Crown Courts may be well over 1,000 per year, and no attempt has been made to estimate the rate in magistrates' courts where over 90 per cent of cases are heard.[54] More recently, the Society of Prison Officers has estimated that there might be up to 700 innocent persons in prisons after conviction.[55] Likewise, the Home Office has revealed that it receives about 700 to 800 petitions per year.[56] Liberty has recently compiled a dossier of 163 cases which it intends to pursue.[57]

Though they may be a small proportion of the total number of miscarriage cases, the Irish terrorism trials stick out as involving the most profound flaws and as being the most susceptible to error. The reasons for their prominence in this catalogue of cases are probably two-fold. First, special powers in the Prevention of Terrorism Act make abuses easier to commit and more difficult to detect. This point will be taken up later.[58] Secondly, miscarriages are in any event more likely because of the nature of these cases, regardless of whether draconian powers are invoked or not. In such prosecutions, the normal due process ideology of the criminal justice system is under pressure, and there is a tendency towards holding a grand 'State' trial.[59] Considerations such as the primacy of the individual and the desire to stack the odds in favour of the innocent in part give way to conflicting goal-based rather than rights-based factors.[60] The goals include the strategy of the criminalisation of terrorists — the policy of the condemnation of the motives and values held by the accused and their kind, together with the reinforcement of the legitimacy of the State. There is also the 'presentational' aspect[61] — the desire to be seen to be taking effective action against terrorists. Even if the action is really worthless, it can still relieve public frustrations and fears. Hence, Lord Denning's comment in response to the *Guildford Four* case that even if the wrong people were convicted, 'the whole community would be satisfied'.[62] These wider societal considerations may also explain why

---

54 But note that disputed confessions are far rarer (perhaps because of the absence of a *voir dire*): CPS, *Submission* to the Royal Commission (1991), vol. I, ch. 10.
55 (1992) *Independent*, 19 March, p. 31.
56 *Memoranda* (1991), para. 4.47.
57 (1992) *The Lawyer*, 17 November, p. 7.
58 See ch. 9.
59 See Kirchheimer, V., *Political Justice* (Princeton University Press, 1961); Allen, F. A., *The Crimes of Politics* (Harvard University Press, 1974).
60 See Packer, H., *The Limits of the Criminal Sanction* (Stanford University Press, 1969); King, M., *The Framework of Criminal Justice* (Croom Helm, London, 1981).
61 See Review of the Operation of the Prevention of Terrorism (Temporary Provisions) Act 1976 (Cmnd 8803, 1983), paras. 207, 208.
62 (1990) *The Times*, 17 August, p. 14.

miscarriages seem so hard to remedy. The problem is not simply stubbornness, but that an acquittal becomes particularly costly to the State in terms of damage to its legitimacy and prestige. These same factors may apply to marginalised groups other than Irish Republicans — the black and deprived accused living on Broadwater Farm display many parallels.[63]

The Common Forms of Miscarriage of Justice in Practice

The JUSTICE *Report on Miscarriages of Justice*[64] highlighted five 'common threads' which ran through most of the allegations made over the years: wrongful identification, false confessions, perjury by witnesses, police misconduct and bad trial tactics. The Runciman Commission is based upon terms of reference which focus upon the following: the conduct of police investigations; the role of the prosecutor; the role of experts; the arrangements for defence; statements by the accused and the right to silence; the powers of the courts and directing proceedings; the role of the Court of Appeal; and arrangements post-appeal. These pointers have in turn been translated into no fewer than 88 specific questions on which views are sought.

Without delineating in detail all these possible issues, it is clear from the cases already cited that there are some common themes, mainly centred upon the first form of miscarriage — namely, treatment in breach of rights.

(1)   The most obvious danger is the fabrication of evidence. It has been recognised for some time that informers who are co-accused may well have self-serving reasons for exaggerating the role of the accused, though this lesson did have to be relearned in response to the 'supergrasses' who emerged in Northern Ireland between 1981 and 1986.[65] The police are also in a powerful position to manipulate evidence, for example by 'verballing' the accused — inventing damning statements or passages within them. The *Birmingham Six, Tottenham Three, Armagh Four*, Darvell brothers and several West Midlands cases all involve allegations along these lines.

(2)   Both the police and lay witnesses may prove to be unreliable when attempting to identify an offender. This has been recognised by the

---

63   See further O'Brien, C. C., 'Legal buffers needed when ethnic groups collide' (1991) *The Times*, 27 July, p. 12.

64   *Loc. cit.*, pp. 3–4. Compare: Sargant, T. and Hill, P., *Criminal Trials* (Fabian Research Series, 1986), ch. 2.

65   See Hogan, G., and Walker, C., *Political Violence and the Law in Ireland* (Manchester University Press, 1989), pp. 123–6.

Criminal Law Revision Committee[66] and the Devlin Committee of Inquiry set up following the case of *Dougherty*, though the implementation of the Committee's recommendations in *Turnbull* leaves much to be desired.[67]

(3) The evidential value of expert testimony has also been overestimated in a number of instances, only for it later to emerge that the tests being used were inherently unreliable, that the scientists conducting them were inefficient or both. The *Maguire Seven, Birmingham Six* and *Ward* cases all fit into this category and are closely related in terms of the techniques used and the technicians using them.

(4) The next common factor concerns unreliable confessions as a result of police pressure, mental instability or a combination of both. The *Guildford Four, Birmingham Six, Judith Ward, Tottenham Three* and *Cardiff Three* cases, *inter alia*, all fall into this category.

(5) A further issue may be the non-disclosure of relevant evidence by the police or prosecution to the defence. The investigation of a case is by and large reliant on the police — they speak to all possible witnesses and arrange for all manner of forensic testing. The defence have neither the financial resources to undertake such work nor the opportunities in terms of access — indeed, approaches to prosecution witnesses might well be construed as attempts to pervert the course of justice. Yet, several cases — the *Guildford Four, Maguire Seven, Darvell brothers* and *Ward* in particular[68] — demonstrate that the police, forensic scientists and prosecution cannot be relied upon fairly to pass on evidence which might be helpful to the accused, despite there being no other agency which might uncover it in the interests of justice.

(6) The conduct of the trial may produce miscarriages. For example, judges are sometimes prone to favour the prosecution evidence rather than acting as impartial umpires, as is alleged in connection with the *Birmingham Six*. A failure to appreciate the defence's submissions either in law or fact can result in unfairness in their rulings or directions to the jury, as in the *Maguire Seven* case. Equally, it must be recognised that defence lawyers are not always beyond reproach. Lack of legal aid funding has made defence work the Cinderella service of the criminal justice system, so it is not surprising that the quality of defence lawyers is not always as good as it should be. Furthermore, the accused choose (or more likely are assigned) lawyers at their own risk. Thus, in *R v*

---

66 11th Report: Evidence (General) (Cmnd 4991, 1972), para. 196.
67 [1977] QB 224. See: JUSTICE Report, *op. cit.*, pp. 24–7.
68 Note also the case of George Lindo: Hansen, O., 'Justice delayed — justice denied' March 1980 *LAG Bulletin* 83.

Ensor,[69] the Court of Appeal said that defence counsel must be 'flagrantly incompetent' before the court will overturn a conviction, not just unwise or mistaken.[70]

(7)   The next problem concerns the presentation of the accused in a prejudicial manner. An insidious way of achieving this effect is the perjorative labelling of them as 'terrorists'. Similarly, the obvious and heavy-handed security arrangements accompanying trips to court and the accused's quarantined appearance in the dock inevitably convey an impression of guilt and menace. These problems could be alleviated by advice to the media and by different physical arrangements in court, but little has yet been done. Prejudice can also arise through comments on the case. The law of contempt may temper excessive behaviour, but the courts should be more concerned about securing a fair trial rather than punishing contemnors. At least in the case of the *Winchester Three* comment did result in the overturning of convictions.[71] However, the commoner response is largely to ignore the possible effects of publications on the fairness of the hearing.[72]

(8)   There are then the problems associated with appeals and the procedures thereafter. Common difficulties include the lack of access to lawyers and limited legal aid funding, so there has to be reliance on extra-legal campaigns which may or may not be taken up by the media dependent upon factors which have little to do with the strength of the case. The Court of Appeal has made life even more difficult because of its interpretations of the grounds for appeal. Once the courts are exhausted, complainants must rely upon a ramshackle and secretive review by Home Office officials rather than on open and independent inquiry.

(9)   Lastly, a miscarriage can occur through the failure of State agencies to vindicate or protect rights, or through laws which are inherently contrdictory to the concept of individual rights. Examples have already been adduced.

This list might be described as embodying the direct causes of concern. However, there are several underlying issues, not all of which can be taken up within the confines of this book and, more disappointingly, virtually none of which figures as part of the agenda of the inquiries

---

69   [1989] 2 All ER 586. See also ch. 7.
70   *Ibid.*, at p. 590.
71   *R* v *McCann* (1991) 92 Cr App R 239. See Woffinden, B., 'The case of the Winchester Three' (1990) 140 NLJ 164.
72   This issue arose on the appeal of those convicted of the Brighton bombing: *R* v *Anderson* [1988] 2 WLR 1017.

envisaged by the Runciman Commission. Such matters include the particular difficulties arising in Northern Ireland and Scotland; police institutional issues such as accountability[73] and the investigation of complaints; the funding of legal aid; and the appointment and training of judges.

Conclusions

Assertions that the British system of justice is the best in the world or that miscarriages of justice are few and far between[74] can no longer be sustained without argument. Criminal justice systems should be judged, *inter alia*, on the number of injustices produced by them in the first place, and, secondly, on their willingness to recognise and correct those mistakes. The British system scores badly on both counts, as will be explained in the following chapters. Whether it performs poorly in comparison with other systems will also be considered (in chapters 10 and 11). More generally, it is hoped that this book will assist the reader to understand the reasons behind the current crisis and to choose amongst the possible solutions to it,[75] including those which will be advanced by the Royal Commission, whose report will eventually provide a temporary conclusion to our debates.

---

73 The current inquiry into working practices is unlikely to stray into such territory: (1992) *The Times*, 21 May, p. 1.

74 Bailey, S. T. (ed.), *Human Rights and Responsibilities in Britain and Ireland* (MacMillan, London, 1988), p. 179.

75 This faith in the value of reform is itself contentious (see McConville, M., Sanders, A. and Leng, R., *The Case for the Prosecution* (Routledge, London 1991) ch. 10, but even sceptics may prefer not to leave the field open to administrative fiat or the powerful clients of government (see Craig, P. P., *Public Law and Democracy in the UK and the USA* (Clarendon Press, Oxford 1990), p. 130.

2

Police Investigative Procedures: Researching the Impact of PACE

Clive Coleman, David Dixon and Keith Bottomley

Introduction

A key question to consider in any discussion of miscarriages of justice is whether the provisions of the Police and Criminal Evidence Act 1984 (PACE) have reduced their likelihood. In addition, are there elements of PACE which can profitably be further developed and extended, or is a radical change of emphasis in the nature and control of procedures in criminal justice required? Answers to such questions require consideration of the impact of the legislation.

This chapter reports the findings of research into some of the early stages of the investigation of crime by the police. It is largely based on a project conducted in a North of England police force, mainly during 1987 and 1988, by means of interviews, analysis of records and extensive observation.[1] It must be stated that what we found will not necessarily apply in other forces; despite the attempt to provide clear and uniform rules to guide practice, the impact of PACE seems to have been variable within and between forces and over time. Where appropriate, we

1 Bottomley, K., Coleman, C., Dixon, D., Gill, M. and Wall, D., *The Impact of PACE: Policing in a Northern Force* (Centre for Criminology and Criminal Justice, University of Hull, 1991).

therefore draw on studies conducted in other locations. A second preliminary point concerns the difficulties in assessing the impact of PACE. Not only are comparable statistics and studies of the situation before PACE sometimes lacking, but it is often difficult to distinguish the specific effects of PACE from those of other changes in law, policy and procedure which were being implemented at about the same time. Examples are the Prosecution of Offences Act 1985 (setting up the Crown Prosecution Service), changes in summonsing policies and the new cautioning guidelines, as well as broader changes in policing styles and culture during the 1980s in which PACE is only one possible factor.

In what follows we discuss the impact of PACE in three areas of police activity which were intended to be regulated by its provisions: stop and search; entry, search and seizure; detention and questioning of suspects in police custody. PACE attempts to control conduct both inside and outside the police station by similar methods (mainly by detailed rules, written records and internal supervision), but we argue that these methods have been more successful within the more limited milieu of the station than in the case of the extensive low visibility activities outside it.

Stop and Search

Police powers to stop and search have been amongst the most controversial of all police powers, with a history of allegations that they (and the earlier 'sus' law powers) have been used in a discriminatory fashion against certain segments of the population, especially young black people. The Scarman Report on the Brixton disorders[2] gave added weight to the proposals of the Royal Commission on Criminal Procedure[3] for the rationalisation of the law and additional safeguards. A major concern, quite clearly, was the attempt to prevent the use of stereotyping as a ground for suspicion and the use of coercive powers, and to make 'reasonable suspicion' an effective necessary condition for the exercise of such powers.

PACE provided the police with a standardised national power to stop and search for stolen or certain prohibited articles, and this and virtually all other statutory stop and search powers were made subject to a Code of Practice. Since many police areas (including the one where we did our research) did not have a general power of the kind introduced by PACE,

---

2   Scarman, *The Scarman Report: The Brixton Disorders 10–12 April 1981* (Penguin Books, Harmondsworth, 1982, para. 177).
3   Royal Commission on Criminal Procedure (RCCP): Report, Cmnd 8092 (HMSO, London, 1981).

this represented a significant formal extension of powers in those areas. The national powers that existed before PACE were confined to specific articles, such as drugs or firearms. The evidence is, however, that the police were already using stop/search in a way that was not justified by the more limited legislation before PACE.[4] Comments were made by officers in our research force about the frequency of stop/searches before PACE and how these were often done 'on a wing and a prayer', 'under the Ways and Means Act' or with 'consent' (on the last, see below).[5]

Although reasonable suspicion was a prerequisite for the exercise of powers that existed before the 1984 Act, Code of Practice A tries to provide guidance on what would and would not constitute reasonable grounds for suspicion.[6] Quite clearly, what is required is suspicion founded on fact about a particular individual, rather than a hunch based on experience. The package of safeguards to protect the public against the risk of random, arbitrary or discriminatory searches was completed by the notification of details to the suspect (including the object of and grounds for the search) and the recording of searches. Such records would be available to the suspect and allow monitoring by supervisors and others. As elsewhere in PACE, faith is placed in the promulgation of detailed rules, the use of written records, and the oversight of senior officers in the attempt to structure discretion. In the case of stop and search, we suggest that such faith was largely misplaced.

The attempt made a number of assumptions: that officers will understand and remember the relevant rules; that they will be willing and able to follow them in actual situations; that they will record diligently and accurately the required details; that supervisors will be willing and able to use the records to monitor practice and ensure that the conduct of searches complies with the rules. Few of these assumptions were well founded. As we have argued elsewhere,[7] the attempt to provide guidance on 'reasonable grounds for suspicion' was an unclear and ineffective control on police discretion. There was also confusion and inconsistency about what to do in cases of stop/search conducted with the 'consent' of the suspect. Attempts in Force Orders, Home Office Circulars and the

---

4   See, for example, RCCP, 1981, para. 3.15.
5   Skogan, W. G., (Home Office Research Study No. 117, *The Police and Public in England and Wales: A British Crime Survey Report*, London, HMSO, 1990) likewise found that PACE formalised unofficial practices rather than created new ones.
6   Code of Practice for the Exercise by Police Officers of Statutory Powers of Stop and Search (1991), paras 1.6, 1.7.
7   Dixon, D., Bottomley, K., Coleman, C., Gill, M. and Wall, D., 'Reality and rules in the construction and regulation of police suspicion' (1989) 17 *International Journal of the Sociology of Law* 185.

revised Code of Practice A to provide guidance here seemed to increase the complexity, and rarely worked their way through to the officer on the street.[8]

The problems that arise here are not simply due to a lack of clarity in the rules, but also to a lack of congruence between the rules and the practical settings of police work and the traditional methods of policing the streets. Stop and search is regarded as a distinct event in PACE, before which officers either must decide whether they have reasonable grounds for suspicion of a specific individual or must establish that individual's informed consent in order to conduct a voluntary search. Real policing is rarely so clear cut. Suspicion is built up and dispersed as officers stop and talk to people. What officers call 'simple street checks' (asking to have 'a quick look' in somebody's bag) are not regarded as 'PACE searches' and will not normally be recorded unless something has happened during the encounter that makes this a useful precaution. In a similar way, consent is not something which is simply established as being present or absent. Instead, what passes for consent for practical purposes is the result of an encounter between two parties of unequal standing in knowledge and power; 'consent' on the streets is the product of a social process and rarely corresponds to the informed consent of legal rhetoric. Lastly, despite the Home Office's concern that voluntary searches should not become a way of avoiding the safeguards that PACE provides, their attractions are fairly obvious. Consent (not legal power, as PACE often appears to assume) is the first resort of policing.

What all this means is that stop/searches recorded under PACE represent the tip of an iceberg of low visibility policing, most of which lies outside the safeguards that PACE provides. Stops and searches are not generally supervised, a point made by over three-quarters of operational officers in our interview sample. Of those that were recorded, the records produced would have limitations as a means of monitoring practice to ensure that reasonable suspicion was present. Leaving aside the relation of the records to the original events, some of the entries were so brief, unclear or mistaken as to make an assessment very difficult. There seemed to be a limited awareness of these forms as a method of

---

8 Dixon, D., Coleman, C., and Bottomley, K., 'Consent and the legal regulation of policing' (1990) 17 *Journal of Law and Society* 345. Note that the original version of Code A (1986, Annex B) reminded police officers that reasonable suspicion for stops and searches should be no less well-founded than for an arrest. This advice was removed in the 1991 version on the pretext that it was confusing, though the effect of removal may itself create a misleading impression as to the degree of suspicion required.

supervision, and apparently no universal expectation that they would be completed meticulously and scrutinised thoroughly afterwards.

Overall our study suggested that, for most officers, it was 'business as usual' after PACE. For example, 71 per cent of officers with experience before PACE said that their practice had not changed. Of the minority who said their practice *had* changed, 40 per cent said that they were now less likely to conduct stop/searches. Such officers, clearly a minority, had been affected by the PACE requirement of reasonable grounds for suspecting a particular individual, which created a tension with the kind of suspicion which had been dominant in police culture. The kinds of arrangements and safeguards introduced by PACE in this sphere were apparently insufficient to produce the kind of change that had been envisaged. The difficulties involved in monitoring practice in this area are illustrated by noting how recorded stop/searches under PACE increased from 109,800 in 1986 to 256,900 in 1990.[9] This apparently substantial increase may reflect more a change in recording practices than a change in the actual practice of stop/search itself.

Entry, Search and Seizure

PACE extended and attempted to clarify and control the wide range of police powers of entry, search and seizure, by placing them on a statutory basis and introducing new procedures for their authorisation, implementation and recording. Particular (and controversial) attention in the formulation of the Act was paid to police powers with regard to 'excluded' and 'special procedure' material of a private and confidential nature. During our research not one instance of the use of these powers was recorded;[10] we were in any case more concerned with the exercise of the far more commonly used powers, which did not attract the same publicity.

One problem with assessing the impact of PACE here is that no routine statistics concerning entry, search and seizure have been collected and published for the period before or after PACE, and very few research studies have been conducted. Our analysis of search registers showed that there was an increase of 65 per cent in recorded searches between 1986 and 1987. The increase was mainly in searches after arrest (s. 18), which constituted the majority of all recorded searches.[11] Such searches

---

9   Home Office (1991), Statistical Bulletin, Issue 14/91 (HMSO, London, 1991).

10   For the national picture, see Bevan, V., and Lidstone, K., *The Investigation of Crime* (Butterworths, London, 1991), para. 4.07.

11   Bevan and Lidstone, *ibid.* report a similar finding in regard to s. 18, though they found rather more searches by consent.

appeared to be an almost routine accompaniment of certain types of arrest, despite the requirements for a connection between the evidence sought and the offence for which the person is arrested and for an inspector's authorisation. Only half a dozen officers interviewed said they had been refused such authorisation.

Searches under warrant comprised 12 per cent of the total recorded. Three-quarters of the searches resulted in the seizure of goods, although in almost half (47 per cent) some property was seized that was not covered by the warrant (a practice that PACE was expected to control), and the reasons for such seizures were not always recorded. In fewer than 10 per cent of cases were illegal drugs seized, although as many as 36 per cent of warrants were issued for drugs searches.

Only 8 per cent of recorded searches in our sample were carried out to effect an arrest (s. 17). In practice it was found that many such searches were done with 'consent' and often not recorded. Recording tended to arise only when force or damage occurred, or where there might be some 'comeback' for the officers concerned. Such under-recording does of course limit the possibility of monitoring or 'after the event' supervision by senior officers.

Similarly, only 15 per cent of recorded searches were with the householder's consent, a figure that our observations and interview responses suggest is an underestimate. One reason for this is that the procedures for such searches were not as clear as with some other types (such as s. 18), so that there was often confusion over whether such searches needed to be recorded in the search register. More important, however, is the fact that police officers often find themselves on private premises for a variety of reasons and might then ask if they could take a 'quick look round'. Such searches would not be seen as 'proper' searches and hence not be recorded. PACE fails to recognise that in such a typical context search of premises is not a clearly defined event but part of a social process.

Such informal searches are likely to occur when police suspicion falls short of the requirements for the exercise of the statutory powers. The very process of obtaining 'consent' is a way of testing police suspicions about a suspect (and the householder will be aware of this, even if aware of the limits of police powers). For the police to inform the householder of the purpose of the search, to offer the option of refusing consent, and to seek that consent in writing would all serve to undermine the basis of the successful negotiation of 'consent'. The point is illustrated by the practice of asking for the householder's signature confirming consent in the officer's note book *on the way out* of the premises (the original Code of Practice did not explicitly state that such consent had to be obtained before entry; the revised Code requires that written consent be given on the new Notice of Powers and Rights before the search takes place[12]). It certainly appeared to us that full and informed consent to a search of premises of a kind apparently envisaged by PACE and the Code of Practice was relatively uncommon. In addition, the adequacy of official records for the purposes of official supervision of these searches must be very doubtful.

In sum, it seems to us that PACE made a rather unrealistic attempt to regularise entry, search and seizure, based on a simplistic notion of the way police searches of premises typically arise and are carried out. Not only were some of the powers and procedures not spelled out clearly enough, but the statutory requirements regarding consent, official authorisation, and the recording of details and outcomes of searches hardly provide adequate safeguards for householders and arrested persons, or a satisfactory basis for supervision and control of police work in this area.

Detention and Questioning of Suspects in Police Custody

The Royal Commission on Criminal Procedure was particularly concerned about the treatment of persons detained in police custody without charge. Therefore, it called for overall limits upon the length of any such detention and for proper arrangements for the care of suspects, including the protection of their rights.[13] Parts IV and V of PACE set out detailed regulations and procedures that can be seen as broadly intended to achieve these objectives.

Pre-charge detention

An attempt was made in PACE to regulate the length of pre-charge detention by specifying maximum duration, introducing a series of formal reviews and establishing the principle that such detention should only be for specified grounds and as brief as possible. Conforming to the Royal Commission's recommendation that police powers should be limited by the principle of necessity, the custody officer receiving the suspect at the station must first 'determine whether he has before him sufficient evidence to charge that person' (s. 37(1)); if such evidence is not

---

12   Para. 4.1.
13   RCCP, 1981, para. 3.94.

forthcoming the person must be released 'unless the custody officer has reasonable grounds for believing that his detention without being charged is necessary to secure or preserve evidence relating to an offence for which he is under arrest or to obtain such evidence by questioning him' (s. 37(2)). The custody officer, created by PACE to be responsible for the care and custody of suspects, is clearly expected to make an informed, independent evaluation of the case before a suspect is admitted into detention.

The practice, we found, was rather different. In common with other researchers,[14] we found that custody officers failed to inquire in any detail into the circumstances of the arrest or the need for detention. The initial authorisation of detention had thus become a routinised formality. One reason for this is the absence of a specific procedure or an alternative recording form to deal with a decision not to authorise detention on reception.[15] A second reason is that PACE requires the custody officer to examine the evidence for detention in the presence of the suspect. A decision not to authorise detention might well imply criticism of the arresting officer in front of the suspect. The likely outcome where grounds for detention are weak or non-existent is a short detention followed by words of advice to the arresting officer to try to ensure that the custody officer is not placed in a similar position in the future. A third reason for the practice here is perhaps that officers bringing suspects to the station now tend to collect more evidence before doing so, so that custody officers are more confident about the likely grounds for deten-tion. Although difficult to confirm conclusively, this was often mentioned by officers as being a major change, and two-thirds of the officers we interviewed thought that arrests based on a hunch were less common since PACE. Lastly, it is worth pointing out that the conditions and pressures that obtain at times at reception often make it difficult to carry out a detailed consideration of the arrest and the grounds for detention at that stage; this, of course, does not explain why non-authorisation of detention virtually *never* occurs.

Length of detention

Turning to the impact of PACE on the length of detention, the mean detention length of persons held before charge or release in our research

---

14 McKenzie, I., Morgan, R., and Reiner, R., 'Helping the police with their inquiries: the necessity principle and voluntary attendance at the police station' [1990] Crim LR 22.

15 *Ibid.* p. 26.

force in 1986 was five minutes longer than it had been before PACE in 1981 and 1984.[16] With the introduction of the package of detention limits and review procedures, it might have been expected that overall detention times would fall after PACE. However, the increase in the take-up of legal advice which it stimulated (see below) counterbalanced this. In one of the few studies also able to look at detention times both before and after PACE (not, however, of a large representative sample of all detentions as ours was), Irving and McKenzie[17] found a drop of over two hours in average detention time between 1979 and 1986. Moreover, while Irving and McKenzie[18] found no statistically significant change in the duration of custody between 1986 and 1987, we found the overall mean had increased by one hour. One reason for this was a further increase in the take-up of legal advice in 1987 (those availing themselves of this right were detained, on average, over four hours longer than those who did not). A second reason was probably the increase in searches of premises of those arrested and in custody mentioned in the previous section, which would increase time in detention before charge. A further factor which was mentioned by a number of officers during interview was a certain 'easing off' in relation to certain procedures after the initial period when PACE was first implemented. As one officer put it:

. . . we tended to do everything by the letter of PACE initially, but not so much now. It's a little less tense and fraught than it was, that is to say chivvying people to get on with inquiries. We have eased off as far as time is concerned to allow more latitude.

This quotation illustrates a point of more general relevance about the impact of PACE: during the early months, custody officers and others were unsure about the elasticity of the new rules and how severely sanctions might be applied, while later on familiarity could lead to controlling procedures becoming routinised and less effective.

The other main effects of PACE on detention times, in our study, especially in 1987, were: a reduction in the proportion of very short detentions (less than two hours); an increase in the proportion released shortly before the six-hour review is due; an increase in the proportion

---

16 Bottomley, K., Coleman, C., Dixon, D., Gill, M. and Wall. D., 'The detention of suspects in police custody' (1991) 31 *British Journal of Criminology* 347.

17 Irving, B., and McKenzie, I., *Regulating Custodial Interviews: The Effects of the Police and Criminal Evidence Act 1984* (Police Foundation, London, 1988), vol. 1.

18 Irving, B., and McKenzie, I., *Police Interrogation: the Effects of PACE* (Police Foundation, London, 1989).

released after six hours but before 15 hours. These findings confirm the pattern suggested by Irving and McKenzie.[19] Very few persons (fewer than 1 per cent of our sample) were detained without charge for more than 24 hours.

These findings reflect to a considerable extent the system of reviews, at regular intervals and by different ranks or authorities as time progresses, that were designed to check the necessity of continued detention. We found that the inspectors' reviews (the first is after six hours) tended to lack substance, with little real opportunity for suspects to make representations and solicitors remarking that their representations rarely influence review officers, who regard early extensions of detention as routine. Reviews by superintendents (after 24 hours) are of a different order, helping to explain why it is rare for suspects to be kept in custody beyond the 24-hour point. This suggests that perhaps the 15-hour review should involve the authorisation of a superintendent, who, unlike the shift inspector, is removed from the investigation of the offence. This might help to ensure that attention is paid to whether further detention is strictly necessary.

For detentions without charge beyond 36 hours, applications must be made to magistrates; during 1990, 405 such applications were made in England and Wales, of which only four were refused.[20] Predictions made in the mid-1980s that detentions for four days would be common under PACE have not been fulfilled, but there is very considerable variation for no obvious reason between forces in the number of applications made, which may indicate inconsistencies in practice in the most serious circumstances.

Intimations and legal advice

Among the main safeguards for suspects that were strengthened by PACE and the Codes of Practice were the right to have someone informed of their arrest ('intimations') and access to legal advice. From our observations, suspects were invariably informed of their right to intimations on arrival at the police station, although this notification was not always recorded on the custody record. After PACE, about 25 per cent of suspects were recorded as having requested intimations, which was almost double the recorded figure for 1981 and 1984. Very few instances of officially delayed intimations were recorded, confirming the findings

---

19   (1988).
20   Home Office, *op. cit.* n. 9 above.

of Brown's national survey in which fewer than 1 per cent were delayed.[21] However, we did find evidence that intimations were at times delayed 'unofficially', both intentionally and unintentionally.

The evidence from our study suggests that PACE has significantly increased the proportion of suspects recorded as requesting and receiving legal advice. Seventeen per cent were recorded as requesting it in 1984, with 9 per cent receiving it. The respective figures rose to 23 per cent and 18 per cent in 1986, and to 26 and 22 per cent in 1987. Our figures after PACE are near the national average, but the latter conceals considerable variations between police force areas, with recorded request rates ranging from 14 per cent to 41 per cent. Such variations have not been satisfactorily explained, and one study suggests that custody records do not record all requests for advice.[22] There is a variety of factors which discourage requests which we have discussed elsewhere.[23] One factor we discovered was that suspects were not routinely made aware that advice in the station is free; it will be interesting to see the impact of the requirement to do this in the revised Code of Practice. A more comprehensive study of this area stresses the role of policy 'ploys' in discouraging access to advice.[24] Certainly officers do deliberately discourage requests and encourage suspects to cancel existing requests. However, in our study more important were suspects' entrenched attitudes towards legal advice and solicitors, and the attempts of officers to give what they considered to be good advice, such as the suggestion that legal advice will extend the detention. To call such advice a 'ploy' implies a particular interpretation of intent on the part of the police which we did not feel was necessarily present.

It is also important to mention issues connected with the nature and quality of legal advice. The legal adviser was frequently not a solicitor but a clerk, or 'runner'. These were often ex-police officers, whose experience may be useful for suspects but there is some danger that their background and connections may result in advice that is not necessarily in the suspect's best interests. Lack of experience and training may handicap solicitors who do not specialise in criminal work. Advice given over the telephone may be limited in its usefulness for suspects. When advisers

21 Brown, D., Detention at the Police Station under the Police and Criminal Evidence Act 1984, Home Office Research Study No. 104 (HMSO, London, 1989).

22 Sanders, A., Bridges, L., Mulvaney, A., and Crozier, G., Advice and Assistance at Police Stations and the 24 Hour Duty Solicitor Scheme (Lord Chancellor's Department, London, 1989).

23 Dixon, D., Bottomley, K., Coleman, C., Gill, M. and Wall, D., 'Safeguarding the rights of suspects in police custody', (1990) 1 Policing and Society 115.

24 Sanders et al., op. cit. and see the following chapter.

did attend interviews, 'advice' as such was seldom in evidence. In the interviews we observed, the adviser mainly adopted a 'watching brief', taking notes of the proceedings rather than intervening. This can, of course, still operate as a check on the way an interview is conducted. Solicitors and clerks do not routinely advise silence, but more frequently encourage confessions. There is no evidence that PACE has substantially increased reliance on the right of silence (claims here were based upon research now acknowledged to have methodological weaknesses[25]).

Vulnerable suspects

PACE requires an additional safeguard in the case of 'vulnerable suspects' — the presence of an appropriate adult. This was deliberately intended to prevent the kind of regrettable sequence of events which occurred in the *Confait* case, which was of major importance in the establishment of the Royal Commission on Criminal Procedure.[26] Our research suggested that the role of the appropriate adult was in need of further clarification and development for it to offer an effective safeguard. Parents were rarely told what their role was and could not be assumed to be protectors of the rights of their children. Even social workers, acting as appropriate adults, are not always given the necessary training or professional guidance on their role, and are not often available on a round-the-clock basis.[27] Some improvements have been made in the revised Code C, such as the requirement that the appropriate adult be informed of the purpose of the role, which is not simply to act as observer,[28] and that a parent estranged from the juvenile should not be asked to act if the juvenile objects.[29]

Questioning of suspects

In addition to the safeguards already discussed, PACE attempted to regulate the questioning of suspects while in custody. The process of

---

25 See Dixon, D., 'Politics, research and symbolism in criminal justice' (1991) 20 *Anglo-American Law Review* 27.

26 Baxter, J. and Koffman, L., 'The Confait inheritance' (1983) 14 *Cambrian Law Review*. See also Introduction.

27 For a detailed discussion of the treatment of juveniles under PACE, based on our research, see Dixon, D., 'Juvenile suspects and the Police and Criminal Evidence Act' in D. A. C. Freestone (ed.) *Children and the Law* (Hull University Press, 1990), pp. 107–29.

28 Para. 11.16.

29 Note for Guidance 1C.

interrogation is monitored by the custody officer, who, among many responsibilities, is required to limit the access of investigating officers to the suspect, ensure that a record is kept on the custody record of details of interviews with the prisoner, and receive reports from the investigating officer on the manner in which PACE and the Codes of Practice have been complied with (s. 39(3)). The other main change was the requirement that an accurate record be made of each interview in the form of contemporaneous notes or tape recordings.

The impact of contemporaneous notes in our force was to increase the total mean time for which suspects were interviewed from less than half an hour (before PACE) to almost three-quarters of an hour in 1987. Fewer persons were interviewed more than once, but the average length of each interview doubled between 1981 (18 minutes) and 1987 (37 minutes). Despite the many complaints about such notes being laborious and deskilling, half of the officers interviewed expressed favourable overall views about them, mainly because of their function in producing less challengeable evidence and fewer complaints of malpractice. For the same reasons (and the fact that contemporaneous notes had preceded it), tape recording was almost universally welcomed. In our research force this appears to have shortened the length of interviews, but increased significantly the time spent subsequently in processing the records. The eventual acceptance of these methods of recording interviews, which had been resisted in the not too distant past, shows how many officers came to realise the benefits of a number of changes introduced by PACE, which was not, after all, simply a 'criminal's charter'.

Nevertheless, such methods of regulating the questioning of suspects have their limitations. There are opportunities to question suspects outside the formal interview rooms and the controlling environment of the station, and suspects may be persuaded to repeat any admissions later in a formal interview. Even with interviews that are being formally recorded, suspects are routinely prepared beforehand (71 per cent of officers said they sometimes, often or always did this), and unrecorded interruptions, clarifications and discussions about other matters persist. These practices are difficult to eradicate when sometimes done at the request of the suspect and with the tacit approval of a legal adviser who may be present. The safeguards here, however, could be strengthened by amending s. 78 so that there would be a statutory presumption of inadmissibility for evidence collected in breach of the Codes.

Role of the custody officer

Finally, we return to the lynchpin in the package of safeguards provided by PACE to regulate detention and questioning: the custody officer. Despite the presumption of independence from the investigation (s. 36(5)) and the priority to be given to the care and custody of suspects, certain factors create difficulties. In one subdivision of our research force, custody officers were also required to perform the roles of station sergeant and communications sergeant. Elsewhere also, serious pressure was created at times by the onerous requirements of the role and the unpredictability of when multiple arrests might occur. Under these conditions the needs of detained persons and the requirements of the Code might be overlooked. Other pressures arose from the custody officers' relationships with investigating officers, particularly those from the CID who might be of higher rank. Although some felt vulnerable to this pressure, it would be wrong to suggest that custody officers routinely collude with investigating officers. Disagreements and conflicts did occur, there were examples of investigating officers' ploys to evade their monitoring and control, and the role had clearly established itself as commanding a certain authority among many officers of all ranks.[30] In general custody officers appeared to take their responsibilities very seriously and routinely carried out such duties as reading detained suspects their rights. However, perhaps owing partly to the pressures mentioned, certain procedures were routinised or even overlooked, such as determining on reception whether sufficient evidence exists to charge a suspect (s. 37(1)) and requiring reports from investigating officers on the observance of the Codes of Practice after interviews. In addition, not only was there variability amongst custody officers in practices, but it did appear that there had been some relaxation from the early months in the strictness and independence with which the custody officers performed their role.

More could be done to enhance the effectiveness of what is seen as a relatively unattractive role; officers complained that it was a very responsible one which could be stressful, and yet it did not count as the kind of operational experience required for promotion. Certainly an attempt should be made to enhance their position *vis-à-vis* investigating officers, and to minimise the conflicting pressures of the role. Custody

---

30 For a rather different view, see McConville, M., Sanders, A. and Leng, R., *The Case for the Prosecution: Police Suspects and the Construction of Criminality* (Routledge, London, 1991).

officers should not be appointed on a shift by shift basis as they are in some forces, or be expected to perform other duties which mean that the principle of independence and their key responsibilities are likely to be compromised or overlooked.

Conclusion

This chapter has discussed the impact of PACE upon some of the earliest stages in the investigation of crime and the processing of suspects. Since events here can be the first steps towards a miscarriage of justice (for example, the *Erroll Madden* case[31] began with a stop and search), it is important to regulate the conduct of the police. Our view is that PACE (in conjunction with other factors) has brought about changes in policing but has had more success inside than outside the station. There is clearly some way to go before we can be confident that the risk of further miscarriages of justice has been minimised. Even within the limitations of the framework provided by PACE, there is, for example, a need for organisational change (such as in the custody officer's role), for more and better training, and more incentives for compliance and greater sanctions for breaches of the rules to counteract the effects of the occupational culture and the routinisation of controlling procedures. Mere changes in the formal rules are limited as a means of reform.

It remains to be seen how PACE will ultimately affect the handling of serious cases of the type in which notorious miscarriages have occurred in the past. One view is that when, as in such cases, professional and/or political incentives and pressures are high, then PACE is likely to be by-passed. Alternatively, it could be that the possibility of losing a case may encourage compliance in such cases (but not perhaps in everyday ones). Given the example set by the *Birmingham Six*, the *West Midlands* and the *Tottenham Three* cases, the latter view may now be more realistic. It would be unfortunate if attention were devoted to circumstances in a number of notorious, but perhaps untypical, cases, while the routine treatment of suspects who are the bread and butter of the criminal justice system is overlooked.

EDITORS' COMMENTS

While accepting the need for reform, the CPS in its submission to the Royal Commission emphasises that PACE has reduced the possibility of

---

31   (1981) *The Guardian*, 9 March.

malpractice.[1] Yet the foregoing chapter finds many faults, and it should be remembered that some of the cases described in the Introduction (such as those relating to the West Midlands Serious Crime Squad) were post-PACE or (as in the case of the *Tottenham Three*) occurred during a period when police regulations were designed to mirror the proposed PACE regime.

Chapter 2 raises the perennial problem of who is to police the police — *'Quis custodiet ipsos custodies?'*. As is pointed out, several safeguards are adopted in PACE, but most — record-keeping, training and supervision by more senior uniformed officers — still rely on the diligence and good faith of the police. Some forms of control mechanism lie outside the hands of the police, such as the complaints system and lay visitors, but their scrutiny is at best fitful and is again dependent on police assistance.[2] The courts provide another source of influence, but consistent and general principles have yet to emerge on ss. 76 and 78 of PACE. Even if they did, there may be some doubt as to whether they would be fully internalised by the police without further ado. More radical solutions must therefore be considered if abuses or misuses of police powers are to be avoided.

In regard to stop and search powers, it is difficult to envisage any form of regulation which will assist. The essence of these powers is that they are street performances. The target encounters only relatively junior officers acting at the limits of their discretion. The officers know that in most cases a blank search will have no repercussions. As chapter 2 explains, the transaction is probably not recorded as a search anyway. Even if it is an official search, only targets found in possession of incriminating evidence will be taken back to superiors at the police station, unlike in the case of arrest, where the vast majority of subjects are documented at the station. Custody officers may not reject many applications for detention, but their oversight may be some deterrent to abusive arrests, and there is always a danger of a quiet ticking off. If supervision cannot be secured, the radical alternative is the abolition of most stop and search powers. After all, most police forces existed without them before 1986,[3] and the charging rate under PACE (which has never

---

1   (1990), para. 3.1.1. The Police Service also view the regulation of PACE as strict: para. 1.1.5.
2   On complaints, see Goldsmith, A. J. (ed.), *Complaints Against the Police* (Oxford University Press, 1991); Maguire, M. and Corbett, C., *A Study of the Police Complaints Sytem* (HMSO, London, 1991). On lay visitors see Kemp, C. and Morgan, R., *Lay Visitors to Police Stations* (Bristol University, 1990); Walker, C., 'Police and community in Northern Ireland' (1990) 41 NILQ 105.
3   The notable exception was the Metropolitan Police Act 1839, s. 66.

exceeded 17 per cent, compared to about 70 per cent charging or cautioning following arrest[4]) suggests that excessive police resources are being diverted into this exercise to no good purpose. The number of searches now being conducted (over a quarter of a million in 1990) does confirm the police's liking for this type of power. It is a flexible, handy power for the purposes of law enforcement, information-gathering and street control.[5] Yet the costs in terms of injustice to most of the individuals stopped for inadequate reasons and the poisoning of community relations are arguably too great. Thus, such powers should be available only in connection with very serious offences, the nature of which would give rise to reasonable suspicion only in very particular circumstances. Examples might include the carrying of firearms or Class A drugs.[6] Otherwise, police officers should rely upon their powers of arrest. Possible adverse consequences flowing from such a change might include an increase in arrests. However, as arrests are much more likely to be well-considered and justifiable, it is more likely the guilty rather than the innocent who are put at greater risk of loss of liberty. Another danger is that the withdrawal of broad stop and search powers will revive a greater reliance upon stops by consent or by bluff. However, as chapter 2 establishes, the existence of formal powers under PACE has not radically reduced such practices, and their withdrawal may serve to make the police more cautious.

In regard to searches of property, the regulatory regime is again deficient. Police rely on search after arrest and so avoid the inconvenience of obtaining a judicial warrant. It would be foolish to invest too much faith in the oversight of magistrates,[7] but there is no evidence that self-authorisation offers any barrier to unjustifiable searches whatsoever. The treatment of individuals in custody in terms of searches of them for incriminating evidence is even more scandalous and seems to stem from English law's blindness to the value of privacy.[8] Accordingly, those powers in ss. 32, 54, and 61 to 63 of PACE which authorise police searches of prisoners should be abolished, except perhaps in a serious

---

4   Liberty, *Submission* (1991), p. 13.
5   See Home Office Research and Planning Unit Paper No. 15, The Use, Effectiveness and Impact of Police Stop and Search Powers (1983); McConville M., *et al.*, *The Case for the Prosecution* (Routledge, London, 1991), p. 94.
6   Thus, the Firearms Act 1968, ss. 47 and 49 could remain and those powers in the Misuse of Drugs Act 1971, s. 23 as amended, but the powers in PACE, the Prevention of Terrorism (Temporary Provisions) Act 1989 and Northern Ireland (Emergency Provisions) Act 1991 should be repealed.
7   Lidstone, K. W., 'Magistrates, the police and search warrants' [1984] Crim LR 449.
8   *Malone v MPC (No. 2)* [1979] 3 WLR 700.

emergency or for items designed to injure or effect an escape. Thus, procedures such as fingerprinting and the taking of other bodily samples should require judicial authorisation, as was the case before 1984.[9] Regrettably, the Police Service and Home Office submissions to the Royal Commission argue in completely the opposite direction, with a particularly strong demand for powers to conduct intimate searches without consent or judicial authorisation.[10]

Next, there is the allegation that the custody officer system fails to protect the rights and welfare of police detainees. The concept is only likely to work if can instill a different occupational culture in custody officers, but the prospects are not good. Police cultures seem remarkably, though not absolutely, obdurate,[11] and the custody officer's eyes cannot be everywhere. Certainly, the analogous system in operation in Northern Ireland since 1979 has not proved wholly effective, albeit in far less propitious circumstances.[12]

One possible response would be to appoint custody officers from higher ranks (or perhaps to create a special rank of custody officer between sergeant and inspector) in the expectation that this will increase their influence and authority.[13] After all, there is evidence in chapter 2 that detention reviews by superintendents are feared. The drawbacks would be that such routine tasks would be resented by the most senior operational officers, and their appointment as such would be expensive and make unrealistic demands on available personnel.

A possible alternative solution would be to divest the police of their responsibilities and powers in relation to the detention of citizens aside from the initial arrest and transportation to a holding centre. The police would remain the investigative agency, but whether the suspect remained in custody pending their investigations would be the decision of a separate detention authority, which would also become responsible for the suspect's well-being during any detention. In this way, this apportionment of responsibilities need not undermine the adversarial nature of the system, but it would advance to a much earlier point non-police

---

9 See Magistrates' Courts Act 1980, s. 49.
10 Police Service, Evidence (1991), pp. 68–71; Home Office, Memoranda (1991), para. 1.14.
11 Compare McConville M., et al, *op. cit.*, p. 42; Dixon, D., 'Legal regulation and policing practice' (1992) 1(4) *Social & Legal Studies* 515.
12 These reforms followed the Bennett Report (Report of the Committee of Inquiry into Police Interrogation Procedures in Northern Ireland, Cmnd 7497, 1979). See Hogan, G. and Walker, C., *Political Violence and the Law in Ireland* (Manchester University Press, 1989), pp. 115–19.
13 Law Society, *Evidence* (1991), para. 1.14.

contact with detainees.[14] The detention agency could be a Next Steps agency,[15] though there may be some attractions to the Government in the introduction of private contractors as part of its civilianisation programme.[16] In any event, the agency must comprise, as well as gaolors, some legally trained officers who can deal with questions of detention, access and searches.

The separation of powers is a common technique in constitutional law to ensure limits on, and accountability for, governmental powers. The separation of detention and investigation would seem ripe for its application, especially as the criteria governing the two functions may conflict at many points. For example, the police often perceive their interests to include the ability to arrest and then to interrogate and pressurise suspects without interruption or outside interference. The interests of society in respect of individual rights demand that arrests be justifiable and that detention time be limited and spent properly. It follows that the police have an interest in frightening and cutting off the detainee from the outside world.[17] A detention authority would have priorities in terms of proper and humane treatment rather than results in terms of confessions. This division of functions could be taken further if the police were also to be divested of their post-arrest investigative role. Continental inquisitorial systems might be categorised as models reflecting this distinction, and so the matter will be discussed in chapter 11.

If, contrary to the foregoing suggestion, the custody officer is to remain, then additional protective measures which might be considered include severer sanctions to ensure compliance with the PACE rules. For example, any serious breach might automatically result in exclusion of evidence so obtained; alternatively, the CPS might interpret any prosecution in those circumstances as contrary to the public interest,

---

14 It would also, in the light of evidence that 99 per cent of detainees are processed within 24 hours (Brown, D., Detention at the Police Station under PACE, Home Office Research Study No. 104, 1989), advance judicial scrutiny to that point. Submissions to the Royal Commission have suggested 12 hours (Legal Action Group, Liberty, p. 17), 24 hours (Law Society, para. 1.100, Justices' Clerks' Society, para. 1.5), 36 hours (Police Service, p. 77).

15 See Prime Minister's Efficiency Unit, Improving Management in Government (1988) (the 'Ibbs Report').

16 Home Office Circular No. 105/1988, Civilian Staff in the Police Service.

17 These realities were recognised and sanctioned by the House of Lords in Holgate-Mohammed v Duke [1984] AC 437.

whether or not based on a confession.[18] Next, even the Police Service submission to the Royal Commission accepts the need for the video-taping of interviews[19] so as to make explicit to the jury any pressurisation by the police or nuances by body language or in the words spoken by the suspect. Some commentators have expressed fears that videos would faithfully record the confession but not the pressures and threats arising from contacts when the camera is switched off or the suspect is in the cells.[20] However, a written or taped confession would be equally damaging in such circumstances — the trouble rests with the custody officer failing to record all contacts rather than with the method of recording when it is activated.[21] A more serious problem which is inherent in video-recording is that it will in most cases present a rather prejudicial contrast between scruffy, nervous and shifty-looking suspects and confident, sharp-suited detectives.[22] Further possible measures include regular medical checks, the greater visibility of lay visitors and readier intervention by the courts. Above all, it is commonly suggested that the availability of legal advice will ensure fair play and proper treatment. The role of solicitors in regard to detainees in police custody will be considered next.

---

18 LAG, *Submission* (1991); Criminal Bar Association, *Submissions* (1991); NACRO, para. 6; Liberty, pp. 6 and 54. Compare JUSTICE, *Evidence* (1991), p. 23, CPS, *Submission* (1990), para. 10.9.1, Police Service, p. 229. Another approach is to create a presumption of inadmissibility: NSW Law Reform Commission, *Police Powers of Detention and Investigation after Arrest* (LRC 66, 1990), para. 8.4.1.
19 At p. 99. See also: CPS, *Submission* (1990), para. 3.11.5; *Justice, Evidence* (1991), p. 10. But see Home Office, *Memoranda* (1991), para. 1.48; Liberty, pp. 23–4.
20 See McConville, M., 'Videotaping interrogations' [1992] Crim LR 532.
21 Recording remains beneficial in that reference is often made to prior exchanges: Baldwin, J., 'Suspect interviews' (1992) 142 NLJ 1095.
22 Baldwin, J., 'Video-taping in police stations' (1991) 141 NLJ 1512.

3

The Right to Legal Advice

Andrew Sanders and Lee Bridges

Introduction

Prior to PACE, access to legal advice was allowed by the Judges Rules only provided that 'no unreasonable delay or hindrance' be thereby suffered by the police. This gave the police considerable latitude for which they were rarely called to account. There are no reliable figures for the numbers of suspects requesting or receiving advice before 1984, but Softley found that 7 per cent of suspects requested advice in the late-1970s in his study of four police stations.[1] Nearly one in five requests was refused by the police. The Judges' Rules also provided that all suspects should 'be informed orally of the rights and facilities available to them'. However, in Softley's study all suspects were informed of their rights in only one station. In that station the request rate was three times as high as in the other three. So, when the police informed suspects of their rights the request rate rose, but the police could not be relied upon to do this. More commonly, the police often broke and 'bent' the law (both on informing suspects of their rights and on allowing access when it was requested).

In this chapter we will be concerned with the changes under PACE which superseded the Judges Rules and how effective those changes have been, both in general and in preventing miscarriages of justice.

---

1   Softley, P., *Police Interrogation: An Observational Study in Four Police Stations: Research Study No. 4* (HMSO, London, 1981).

Exercising the right

The effect of PACE on request rates

PACE, s. 58(1) provides that 'A person arrested and held in custody . . . shall be entitled, if he so requests, to consult a solicitor privately at any time.' The proviso in the Judges Rules has been replaced by s. 58(6) and (8), which allow the police to delay access, rather than to deny it, and to do so only in very restricted circumstances. Further, the Code of Practice for the Detention, Treatment and Questioning of Persons by the Police (COP) obliges the police to inform suspects of their rights. This is done orally by a custody officer and by a written notice. Apart from the fact there is no specific remedy or enforcement mechanism, there is now, for the first time, an absolute right to legal advice and to be informed of that right.

Moreover, s. 59 (as amended by the Legal Aid Act 1988, sch. 6) provides free legal aid for suspects, enabling duty solicitor schemes to be established. Far more suspects are now able to see solicitors than could those prior to PACE. However, it is little use ensuring the ready availability of solicitors free of charge without also informing suspects of that facility. The written notice provided under the original version of COP did not mention it. The revised Code, which came into operation in April 1991, does require full information to be provided and, as we shall see, makes a number of other detailed but important changes.

In addition to the right to advice in s. 58, there are important new rights to consult the COP (para. 1.2), to have someone informed of one's arrest and to speak to someone on the phone (s. 56). All these rules apply to every arrested person, regardless of age or suspected offence (and extra protections are provided for juveniles and other vulnerable individuals), with two exceptions. The first is a suspect who is 'incapable . . . of understanding what is said to him or is violent or likely to become violent' (COP, para. 1.8). The second is that rights are severely curtailed in respect of suspects detained under the Prevention of Terrorism (Temporary Provisions) Act 1989. Since this is covered in chapter 9, we will not discuss it here. It is worth observing, however, that these categories of suspect remain as vulnerable as all suspects were in the 1970s and early-1980s.

Since there are no national data on requests for advice, we have to rely on research studies of particular police stations for a picture of the working of these rights. Brown found that, on average, around 25 per cent of all suspects requested advice, and that around 21 per cent secured it (although only 17.5 per cent did so prior to charge).[2] In subsequent research, in which we observed the processing of suspects and interviewed officers, solicitors, and suspects, in 10 police stations for 45 days each throughout 1988, we secured similar results. Interestingly, both Brown and ourselves found great variations between different stations which we could not explain.[3] Although a 25 per cent request rate represents a dramatic increase over the pre-PACE situation, three out of four suspects still appear to be refusing a free gift, and a further 6–8 per cent who accept the offer fail to receive it in time or do not receive it at all.

Factors influencing request rates

Out of the 103 suspects we interviewed, 60 said that they knew that they had a right to legal advice, and only two said that they did not. However, 14 of the 60 (23.3 per cent) only knew this because the police had told them, and 12 out of 38 (31.6 per cent) still remained ignorant that the service was free.[4] It is clearly still important that suspects be given all relevant information by the police if they are to make informed decisions, yet around 10 per cent of all suspects were not accorded their rights on reception. Only 16.1 per cent of this group requested a solicitor, according to the custody records, as compared to 25.5 per cent of the suspects who were fully informed of their rights.

Failure to inform suspects that advice would be free did not seem to have such a marked impact, perhaps because when that information was provided — in most cases, via a badly written and complicated leaflet alone (since revised) — that had little effect either. However, many suspects who declined advice because of the triviality of their offences may not have done so had they realised that it would be free, as the following explanations given to us suggest:

> Something like drunk and disorderly is not really worth it because you don't get legal aid for things like that.

> It's not a serious offence anyway . . . not worth seeking advice and spending money for in my opinion.

---

2 Brown, D., *Detention at the Police Station under the PACE Act 1984* (HMSO, London, 1989).

3 Sanders, A., Bridges, L., Mulvaney, A., Crozier, G., *Advice and Assistance at Police Stations and the 24 Hour Solicitor Scheme*, (Lord Chancellor's Department, 1989).

4 The numbers do not 'add up' because in a large number of interviews no comprehensible responses could be secured.

. . . I work and I'd have to pay for a solicitor.

Notwithstanding the above concern, many suspects would not have wanted a solicitor under any circumstances. Some are too fatalistic, while others are remarkably confident. Here are some typical responses:

There was nothing to hide.

I think they [the police] have been very good to me and I'm quite happy.

I don't see the point . . . I was going to admit to it.

I knew what I was going to tell them . . . I was involved but I didn't put it into his face. They [the police] were trying to tell me that I had stuck it into his face.

Q. 'Do you think a solicitor could have helped?' A. 'No.' Q. 'Did you actually admit the offence?' A. 'They sort of put words into my mouth.'

As some of these examples indicate, confidence (or, indeed, fatalism) may sometimes be misplaced. Many suspects are unaware of how helpful a solicitor could be in ensuring that their stories are told properly.

For some suspects it is not that legal help is unwelcome in principle, rather, that solicitors as such are disliked and distrusted:

They [solicitors] are a waste of time . . . most are there just to earn their money.

Some suspects differentiate duty solicitors from their own solicitors. As we shall see, there is some basis in fact for this view, and the following suspects capture the feelings of many:

Q. 'Would you ask for a duty solicitor again?' A. 'No, I'd ask for my own.' Q. 'Why?' A. 'Because he weren't no bloody good!'

. . . I told my mother to get me one . . . When I was arrested before, the police put their own man in . . . and he acted like a policeman.

Perhaps the most important influence on suspects is the time factor. Suspects who believed that a solicitor would shorten their time in custody (for example, by securing bail) usually asked for one, while those who believed the opposite (perhaps because they would have to wait for one to arrive) usually did not:

Suspect: 'Is it going to take time to get one [a solicitor]?'
Officer: '. . . I haven't got one in the cupboard . . . I'll call one . . .'

Suspect: 'I'll have one when I'm charged . . .'
Officer: 'I asked you if you wanted a solicitor.'
Suspect: 'It depends how long I'm in here . . .'

One thing that put me off seeing a solicitor is that I would have been longer here.

One suspect wrote on the custody record 'I agree to be interviewed without the presence of a solicitor only on provision that I am released a.s.a.p.'. Needless to say, she was not. It follows from all this that suspects who do ask for solicitors usually do so if they are scared of the police, afraid of being detained overnight, or if they recognise specific problems with which they need immediate help. Only occasionally do suspects (usually the more experienced ones) ask for advice simply because it is free or in an attempt to obstruct the police. Many suspects are so indecisive that they seek advice from the police on whether they should seek advice!

The conundrum, then, is this: why is only one out of every four suspects afraid of being unaided? Why are three out of every four suspects so trusting of the police, distrustful of solicitors or confident of their own abilities, when objectively so many could benefit from advice? The answer lies, in part, with the police: as we shall see, they often play on fears about delay and cost. It also lies with solicitors: many do take time to arrive, many more do not arrive at all, and yet more simply 'advise' suspects to confess. But most important of all is a joint message from both: that what happens in the station is really not that important, and court is where guilt and innocence is decided. This is far from the truth, as the centrality of 'confession evidence' in the recent miscarriage cases shows, but it suits the police, the legal profession, and the State to maintain this ideology.[5]

---

5 McConville, M., Sanders, A. and Leng, R., *The Case for the Prosecution* (Routledge, London, 1991).

The Police

Under PACE, access to a solicitor is not automatic. It has to be positively requested by the suspect. This requires the negotiation of several obstacles. First, suspects need to know their rights. Secondly, they need to make and then maintain their requests unambiguously in the face of possible police obstruction. Thirdly, they need the police to act on those requests by actually contacting a solicitor. Since we have discussed these matters at length elsewhere,[6] we shall discuss them only briefly here.

We observed the processing of 801 suspects. Custody records chart the provision of their rights in 93.9 per cent of cases. Seemingly, 2.9 per cent were unlawfully denied their rights (the rest were deemed 'incapable' due to drunkenness or violence). Yet we observed only 87 per cent to be given the required written notice, and 85.4 per cent to be informed orally. Apart from the sheer failure to provide information to so many suspects according to the law, there are two issues here. First, as we have seen, failure to notify suspects of their rights makes it less likely that those rights will be asserted. Secondly, the level of unlawful failure to notify suspects of their rights was over three times as high on our observations than custody records reveal. These figures show that the police do in practice either falsify or wrongly complete custody records, making it appear that they are more law abiding than they really are. For instance, rights were read to only eight of the 13 suspects observed by us who allegedly 'refused to sign'. Overall, rather than breaching COP in 2.9 per cent of cases (according to custody records), we found that the police actually breach it in 10.5 per cent of cases.

Police ploys

It would be misleading simply to concentrate on formal compliance. Being *informed* of one's rights is not the same as *understanding* those rights. Gudjunsson has found that the official leaflet was too complicated for most suspects with a lower than average IQ to understand.[7] Furthermore, we found that the oral provision of information by custody officers was often too garbled and/or hurried to be understood. Among various 'ploys' used by the police to dissuade suspects from seeking advice, the incomplete or incomprehensible reading of rights (ploys 1 and 14) were the most common (see Table 3.1). We observed one or more

---

6   Sanders, A. and Bridges, L., 'Access to legal advice and police malpractice' [1990] Crim LR 494.

7   Gudjonsson, G., 'Understanding the notice to detained persons', (1990) 43 LS Gaz 24.

ploys being used in 41.4 per cent of cases, and two or more in 9.3 per cent. All of our 10 stations used these ploys, though some did so more than others.

Table 3.1: Types of ploy

Ploy	Frequency (Principal ploy only)	
1. Rights told too quickly/incomprehensibly/ incompletely	142	(42.9%)
2. Suspect query answered unhelpfully/incorrectly	5	(1.5%)
3. Inability of suspect to name own solicitor	2	(0.6%)
4. 'It's not a very serious charge'	1	(0.3%)
5. 'You'll have to wait in the cells until the solicitor gets here'	13	(3.9%)
6. 'You don't have to make up your mind now. You can have one later if you want to'	27	(8.2%)
7. 'You're only going to be here a short time'	25	(7.6%)
8. 'You're only here to be charged/interviewed'	14	(4.2%)
9. (To juvenile) 'You'll have to [or 'do you want to'] wait until an adult gets here'	18	(5.4%)
10. (To adult) '[Juvenile] has said he doesn't want one'	8	(2.4%)
11. Combination of 9 and 10	4	(1.2%)
12. 'We won't be able to get a solicitor at this time/none of them will come out/he won't be in his office'	6	(1.8%)
13. 'You don't need one for this type of offence'	2	(0.6%)
14. 'Sign here, here and here' (no information given)	7	(2.1%)
15. 'You don't have to have one'	4	(1.2%)
16. 'You're being transferred to another station — wait until you get there'	6	(1.8%)
17. Custody officer interprets indecision/silence as refusal	9	(2.7%)
18. 'You're not going to be interviewed/charged'	1	(0.3%)
19. 'You can go and see a solicitor when you get out/at court'	9	(2.7%)
20. 'You're (probably) going to get bail'	6	(1.8%)
21. Gives suspects Solicitors' Directory or list of solicitors without explanation/assistance	3	(0.9%)
22. Other	19	(5.7%)
TOTAL	331	(100.0%)

Not only do ploys obstruct suspects' understanding of their rights (misleading suspects as to the cost of advice being another example), but they are also designed to dissuade suspects from making requests and to persuade them to cancel those requests. Being told to 'sign here, here and here' (ploy 14) is difficult to resist even when one knows one may be signing away one's rights. Moreover, some ploys reinforce the negative aspects of seeking advice (such as having to wait: ploy 5). Others, by reassurance, bolster the naive feeling of confidence possessed by many suspects (telling suspects that they can have a solicitor later (ploy 6), even though the police rarely repeat the offer later). Other ploys crucially underplay the importance of police station procedures (ploys 4, 7, 8, 13, 18, 19, 20).

These ploys have not been perceived as being so Machiavellian by all researchers.[8] Others see much of what we describe as 'ploys' as simply the provision of information (the likely delay in securing a solicitor, for instance). At one level we would not disagree. And as we observed earlier, the police cannot be faulted for engaging in discussion when so many suspects ask their advice! The problem is the information which is *not* provided by the police. Suspects are *not* told the advice will be free. Suspects are *not* told that they will spend hours in the cells awaiting interview regardless of whether or not they request advice. Suspects are *not* told that telephone advice can be secured with virtually no delay at all. Suspects are *not* told that a solicitor is far more useful in the station than in the court. Inarticulate, confused and indecisive suspects are not assumed to want, or told that they should seek, advice.

On closer inspection, Dixon et al. found police practices similar to those we observed, although they did not attempt to quantify them. Morgan et al. found 'active discouragement, leading questions or incomplete statement of rights . . . in about 14 per cent of observed cases'.[9] In the 'overwhelming majority of cases', they say, rights are stated in a way that anyone in a reasonable state of mind would comprehend. But they concede that 'few suspects are in a "reasonable" frame of mind at the time. There is usually no attempt to make sure the statement has been understood'.[10] Behind the different emphasis of other researchers there is, then, no fundamental disagreement: in many cases — perhaps the

---

8   Morgan, R., Reiner, R. and McKenzie, I., Report to ESRC: A Study of the Work of Custody Officers (unpublished); Dixon, D., Bottomley, K., Coleman, C., Gill, M. and Wall, D., 'Safeguarding the rights of suspects in police custody' (1990) 1 *Policing and Society* 2.

9   Morgan, R. et al., *op. cit.*, p. 22.

10 *Ibid.*, p. 23C.

majority — the police allow suspects who are unsure of their rights to remain unsure.

We found little correlation between the use of just one ploy and requests for advice. However, when police officers have a particular interest in preventing or delaying access, they tend to use several ploys to discourage a request or, if a request has already been made, to secure cancellation or a waiver of the suspect's right to delay interrogation until the solicitor's arrival. We found a strong correlation between the use of multiple ploys and failures to request/cancellations/waivers. We also suspected that police behaviour was modified when we were observing them, although, worryingly, not as much as one would expect. However, some suspects who initially insisted on seeing a solicitor were hustled out of our sight, only to be returned a few minutes later with a new willingness to waive their rights!

Lastly, in a small but significant number of cases the police failed to record requests (for instance by crossing out the wrong line on the custody record) and failed to secure legal advice when requested and recorded. Now that outright refusal of access is unlawful, and delay under s. 58(6) and (8) is restricted to exceptional circumstances (3 per cent of requests or fewer), it seems that the police resort to less overt, but equally effective, denials of access.[11]

The revised Code of Practice

Since our research (and that by the other teams mentioned) was completed, COP has been revised. Several ploys are now outlawed. For instance, rights must be read 'clearly' and must include the fact that advice is free (para. 3.1); the written information provided also now includes this fact (para. 3.2); the custody officer is responsible for ensuring that suspects sign 'in the correct place' and he 'must act without delay to secure the provision' of advice when requested (para. 3.5); and the right of juveniles and other vulnerable suspects to advice prior to the arrival of an 'appropriate adult' has been clarified (note 3G). These changes were recommended in our original report to the Lord Chancellor's Department. But we also stated there that:

A key problem is that the presumption in PACE and in actual police behaviour is against having advice . . . If PACE required a positive decision to refuse advice . . . the take up rate would probably rise considerably.[12]

---

11   See, for details, Sanders, A. and Bridges, L., *op. cit.* Also see Maguire, M., 'Effects of the PACE provisions on detention and questioning' (1988) 28 *British Journal of Criminology* 19.

12   Sanders, A. et al., *op. cit.*, p. 80.

Needless to say, this recommendation was not implemented. The result is that access is still sought by only a minority of suspects. Moreover, since the police were prepared to break the law under the old Code in the ways we have described, it would not be surprising to find that they continue to do so now. Having said this, we have never argued that the police strongly discourage access in all (or perhaps even most) cases, and there are even suspects and solicitors whom the police wish to put together prior to interrogation.[13] Thus the changes to COP would be expected to influence police behaviour at the margins. The result is an increase of around one-third in the numbers requesting duty solicitors between 1 April 1991 and 1 September 1991.[14]

However welcome this is, we should not forget that when the police strongly wish to confront suspects on their own, they have every opportunity to do so — before a request is made, before the solicitor arrives, and between interrogations. In addition, 'informal' interviewing — uncontrolled interrogation outside the surveillance of tape recorders — still goes on.[15] The revised COP attempts to restrict it but, crucially, provides several loopholes for the police. The small number of cases where this happens may make little statistical impact on rates of access, but if miscarriages arise from the police's determination from the moment of initial detention to secure incriminating statements from selected suspects in major crimes, clearly the current arrangements for access will not stop this. It is worth remembering that none of the suspects in the *Birmingham*, *Guildford* or *Tottenham* cases, and very few in the *West Midlands Serious Crime Squad* cases, were allowed to see a solicitor.[16]

The Response of Solicitors

It is no use having a right to a solicitor if none can be found when needed or if the service is too expensive. This was recognised by the Government, which provided for free advice and assistance from either one's

---

13 Dixon, D., 'Common sense, legal advice, and the right of silence' [1991] *Public Law* 233.

14 Unpublished Legal Aid Board figures. Our thanks to Simon Hilliard for providing them.

15 See Kaye, T., *Unsafe and Unsatisfactory? Report of the Independent Inquiry into the Working Practices of the West Midlands Police Serious Crime Squad* (Civil Liberties Trust, London, 1991). Also see Evans, R. and Ferguson, T., *Comparing Different Juvenile Cautioning Systems in One Police Force Area*, Report to Home Office (1991); McConville, M. et al., *op. cit.*; Sanders, A. and Bridges, L., *op. cit.*

16 Kaye, T., *op. cit.*

own solicitor or a duty solicitor.[17] Duty solicitor schemes for nearly every magistrates' court area have now been established. On a rota scheme there is always someone on duty who is obliged to provide advice and who receives a 'stand by' payment as well as specific payments for each suspect assisted. With panel schemes no one solicitor is on duty, and there is no 'stand by' payment. When suspects request duty solicitors, custody officers contact an answering service (previously Air Call, but the AA since 1 January 1992), which attempts to find a duty solicitor. That solicitor will then phone the station and speak to the custody officer and/or the suspect.

Of the 25 per cent approximately of suspects who requested advice prior to 1 April 1991 (when the revised Code took effect), around 19 per cent actually secured advice prior to charge. As we have seen, police malpractices (sometimes blatant law-breaking) explain the gap in part. However, the contribution to miscarriages of justice made by the absence of meaningful legal assistance cannot be blamed on the police alone. The legal profession is equally responsible.

Delay

Some requests fail because suspects will not wait for the solicitor. Of those solicitors who attend the station, fewer than 60 per cent manage it within one hour of being contacted (and contact itself takes over one hour in 7 per cent of requests). This cannot be entirely the fault of the profession but, significantly, suspects' own solicitors tend to be quicker at getting to the station than do duty solicitors. If delay were a product solely of factors beyond the lawyers' control, it should be randomly spread rather than patterned in this way. The inference is that if the suspect is not the client of the solicitor in question, the suspect is given a low priority.

Delay is a problem not just because it leads to overall dissatisfaction with the legal profession and an unwillingness to wait for, or even to request, a solicitor. It also leaves suspects vulnerable to police malpractice. In particular, the police are more easily able to 'get at' a suspect and secure incriminating statements if the suspect is anxiously waiting for his solicitor, not knowing when (or if) he or she is going to turn up.

No solicitor available

The second problem is that there is sometimes no solicitor available (or willing) to advise. Suspects' own solicitors are unavailable more often

---

17   Originally provided in PACE, s. 59. Now see the Legal Aid Act 1988, sch. 6.

than duty solicitors, though the difference is not as great as one would
expect, for duty solicitor unavailability ought to approach nil. Anyone
unavailable when on duty on a rota could be excluded from the scheme,
which ought to be an important deterrent. In practice, though, local
administrators are afraid of alienating their duty solicitors in case so few
remain that schemes become unviable, as these comments about unavailability, made to us by two different administrators show:

> I will certainly mention the matter at an appropriate local committee
> meeting. I am not convinced that there is a great deal I can do about
> the matter or indeed that it would be politic for me to write to the
> individual participants. I fear that a letter from me might be wrongly
> construed as a criticism.

> I am quite relieved that there were only four occasions, given the
> number of solicitors now participating in the scheme. Looking at my
> list, F, S, G, V, M and S all prosecute one or two days a week and I am
> thus not at all surprised that Air Call had difficulty in getting anybody.

One of these schemes, covering a large town, had dropped from 30
participating solicitors to 13. Another scheme was down to three solicitors.

Phone advice

The third problem is the manner in which advice is delivered. Solicitors
may advise on the phone or attend the station (or both). When at the
station they are entitled to advise the suspect privately, to attend the
interrogation and provide support for as long as the suspect is in police
custody. None of this is possible via the phone, yet around 30 per cent of
advice is by telephone alone. Even in serious cases phone advice alone is
used in 20 per cent of cases. Moreover, duty solicitors provide phone
advice far more frequently than do suspects' own solicitors. In some
areas, such as South London or Leicester, telephone advice only is given
in a substantial majority of referrals to duty solicitors.

According to the Law Society,[18] solicitors should decide what type of
advice and assistance is required and then decide whether to attend in
person or not (or send a representative or not, as discussed below) on that
basis. In fact, financial factors are at least as influential. Solicitors broadly
do what is in their economic interest, as one would expect of a small
business. While advice in person is paid at a higher rate than advice on

---

18   Law Society, *Advising a Suspect in the Police Station* (Law Society, London, 1991).

the phone, part of the 'stand by' payment is clawed back out of fees earned when on duty. There is therefore less incentive for duty solicitors to advise in person than there is for suspects' own solicitors to do so. Also, unless they are avidly looking for more clients, there is less reason for duty solicitors, as compared to suspects' own solicitors, to satisfy suspects in police stations (who often would return to their own solicitors anyway). This became apparent in conversation with solicitors, one of whom referred to attending his own clients as 'a public relations exercise'. Another told us that:

> I would always go down for my own clients purely because they are my seed-corn, if you like. With the DS scheme I don't feel the same level of loyalty although I wouldn't like to think that people didn't get proper service.

Another solicitor was critical of colleagues:

> I fear that there are certain people . . . who would just speak to everyone on the phone.

Many suspects, not surprisingly, flounder when confronted with the police. A phone conversation, often with an anonymous voice to which neither name nor face can be put, is not much help. As one put it, had his solicitor attended, 'you could have talked to him, you know, tell him more things you wouldn't say on the phone . . . If you met him face to face you could talk.' Another said,

> . . . he gave me a certain amount of advice. But obviously I wasn't going to say a lot over the phone to anybody . . . Well you never know do you? I could have been speaking to another policeman, you never know.

The phone advice which was provided was often valueless:

> He said basically stick to your story and hopefully you'll get bailed and that was most of what he said . . . If I got charged with it I was to take the charge-sheet down to him.

> I thought they automatically came down but we only spoke on the phone. He said 'You're making a mountain out of a molehill. Probably what you'll be fined is £10 . . . It's only a minor offence'. I suppose it is minor but these people are making a big issue out of it saying 'It's a

criminal offence' . . . I think if it happened again I would arrange to have a solicitor with me at all times because the ordinary man in the street doesn't stand a chance once they get their teeth into him.

A particular point made in all the official guidance and by solicitors in conversation is the importance of a solicitor in the interrogation. Yet not only do solicitors fail to attend one-third of those suspects who ask for advice and who are interrogated, they also attend only 80 per cent of the interrogations in cases where they do attend the station. This means that, overall, only 14 per cent of interrogated suspects have a lawyer (or a representative) with them in the interrogation.

The distress caused by solicitor responses is sometimes harrowing. We saw far more suspects upset by the failures of lawyers than by police action, although we cannot discount the fact that the police knew we were watching and the lawyers did not. Many suspects were advised on the phone to stay silent, but of course they rarely did once under police pressure. Some of these suspects tried refusing interrogation on the ground that their solicitors were not there, but of course the police refused to accept this. Other suspects were hardly advised at all. We asked the mother of one suspect what advice the solicitor provided, and she replied, 'Not a lot really. Mainly her choices: she could either say nothing in the interview or she could make it easy on herself.'

Advice and advisers

The fourth problem is the competence and approach of the legal adviser. Legal executives, articled clerks, and other 'representatives' are used in over one-third of all cases. In our research, over 55 per cent of own solicitor cases that entailed a visit to the station, and where the status of the adviser could be determined, were dealt with by representatives. While not all representatives are necessarily worse than qualified solicitors, one can have little confidence in the 'runners' with no training who are often used in this type of work. Moreover, few solicitors assess the case in question and then decide whether it is suitable for a representative. Most simply send representatives wherever possible, and sometimes in breach of the rules of their local scheme.

Whether the solicitor or representative has an adversarial attitude is more important than qualifications and status. Few advisers seem to be adversarial, as is apparent from the dissatisfaction of the suspects we listed in the previous section. Even advisers who attend are generally passive and let the police set the agenda. They rarely intervene in interrogations, to remind clients of their rights or to prevent them being brow-beaten. Their advice to their clients is often to confess, and rarely to remain silent.[19] In one typical case, when we asked what advice the solicitor provided the suspect replied 'He just asked me to plead guilty'. In another the suspect actually argued with her solicitor who put the police case to her. As she put it in interview with us, 'But I hadn't admitted it. . . . it was all hearsay.' The custody officer told us that 'nine times out of 10 . . . he says "well do as the policeman says and be a good boy and you'll be out soon".'

Duty solicitor committees have been largely unconcerned with the most important issues affecting the quality of legal representation (phone advice, stance), and more concerned with numerically smaller issues (unavailability) and issues of professional concern alone (ensuring that duty solicitors do not 'poach' other solicitors' clients). This may reflect a lack of interest in the quality of advice because of the absence of financial incentive, or, as with unavailability, reflect fear that the imposition of high standards could lead to even smaller numbers of solicitors being willing to participate in local schemes.[20] It may also reflect the more fundamental problem that most defence lawyers do not, in reality, subscribe to the due process adversarial values that supposedly underpin the system. They rarely operate with a presumption of innocence and are loath to make the police prove their case, unless the client convinces them that he or she is innocent.[21]

New duty solicitor rules

As a result of our original report, there have been some new developments. The Legal Aid Board (LAB) now requires duty solicitors to attend the station when there is to be an interrogation (although not necessarily to attend the interrogation), if there are complaints of police mistreatment (another circumstance in which we found non-attendance problems), and so forth. Duty solicitors who do not attend in these circumstances have to explain why on the claim form. Suspects' own solicitors may continue to act as they wish. Although, as we have seen, failures of service are more common among duty solicitors, suspects' own solicitors could hardly be regarded as so superior as to be above the need for regulation.

---

19   Dixon, D., *op. cit.*
20   Cape, E., 'New duties for duty solicitors' (1991) 13 LS Gaz 19.
21   McConville, M. et al., *op. cit.*

To change rules in ways which benefit suspects but not those operating those rules (be it police officers or solicitors) is no guarantee that adverse practices will cease. We have seen that, in relation to the revision of COP, adverse police practices have probably been reduced. However, the average legal aid bill per suspect increased by only 5.8 per cent between August 1990 and August 1991, which is, in fact, a smaller percentage than the rise in the rate of renumeration which also took effect from 1 April 1991.[22] This suggests that solicitors are neither attending stations in a higher proportion of calls, nor spending longer there when they do attend. It seems that it is easier to change police practices than the iron laws of private enterprise economics.

This has not stopped solicitors protesting about the new rules. Merseyside duty solicitors actually refused to implement them, forcing the LAB to water down the attendance requirement.[23] When we did our research (1987–9), duty solicitors avoided attendance because it was uneconomic and disruptive; now many just refuse to implement the rules, pull out of the scheme or go on 'strike' (albeit that duty solicitor 'strikes' in December 1991 and January 1992 were protests against other developments in the criminal legal aid system).[24] These were precisely the fears of local administrators which we reported earlier.

Another ingenious way of avoiding the personal commitment required in providing a full service to clients is a new scheme devised by Health Call (previously Air Call, which lost its LAB contract to the AA in 1991). The clients of solicitors subscribing to Health Call's 'own solicitor service' will find that telephone calls will not go to their chosen solicitor at all. Instead they will go to Health Call's own solicitors who will provide phone advice. The suspect's solicitor will be roused from his or her cocktail party or home video only if attendance is deemed necessary by a Health Call solicitor. This is a worrying development, because solicitors will subscribe to this service precisely in order to reduce the number of suspects on whom they are required to attend during unsocial hours.[25]

Conclusion

We have seen that the practices of both police officers and the legal profession have led to a minority of suspects securing legal advice prior

---

22 Unpublished Legal Aid Board figures.
23 Now see the Duty Solicitor (Amendment) Arrangements 1991, amending para. 55 of the 1990 arrangements.
24 *Guardian*, 13 December 1991, 12 January 1992.
25 May 1991 *LAG Bulletin* 4.

to interrogation. Attempts to tighten the rules have led to more suspects securing advice, but the proportion of those advised who actually see a solicitor or clerk does not seem to have risen. When we did our research, 14 per cent of suspects were accompanied by a legal adviser in interrogation. It is doubtful whether that figure has risen to even 20 per cent. It is true that many suspects choose not to seek advice or to wait for it. However, the practices which we have described are bound to increase the numbers who do not consider it worth asking or waiting for. Even when a solicitor is secured speedily, does come to the station, and does attend the interrogation — and at each stage the numbers get smaller — if the solicitor adopts an entirely non-adversarial stance, it really will not have been worth the effort.

It is not clear to us why solicitors are so non-adversarial. It is possible that it is not in the financial interest of lawyers to be adversarial in the station. The problems of delay, unavailability, phone advice and unqualified 'runners' arise from the inevitably low priority given to relatively low paid work. Only a minority of practices specialises in criminal work and, with very few worthy exceptions, these need to adopt bureaucratic, rather than adversarial, procedures to keep themselves afloat financially. It may also be that many solicitors, including some in the notorious miscarriage cases, are out of sympathy with the suspects and/or are convinced of their guilt because of the power of the police/media machine.

In so many miscarriage cases, 'confessions' are virtually the only evidence.[26] If the falsification of evidence by the police and/or the dubious circumstances in which it is obtained is to be prevented or uncovered, then at a minimum a solicitor must be present prior to interrogation. The link between miscarriages and lack of access to lawyers should now be obvious for anyone — including the Royal Commission on Criminal Justice — to see. Equally clear is the crucial importance for the outcome of any case like this of support from a lawyer in the station.[27] Waiting until after the charge is too late. Yet, as many of the extracts in this chapter indicate, police officers and lawyers often suggest that suspects can see lawyers 'later', or 'in court' or 'if we charge you'. One suspect, when asked how he felt about the non-appearance of his lawyer, replied that he did not mind as 'nothing happened'. In fact he had been interrogated and had been charged as a result of what he had told the police!

---

26 Kaye, T., *op. cit.*, p. 4.
27 The latest disgrace to come to light is that of Stephen Kiszko, convicted of murder in 1976: *Guardian*, 23 February 1992.

The police still have all the opportunities they need to 'get at' suspects, when they really want to, in the absence of a solicitor. Police freedom here is not unfettered but is made considerably wider by the practices of solicitors. These practices stem in large measure from the private enterprise nature of this work. Because it is voluntary, and solicitors will do it thoroughly only if it pays reasonably well, the rules cannot be as tight as the LAB, and even some local administrators (who are simply local solicitors), would like them to be.

The picture we have portrayed of professional self-interest is as predictable as the way the police obstruct access when they believe that so doing will make their own working lives easier. If it was a mistake to graft the 24-hour scheme on to the existing structure of private practice, what alternatives are there? A fully fledged 'public defender' institution on American lines would not necessarily be better.[28] Another alternative would be to replace the duty solicitor scheme with a salaried service, probably combining qualified solicitors and well-trained para-legals, to provide 24-hour cover for police station advice (although it would be important to retain, as a safe-guard against poor quality, the right of suspects to choose their own solicitors who would be paid out of the legal aid fund). It might be argued that this would institutionalise 'second class' professionals for what are regarded as 'second class' citizens. But, against this, it might be countered that this would be an improvement over the 'third class' service so often provided at the moment through the private enterprise-based schemes examined in this chapter.

The need for further change is clear when we compare the effects of the revised COP with the revised duty solicitor rules. The former, affecting the adversaries of the suspects, actually had more of an impact than the latter, which are aimed at encouraging the supposed defenders of the suspect! It seems that duty solicitor schemes, as currently constituted, are not reformable. Until they are fundamentally restructured the potential for miscarriages will lie with the legal profession as much as with the police.

EDITORS' COMMENTS

In an adversarial system, the protection of the interests of the detainee is as much a matter for the individual as for the State. However, the State has a duty to ensure equality between the parties. Fairness surely requires

---

28 See McConville, M. and Mirsky, C., 'The State, the legal profession, and the defence of the poor' (1988) 15 *Journal of Law and Society* 342.

that professionalisation within the police and prosecution services be matched by the defence. The principle of equality of arms is especially relevant to the provision of adequate legal assistance. Changes within the PACE regime are therefore necessary to achieve this goal. Aside from those considered in chapter 3, others might include police notification of rights at the moment of arrest rather than on arrival at the police station,[1] a lawyer's right to see the custody record and record of interview,[2] any waiver of the right to legal advice to be effective only after speaking to a solicitor[3] and denial of access to be confirmed by a judge.[4] There may be a host of other reforms necessary to make legal assistance effective, such as legal aid funding at adequate levels,[5] the extension of rights of audience so that solicitor-advocates can develop their careers properly[6] and encouragement by the Law Society and universities to students not to gravitate unthinkingly towards highly-paid commercial law.[7] At the later stages of the process, the propensity of barristers to inflict late changes in personnel on the hapless accused should come under scrutiny.[8] The problem may be alleviated by better trial listing practices and greater use of pre-trial reviews (discussed further in chapter 7).

Even when well-qualified and experienced lawyers do deign to make an appearance at the police station, chapter 3 grieves their lack of an adversarial approach. This phenomenon has been recognised in other contexts and is said to result from the 'local legal culture' that inevitably arises.[9] The effect is that the practices of actors within the criminal justice system are to be understood in terms of their common expectations, workgroup practices and social relations, which means that they strive for

---

1   Amnesty International, *Submission* (1991), para. 4.1.1, Law Society, *Evidence* (1991), para. 1.118; compare, CPS, *Submission* (1990), para. 3.6.11; Police Service, *Evidence* (1991), p. 83. The Law Society (para. 1.14) also calls for a video record to be made of the processing of the suspect on arrival at the station.

2   Law Society, *Evidence* (1991), paras 1.38, 1.106; Crimial Bar Association, *Submission* (1991); Liberty, p. 26.

3   Law Society, *Evidence* (1991), para. 1.24; Liberty, p. 21.

4   Amnesty International, *Submission* (1991), para. 4.2.3.

5   The Law Society, *Evidence* (1991), para. 6.56 calls for an independent review body.

6   Courts and Legal Services Act 1990, s. 67.

7   The current proposals will be wholly counter-productive. See Law Society, *Training Tomorrow's Solicitors* (1992).

8   Zander ('The Royal Commission's Crown Court survey' (1992) 142 NLJ 1730) found that 50 per cent of barristers were first briefed within 24 hours of the trial, though 95 per cent of the accused felt they had been properly represented.

9   See Blumberg, A., 'The practice of law as a confidence game' (1967) 1 *Law and Society Review* 15; Skolnik, J., 'Social control in the adversary system' (1967) 11 *Journal of Conflict Resolution* 52; Baldwin, J. and McConville, M., *Negotiated Justice* (Martin Robertson, London, 1977); McConville M. et al., *The Case for the Prosecution* (Routledge, London, 1991), p. 167.

cooperation and negotiation rather than conflict and confrontation. By comparison, the client is a transient and socially remote character who is unlikely to influence the prevailing outlook. Another factor to be considered is the sheer inconvenience of visiting the police station, often at unsocial hours, despite the fact that most cases are effectively determined at that time rather than in a comfortable office or in court. The lesson would seem to be the importance of constant retraining in the ethos of the defender, so as to achieve some distance between lawyer and police and greater commitment to the client. Further, one wonders whether, in the era of empowerment via the Citizen's Charter,[10] some mechanism could not be found for an element of incentive legal aid payment based on client satisfaction. A public defender system, as in the USA,[11] presents a more radical solution. Such a system may have benefits in terms of the commitment and availability of its personnel but is vulnerable to State manipulation in terms of funding, and so may not be able to attract the calibre of recruit necessary or may not equip them with adequate resources. The Legal Aid Board's proposals for franchising specialist private practices[12] may be a better compromise, by reducing the dangers of financial manipulation as well as preserving choice for the accused. If, at the end of the day, the accused has failed to receive competent legal assistance through no fault of his or her own (such as failure to give full instructions), then the equality of arms necessary to the working of an adversarial system has not been secured. Accordingly, significant mistakes or failures by lawyers who are said to be 'gravely at fault', as in the *Cardiff Three* case,[13] should provide a ground for appeal.[14]

Most of the safeguards for the accused, including those just proposed, only bite in the context of a regulated detention in the police station. Where interrogation takes place outside that context, especially at the scene of a crime or in a police car following 'the scenic route' back to the police station, then few checks and balances are posssible.[15] It is then arguable that a confession alone should not be sufficient evidence for a conviction and that some form of corroboration should be demanded.

---

10 Cm 1599, 1991.
11 See McIntyre, L., *The Public Defender* (University of Chicago Press, 1987).
12 See Appleby, J., 'Autonomy for franchises' (1992) 39 LS Gaz 2.
13 *R v Paris, Miller, Abdullahi* (1992) *The Times*, 24 December.
14 LAG, *Submission to the Royal Commission* (1991).
15 The most recent version of PACE, Code C, para. 11.1 attempts to combat this problem but is subject to a restrictive definition of 'interview', is subject to exceptions and is not automatically enforceable by exclusion of evidence. The CPS (para. 3.6.3) and Law Society (para. 1.120) suggest that the suspect should be invited to repeat any admission on tape in the station; compare Police Service, *Evidence* (1991), p. 217.

This matter will be considered further in chapter 7. In the meantime, attention will be turned to the exercise of 'the right to silence', which is often linked to the availability of legal advice. That link has now been touched upon, but the fundamental worth of a right to silence is yet to be determined.

4

The Right to Silence

Fiona McElree and Keir Starmer

Introduction[1]

The privilege against self-incrimination, often referred to as the 'right to silence', embraces both the right of a suspect not to answer police questions and the right of an accused not to testify at his/her own trial. The extent of the privilege is circumscribed by rules of evidence and procedure, primarily the following:

(a) that answers to police questions should not be admitted in evidence unless given voluntarily and without oppression or inducement;[2]

(b) that an accused may testify in his/her own defence at trial, but only if she/he chooses to do so;[3]

(c) that only limited comment can be made if a person chooses to exercise the right to silence;[4] and

---

1 For other studies, see Galligan, D., 'The right to silence reconsidered' (1988) 40 *Current Legal Problems* 69; Dennis, I., 'Reconstructing the law of criminal evidence' (1989) *Current Legal Problems* 21; Greer, S. and Morgan, R. (eds.), *The Right to Silence Debate* (Bristol Centre for Criminal Justice, 1989); Wood, J., and Crawford, A., *The Right of Silence* (Civil Liberties Trust, London, 1989); Easton, S. M., *The Right to Silence* (Avebury, Aldershot, 1991).
2 Police and Criminal Evidence Act 1984, ss. 76, 78 and 82.
3 Criminal Evidence Act 1898, s. 1.
4 Criminal Evidence Act 1898, s. 1; *R v Bathurst* [1968] 2 QB 107; *R v Mutch* [1973] 1 All ER 178; *R v Sparrow* [1973] 1 WLR 488; *R v Chandler* [1976] 1 WLR 585; *R v Brown and Routh* [1983] Crim LR 38.

(d) that no inference of guilt should be drawn from the fact that a person has exercised the right to silence[5] (the common-law rule regarding the evidential significance of silence in response to questioning by persons other than police officers or those in authority is less protective: where an individual is accused of a crime by someone on equal terms, his/her silence may be admitted to show acceptance of the charge made[6]).

The right to silence is not of universal application but has been restricted in many instances.[7] Moreover, it is very rarely invoked in practice. The Royal Commission on Criminal Procedure which, in its 1981 report, emphasised the importance of empirical evidence, found that most suspects did in fact account for their conduct while undergoing police interrogation.[8] This was confirmed by subsequent studies, both before and after the enactment of the Police and Criminal Evidence Act in 1984.[9] The more recent study, carried out by Sanders, Bridges, Mulveny and Crozier in 1989, established that only 2.4 per cent of suspects in their sample exercised their right to silence during police interrogations.[10] An investigation by Zander for the Royal Commission found that 10 per cent of accused persons were silent altogether and at least 10 per cent more (the police claimed 17 per cent) were silent in response to some questions.[11] It should be noted that the survey was confined to cases heard before the Crown Court and that the data were based on the opinions of participants rather than court records.

Nevertheless, the right to silence has both symbolic and practical importance. Symbolically it defines the nature of the relationship between the individual and the State and preserves human dignity. In practice, it provides a safeguard for the vulnerable against wrongful convictions. The trials of those charged with offences arising out of the disturbances in October 1985 at Broadwater Farm Estate in Tottenham,

---

5   *R v Whitehead* [1929] 1 KB 99; *R v Keeling* [1942] 1 All ER 507; *R v Bathurst*, above.
6   *R v Mitchell* (1892) 17 Cox CC 503; *Parkes v R* [1976] 1 WLR 1252.
7   See *infra*.
8   Royal Commission on Criminal Procedure Cmnd 8092, 1981, para. 4.43; Softley, P., *Police Interrogation: An Observational Study in Four Police Stations: Research Study No. 4* (HMSO, London, 1980).
9   Baldwin, J. and McConville, M., *Confessions in Crown Court Trials, London: Research Study No. 5* (HMSO, London, 1981); *Courts, Prosecution and Conviction* (Clarendon, Oxford, 1981); Smith, D. J. and Gray, P., *Police and People in London* (Policy Studies Institute, 1983); Mitchell, B., 'Confessions and Police Interrogation of Suspects' [1983] Crim LR 596.
10 Sanders, A., Bridges, L., Mulvaney, A. and Crozier, G., *Advice and Assistance at Police Stations and the 24 Hour Duty Solicitor Scheme* (Lord Chancellor's Department, 1989).
11 'The Royal Commission's Crown Court survey' (1992) 142 NLJ 1730.

North London, provide graphic examples of the dangers of disregarding such safeguards.[12] In the wake of cases such as the *Guildford Four*, *Maguire Seven*, and *Birmingham Six*, in which false confessions led either alone or in large part to wrongful convictions, it is paradoxical that the Royal Commission on Criminal Justice set up in 1991 is being urged to recommend comprehensive restrictions regarding the right to silence.[13]

Historical Background

Historically, the right to silence had become embedded in English jurisprudence well before the beginning of the 19th century.[14] The common law courts prohibited a defendant from giving evidence on oath until 1898.[15] However, the prerogative-based Star Chamber and the ecclesiastic court of High Commission, whose operations included the investigation and suppression of 'crimes against the State', were empowered to compel individuals to come before them and to answer questions on oath. Interrogations were usually arbitrary and often brutal. Religious groups objected vehemently in principle to the administration of oaths, and many individuals suffered torture, mutilation and imprisonment rather than comply with forced questioning. Gradually opposition to these courts grew, and by 1641 the momentum of this opposition was such that both courts were abolished. Resistance to the methods of the Star Chamber and the High Commission were translated into a general popular demand for the right not to incriminate oneself, to which the common law courts acquiesced.[16]

As pre-trial questioning developed in the 19th century, particularly with the emergence of professional police forces throughout the country, the right to silence was accommodated by the rules of criminal evidence and procedure. In 1848, justices were prohibited from questioning an accused person during preliminary inquiries,[17] though it was not until 1912 that it became clear that evidence collated by the police during questioning could be admitted in evidence at trial. In that year, in

---

12 The First and Second Reports of the independent inquiry into the disturbances of October 1985 at the Broadwater Farm Estate, Tottenham, chaired by Lord Gifford QC (1986 and 1989).
13 Its terms of reference include a duty to consider whether changes are needed in 'the opportunities available for an accused person to state his position'.
14 See Macnair, M. R. T., 'The early development of the privilege against self-incrimination' (1990) 10 OJLS 66.
15 Criminal Justice Act 1898, s. 1.
16 *Per* Brennan J in *Brown* v *Walker* (1896) 161 US 591, at pp. 596–7.
17 11 & 12 Vict., c. 43.

response to a request from the police for clarification, the Home Secretary asked the judges of the King's Bench Division to formulate rules of guidance. These became known as the 'Judges' Rules' and (with some revision) remained the main form of control in respect of police interrogation evidence until the Police and Criminal Evidence Act was passed in 1984.[18] The Judges Rules provided that suspects could only be questioned after arrest if they were warned that they need not answer, but that if they did, their answers would be taken down and might be given in evidence against them. The famous words of the caution amounted to a recognition that the right to silence was meaningless unless a suspect was made aware of it before questioning.

The Judges Rules were distinctly double-edged. Although they provided protection in writing for the suspect, they were also effectively the first real permission for the police to question suspects: if interrogations were conducted according to the Rules, then they would inevitably be admitted in evidence. The converse did not apply: if the Rules were broken, it did not automatically mean that the evidence obtained would be excluded. That would depend on the decision of the individual trial judge.

Justice in Error

By the time the Judges Rules were revised in 1964, the questioning of suspects in police stations was not only commonplace but had also become inevitable in most investigations. This development in the criminal justice process over the past 80 years has alone had profound effects on the other safeguards afforded to suspects in police custody and discussed elsewhere in this book. For if a suspect could be made to confess, the process of investigation could be concluded. The evidence at trial would be cogent and difficult to refute — so difficult, indeed, that a guilty plea would be more than likely. The incentive for police to delay access to courts and lawyers, to rely upon inducements or simply to resort to actual or threatened physical violence has been considerable.

When it proposed that the police should be forbidden from questioning suspects in custody at all, the 1929 Royal Commission on Police Powers and Procedures reasoned that:

> . . . a right to ask questions gives rise to an impression of a right to an answer, and . . . the right to an answer seems to create 'a right to the

---

18 See Leigh, L. H., *Police Powers in England and Wales*, 1st ed. (Butterworths, London, 1975), ch. 8.

expected answer', that is a confession of guilt. The simple and peaceful process of questioning breeds a readiness to resort to bullying and physical force and torture.[19]

The revelations which have recently emerged concerning police malpractice over the last 25 years[20] have given considerable force to this reasoning. Yet during the same period the trend has been one of significant restrictions of the right to silence and numerous proposals for further constraint. It appears unlikely, despite its *raison d'être*, that the current Royal Commission on Criminal Justice will reverse this trend.

Restrictions on the Right to Silence

The restrictions on the right to silence over the last 25 years have arisen by both express and implied statutory provision. The most significant express statutory provisions are as follows:

(a)   The Theft Act 1968, s. 31, which provides that a person shall not be excused, by reason that to do so may incriminate that person of an offence under that Act, from answering any question put to that person for the recovery or administration of any property, for the execution of any trust or for an account of any property or dealings with property, or from complying with any order made in such proceedings. However, it is expressly conceded that no statement or admission made by a person in answering such question or complying with any such order shall, in proceedings for an offence under the Theft Act 1968, be admissible evidence against that person.

(b)   The Supreme Court Act 1981, s. 72, which provides that, in civil proceedings in the High Court relating to infringement of rights pertaining to any intellectual property or for passing off, a person shall not be excused, by reason that to do so would expose that person to proceedings for a related offence or for the recovery of a related penalty, from answering any question put to him/her in the first-mentioned proceedings or from complying with any order made in those

---

19   Cmd 3297, para. 164.
20   See, in particular, the First and Second Reports of the independent inquiry into the disturbances of October 1985 at the Broadwater Farm Estate, Tottenham, chaired by Lord Gifford QC (1986 and 1989); Kaye, T., *Unsafe and Unsatisfactory?, Report of the Independent Inquiry into the Working Practices of the West Midlands Serious Crime Squad* (Civil Liberties Trust, London, 1991); and generally the cases of the *Guildford Four* and the *Birmingham Six*.

proceedings. However, it is also recognised that no statement or admission made by a person in answering such a question or in complying with such an order shall be admissible in evidence in proceedings for any related offence, or for the recovery or any related penalty, save proceedings for perjury or contempt of court.

(c) The Criminal Justice Act 1987, s. 2 (under which Act the Serious Fraud Office was established), which provides for the questioning of suspected offenders. Although a statement by a person in response to a requirement imposed by s. 2 may only be used for the prosecution of specified offences under the Act, or where in a prosecution for some other offence she/he makes a statement inconsistent with it, the House of Lords has recently held that the powers to interrogate of the Director of the Serious Fraud Office do not cease when the suspect is charged. Thus, the general provisions of the Police and Criminal Evidence Act 1984 yielded to the later provisions of the Criminal Justice Act 1987.[21]

(d) The Criminal Evidence (Northern Ireland) Order 1988, which provides that the court or jury, in determining whether the accused is guilty of the offence charged, may draw such inferences from the accused's silence as appear proper and, on the basis of such inferences, treat the silence as, or as capable of amounting to, corroboration of any evidence against the accused which is material. For the purposes of the Order, 'silence' arises from any of the following omissions: a failure to mention particular facts when questioned, charged, etc. (Art. 3); a refusal to be sworn in court or, having been sworn, to answer questions without good cause (Art. 4); a failure or refusal to account for objects, marks on person, clothing, etc. (Art. 5); or a failure or refusal to account for presence at a particular place (Art. 6). The Order also provides certain 'safeguards': that the accused cannot be convicted of an offence solely on an inference from silence (Art. 2(4)); that a fact not mentioned when questioned, charged, etc. must be one which the accused could reasonably have been expected to mention (Art. 3(1));[22] and that the accused cannot be compelled to give evidence in court on his/her own behalf and, accordingly, in the event that she/he refuses to be sworn, she/he is not guilty of contempt (Art. 4(5)). The implementation of the Criminal Evidence (Northern Ireland) Order 1988 incidentally demonstrates the arbitrary way in which delegated legislation can be used to take away established rights. The Order was not presaged by any empirical research

---

21 *R v Director of the Serious Fraud Office, ex parte Smith* [1992] 3 WLR 66. See also *Ex parte Saunders* [1988] Crim LR 837; *Ex parte Nadir* (1990) *Independent*, 16 October.
22 The effect of legal advice to remain silent is unclear. See Jackson, J. D., 'Curtailing the right to silence' [1991] Crim LR 404.

or forewarning of its arrival and was aired in Parliament for no more than a couple of hours within a space of a week before its approval. Furthermore, the Order is part of the general criminal law and so applies in relation to any offence, whether connected with the 'troubles' or not.

In addition to statutory provisions, the courts have increasingly been prepared to interpret various statutes as impliedly restricting the right to silence. This tendency has been particularly marked in the last few years in respect of so-called 'economic crime'. Hence, there is no right to silence in inquisitorial proceedings by the Commissioner of Customs and Excise established by the Purchase Act 1963,[23] during examination by inspectors appointed by the Department of Trade and Industry under the Companies Act 1985,[24] during examination by the Bank of England under the Banking Act 1987[25] or where company office holders are questioned by a liquidator under ss. 235 and 236 of the Insolvency Act 1986.[26] The courts have been correspondingly slow to infer safeguards similar to those set out above in relation to the express statutory provisions to delimit the uses to which evidence can be put.

Proposals for Change

Pressure for further restrictions on the right to silence has been a constant feature of the last 25 years. Two official bodies have recommended comprehensive amendments to the law of criminal evidence and procedure, and some senior judges have made clear their hostility. For example, in the case of *Alladice*,[27] Lord Lane, the then Lord Chief Justice, said that the effect of s. 58 of PACE (which gives the suspect the right to legal advice) was such that the balance between the prosecution and defence could not be maintained 'unless proper comment is permitted on the defendant's silence in such circumstances', and that 'it is high time that such comment should be permitted together with the necessary alteration to the words of the caution'.

The two official bodies to have recommended curtailment of the right to silence were the Criminal Law Review Committee (CLRC), which

---

23 *R v Harz; R v Power* [1967] 1 AC 760.
24 *R v Seelig* [1991] 4 All ER 429; *In re London United Investments plc* [1992] 2 WLR 850.
25 *Bank of England v Riley* [1992] 2 WLR 840.
26 *Bishopsgate Investment Management Ltd (in provisional liquidation) v Maxwell & Anor; Mirror Group Newspapers plc & Anor v Maxwell & Others* [1992] 2 WLR 991; *Re Jeffrey S. Levitt Ltd* [1992] 2 All ER 509; *In re Arrows Ltd* [1992] 2 WLR 923; *In re British & Commonwealth Holdings (Nos 1 & 2)* [1992] 2 WLR 931.
27 *R v Alladice* (1988) 87 Cr App R 380, at p. 385.

proposed its abolition in 1972,[28] and the Home Office Working Group, which reported in 1989.[29]

The CLRC was made up as follows: three Lord Justices of Appeal, two High Court Judges, the Common Sergeant (the Chief Judge at the Old Bailey), the Chief Metropolitan Stipendary Magistrate, the Recorder of Southend, the DPP, the legal adviser to the Home Office, three Professors of Law and one practising solicitor. All members were male, all were over 50 and the average age was 65. It is difficult to conceive a more narrowly-based group of people to deliberate on the privilege against self-incrimination. It contained no practising criminal lawyers, criminologists, sociologists, probation officers, social workers or representatives of human rights or civil liberties groups. Notwithstanding that the Committee did not commission or consider any empirical research, it nevertheless ventured that the present rules were 'much too favourable to the defence'. So its proposals contained a restrictive draft Criminal Evidence Bill, cl. 1(1) of which read as follows:

Where in any proceedings against a person for an offence evidence is given that the accused:

(a)   at any time before he was charged with the offence, on being questioned by a police officer trying to discover whether or by whom the offence had been committed, failed to mention any fact relied on in his defence in those proceedings; or

(b)   on being charged with the offence or officially informed that he might be prosecuted for it, failed to mention any such fact,

being a fact which in the circumstances existing at the time he could reasonably have been expected to have mentioned when so questioned, charged or informed, as the case may be, the court, in determining whether to commit the accused for trial or whether there is a case to answer, and the court of jury, in determining whether the accused is guilty of the offence charged, may draw such inferences from the failure as appear proper; and the failure may, on the basis of such inferences, be treated as or as capable of amounting to, corroboration of any evidence given against the accused in relation to which failure is material.

The draft Bill (cl. 5(3)) also dealt with the exercise of the right to silence during trial as follows:

---

28   Criminal Law Revision Committee, Eleventh Report, Evidence, General, Cmnd 4991 (HMSO, London, 1972).
29   Report of the Working Group on the Right to Silence, Home Office, C Division (London, 1989).

If the accused . . .

(a)   after being called upon by the court to give evidence . . . refuses to be sworn; or

(b)   having been sworn, without good cause, refuses to answer any question,

the court or jury, in determining whether the accused is guilty of the offence charged, may draw such inferences from the refusal as appear proper; and the refusal may, on the basis of such inference, be treated as, or capable of amounting to corroboration of any evidence given against the accused.

The proposals of the CLRC have yet to be acted upon in England and Wales, having aroused vehement opposition from many quarters when they were published. However, the Criminal Procedure Code (Amendment) Act 1976 in Singapore was modelled on the CLRC's draft Bill. The impact of this Act was assessed in 1983.[30] So far as pre-trial exercise of the right to silence was concerned, it was found that there had been no substantial change in the numbers exercising the right before and after implementation of the Act. As for the exercise during trial itself, the percentage of cases in which the accused did testify was actually higher before the Act was passed.

The second official body to recommend restrictions on the right to silence was the Home Office Working Group, which was set up in May 1988 by the then Home Secretary, Douglas Hurd. Significantly, its terms of reference were not to consider the merits of the right to silence but to formulate the changes in the law necessary to abolish it. Its work was further undermined by the introduction of the Criminal Evidence (Northern Ireland) Order 1988 in November 1988 (before the Working Group had even begun to receive evidence) and the statement made by the Home Secretary around the same time to the effect that the Government's aim was to extend the changes set out in the Order to England and Wales.[31]

When the Working Group reported in July 1989, its main recommendations were as follows:

(a)   that statutory guidelines ought to be drawn up setting out factors

---

30   Yeo, M. H., 'Diminishing the right to silence: the Singapore Experience' [1983] Crim LR 89. Curtailment of the right to silence in the Republic of Ireland's Criminal Justice Act 1984, ss. 15, 18 and 19 also remains unused: SACHR, 14th Report (1988–89 HC 394), Annex A.

31   See Easton, S. M., *op. cit.*, p. 24.

to be taken into account by courts in respect of which inferences may properly be drawn;[32]

(b) that in the Crown Court, prosecution, defence and judge ought to be able to comment on the accused's failure to mention a fact on which she/he later relied and that the prosecution ought to be able to cross-examine the accused about this;[33]

(c) that the judge should give guidance to the jury as to which factors they should take into account in assessing the veracity of the evidence at trial;[34]

(d) that a new caution be introduced with the following wording: 'You do not have to say anything. A record will be made of anything you do say and it may be given in evidence. So may your refusal to answer any questions. If there is any fact on which you intend to rely in your defence in court, it would be best to mention it now. If you hold back until you go to court you may be less likely to be believed.';[35]

(e) that the main inference to be drawn from an accused's previous failure to answer questions, or to mention a fact later relied upon at trial, is that the subsequent line of defence is untrue and that it may have an adverse effect on his/her general credibility;[36]

(f) that in the Crown Court advance disclosure ought to be required where there is a risk of an 'ambush' defence, and that it should be modelled on s. 9 of the Criminal Justice Act 1987.[37]

Key Factors in the Right to Silence Debate

A few months after the Working Group reported, the appeal of the *Guildford Four* was allowed. There followed a stream of litigation involving miscarriages of justice, including the *Maguire Seven*, the *Birmingham Six*, the *Tottenham Three* and numerous cases involving the West Midlands Serious Crime Squad. It will be for the current Royal Commission on Criminal Justice to assess the proposals of the Working Group in the light of these cases. Several key factors ought to be taken into account.

The first is that silence should not be equated with guilt. Silence by its very nature can prove nothing. There are numerous innocent reasons

32 *Loc. cit.*, para. 3.64, 126(i) and Appendix D.
33 *Ibid.*, para. 65, 126(ii).
34 *Ibid.*, para. 65, 67, 126(iii), 126(iv).
35 *Ibid.*, para. 71, 126(v).
36 *Ibid.*, para. 86, 126(vii).
37 *Ibid.*, para. 102, 127(xi).

why people in custody may refuse to answer questions, as was recognised by the CLRC in 1972.[38] Even in Northern Ireland, plausible, exculpatory pretexts for silence can be suggested. The low proportion of charges arising from Prevention of Terrorism Act detentions[39] indicates that the police often select for interrogation persons who have no direct knowledge of terrorism but who may be too intimidated by terrorists to cooperate in any way with the police. In conclusion, once the possibility that there is even one innocent reason for silence is conceded, the risk of a miscarriage of justice arises if silence is equated with guilt.

A second point is that the right to silence has not resulted in large numbers of (guilty) people being acquitted. Most people do not exercise their right to silence, as already described. Nor is it common practice for solicitors to advise silence when visiting clients in police stations.[40] In addition, Zander found that of those suspects who did stay silent, the great majority were convicted.[41] Furthermore, the assumption underpinning the 'wrongful acquittals' argument, that juries who have heard all the admissible evidence and seen the witnesses undergoing cross-examination make the wrong decision, is disturbing.[42] The Report of the Working Group pointed to professional criminals as causing the most difficulties.[43] However, if the rules were changed for all suspects, as it suggests, such criminals would no doubt have the training and experience to concoct plausible cover stories and alibis. The losers would be the inarticulate, unintelligent and inadequate who are innocent of any crime.

Thirdly, it must be remembered that the right to silence had already been restricted in many key instances. Moreover, s. 11 of the Criminal Justice Act 1967, which requires an accused to give notice to the prosecution of his/her intention to adduce alibi evidence (which includes any assertion that the accused was not at the scene of the offence at the relevant time, whether or not supporting witnesses are to be called) within seven days of committal proceedings, has largely dealt with the perceived problem of 'ambush' defences.

---

38 *Loc. cit.*, para. 35.
39 See ch. 9.
40 See Dixon, D., 'Common sense, legal advice and the right to silence' [1991] *Public Law* 233; Lethem, C., *Police Detention* (Waterlow Publishers, London, 1991) pp. 50, 62.
41 Zander, M., 'The investigation of crime, a study of contested cases at the Old Bailey' [1979] Crim LR 203; Zander, M., 'No case for destroying the right to silence' (1988) 22 January *Law Magazine* 16.
42 Easton, S. M., *op. cit.*, p. 52.
43 *Loc. cit.*, Appendix C. The Appendix is based on research by Williamson, T. M., 'Strategic changes in police interrogation' (Ph.D., Kent, 1990). The research was significantly flawed in terms of questionnaire design and the calculation of silences.

Next, any restriction on the right to silence disturbs the delicate balance between the State and the individual. If inferences of guilt can be drawn from a person's refusal to answer questions, the rule that the prosecution must both bring and prove the case becomes a nonsense. This was recognised by the Royal Commission on Criminal Procedure in 1981. Its membership and methodology stand in stark contrast to those of the CLRC. The members of the Commission were drawn from a wide base and included the judiciary, the legal professions, the magistracy, the church and the trade union movement. It commissioned and subsequently published large quantities of empirical research on the right to silence. It recommended the retention of the right to silence on the basis that:

> There is an inconsistency of principle in requiring the onus of proof at trial to be upon the prosecution and to be discharged without any assistance from the defence and yet in enabling the prosecution to use the accused's silence in the face of police questioning under caution as any part of their case against him.[44]

In the light of this recommendation, the argument that the right of silence should be abolished because the Police and Criminal Evidence Act 1984 has increased the protection for suspects in other ways should equally be rejected. Aside from grave doubts about the strength and efficacy of those protections,[45] the argument may be dismissed as a form of double-counting: the increased safeguards were supplied as a counter-balance to the massive increase in police powers which the Act also wrought.

The need to maintain a balance between State and suspect also suggests that if compulsory disclosure of relevant, known facts is imposed on the accused, it should also be imposed at the time of interrogation on the police, so that suspects are aware of the relevance and meaning of each question and can make an informed choice as to whether to respond or not. However, no official body has made such a recommendation, nor have the courts implied such a requirement in those exceptional situations where there is a restriction on the right to silence.[46]

Next, changes to the right to silence will further augment the importance of interrogation in the police station as the common mode of investigation of crime. Yet the reliability of confessions, the fairness of

---

44   *Loc. cit.*, para. 4.51.
45   See chs 1 and 2.
46   *Re Barlow Clowes Gilt Managers* [1992] 1 All ER 385.

police interrogation techniques and the reliability of the record of the exchanges have all been exposed as highly problematical in recent miscarriage of justice cases. Many conclude that a greater emphasis should be placed on police detection through forensic science or independent witnesses.

Lastly, the operation over the last four years of the Criminal Evidence (Northern Ireland) Order 1988 demonstrates that the erosion of the right to silence involves more than a mere technicality. Thus, while the initial approach of the judiciary was only to draw an inference from silence in an otherwise finely balanced case, this stance has gradually relaxed to the point where inferences are now drawn from silence in cases where they merely add weight to the prosecution case, as will now be explained.[47]

Although the Criminal Evidence (Northern Ireland) Order 1988 came into effect on 15 December 1988, it was not until October 1989 that the Order was invoked to support a conviction.[48] Before then, both Nicholson and Kelly LJJ had set themselves guidelines which reflected their initial concerns. In *R* v *MacDonald*,[49] Nicholson LJ held that an inference should not be drawn under the Order unless the other evidence in a case 'at least' amounted to evidence of 'probable' guilt. Lord Justice Kelly went further. In his judgment in *R* v *Smyth*,[50] he stated that an inference under the Order should only be taken into account where the standard of evidence adduced by the prosecution without the inference rested on the brink of being 'beyond reasonable doubt'. The inference was only to be used as the final 'weight' in an otherwise finely balanced case.[51]

Within a relatively short compass of time, the judiciary in Northern Ireland overcame its initial caution in respect of drawing inferences and demonstrated a willingness to broaden its application. In the first case in which the Order was actually applied, *R* v *Gambrel*,[52] Caswell J drew an inference not from the accused's refusal to answer police questions (he had done so) but from his decision not to testify in court. There was a strong expectation when the Order was introduced that, given the historical importance of the right not to testify, inferences in such circumstances would be less readily drawn than when an accused person

47   Haldane Society of Socialist Lawyers, *Upholding the Rule of Law?*, *Northern Ireland: Criminal Justice under the 'Emergency Powers' in the 1990s* (London, 1991).
48   *R* v *Gambrel, Douglas, McKay, Boyn & Others*, 27 October 1989, reported in Haldane Society of Socialist Lawyers, *loc. cit.*, p. 44.
49   (1989) reported *ibid*.
50   20 October 1989, unreported, but cited in Ruddell, G., 'A summary of recent judicial decisions in Northern Ireland', in Greer, S. and Morgan, R., *op. cit.*, p. 44.
51   *Loc. cit.*, at p. 44.
52   *Loc. cit.*

refused to answer police questions. Next, in the case of *R* v *McClernon*,[53] an accused charged with possession of a firearm had refused to answer police questions for six days before making a partial confession on the seventh. In allowing an inference to be drawn, Lord Justice Kelly said that he had never intended his judgment in *R* v *Smyth* (above) to limit the application of the Order — a refusal to answer questions may be taken into account where it merely adds weight to the prosecution case. Lord Justice Kelly's change of approach was completed in the case of *R* v *Murray*.[54] Thumb-prints of the accused and fibres from his clothing had allegedly been found on the car of a murder victim. Lord Justice Kelly formed the view that at common law an inference could be drawn, relying on the case of *R* v *Mutch*.[55] However, he went on to assert that the Order was not limited to situations of 'confess and avoid' (in other words, where an explanation was clearly called for on the evidence) but that it might be used, and Parliament had intended it to be used, more generally. This stronger discretion seems to have resulted in some confusion in later cases as to what level of evidence must be established before the Order can be applied.[56]

The case of *R* v *Danny Morrison*[57] demonstrates very well the current thinking of the judiciary in Northern Ireland. The accused had been charged with an offence of false imprisonment and conspiracy to murder. The evidence against him was that he had been arrested in the house next door to the house in which the victim had been falsely imprisoned by the IRA, and had visited that house while the victim was being held there. The accused refused to answer police questions but did give evidence during the trial. His reason for refusing to answer questions was that, as a local politician, he had repeatedly advised suspects not to answer questions and that it would be hypocritical for him to do otherwise himself. His counsel urged that where an innocent explanation is put forward, no adverse inference should be drawn at all. On appeal in *R* v *Murray*, Lord Chief Justice Huton refused to accept this proposition, stating that Parliament had intended judges using the Order to apply their own common sense and that this was the only fetter on the discretion to be exercised.[58]

---

53 (1992) 5 BNIL n. 38.
54 18 January 1991, (1992) 2 BNIL n. 45 (Court of Appeal).
55 (1972) 57 Cr App R 196.
56 See Committee on the Administration of Justice, *The Casement Trials* (Belfast, 1992), pp. 36, 37.
57 Reported *sub. nom. R* v *Martin and others* (1992) 7 BNIL n. 42.
58 7 July 1992, affirmed 29 October 1992 (House of Lords).

Conclusion

The right to silence is a fundamental feature of our adversarial criminal justice system. It protects the individual from excessive and arbitrary State power. There is little evidence to support the proposition that the right to silence permits the guilty to go free. Conversely, there is a great deal of evidence to support the proposition that to compel answers to questions, whether directly or discreetly (by the drawing of inferences), leads to injustice, repression and, in some instances, to tyranny.

EDITORS' COMMENTS

As has been pointed out elsewhere,[1] the role of the right to silence in a criminal justice system ultimately depends on whether it is recognised as a fundamental right or is viewed in instrumental, often utilitarian, terms. English law has been traditionally reluctant to confer a meta-legal status upon any claim against the State. However, the vital nature of the privilege against self-incrimination in a common-law adversarial system[2] is confirmed by its expression in the Fifth Amendment to the US Constitution — 'no person . . . shall be compelled in any criminal cases to be a witness against himself . . .'. If the case for the right to silence in rights terms is accepted, then it is clear that it should not be restricted or abolished for utilitarian gain — such as to make the police more efficient. However, even if a utilitarian approach were adopted, one may still doubt on the evidence whether the benefits are certain or substantial enough to outweigh the costs of aggressive police forces and miscarriages of justice. The current proposals before the Royal Commission neatly illustrate this divergence of viewpoints.

On the one hand, the document from the Police Service reveals its continuing hostility. It regards the right to silence as not only benefiting the guilty but also entrapping the innocent because their later explanations will not be credible to jurors.[3] Of course, if the latter assertion were true, it would provide an argument for reversing the Criminal Evidence Act 1898. Arguments against it along the lines suggested by the police were

---

1 See Walker, 'An exploration of the right to silence' (1980) 9 Anglo-Am L Rev 257; Easton, S. M., *The Right to Silence* (Avebury, Aldershot, 1991), ch. 6.
2 Compare its omission from the European Convention on Human Rights (1950), Art. 6.
3 Submission (1991), para. 1.2.2. By contrast, the Home Office states that it is undecided (para. 3.53).

indeed made at the time and were particularly strong in Ireland,[4] where the change in rules did not occur until 1923 in Northern Ireland and 1924 in the south.[5] Next, the police submission resurrects the discredited belief that it is standard practice for solicitors to advise silence, thereby wasting legal aid funds.[6] While it is true that silence and the presence of a solicitor correlate,[7] it is not shown that silence with or without legal advice is adverse to a just resolution of the police inquiry. Rather, the police simply assume once again that silence prevents the effective working of the criminal justice system in terms of the conviction of the guilty and acquittal of the innocent. Despite the shortcomings of their arguments, the police submission floats the idea of at least one 'formal interview' with every suspect to be prosecuted. The accused would be asked for an explanation, and there would be a right to comment at trial on silence at that hearing.[8] In addition, the police wish to be able to adduce evidence of questions asked in police stations to which there is no response — tantamount to an inference of guilt.[9] Similarly, courts should be permitted to draw inferences from failure to mention earlier facts relied on at trial.[10] Lastly, adverse inferences derived from silence should be capable of being corroborative.[11] Throughout the document, there is no recognition that the right to silence might be an important constitutional safeguard or that other, new safeguards might be necessary if it is abolished.

On the other side of the theoretical divide are organisations such as Amnesty, JUSTICE, Liberty and NACRO, which advocate no change.[12] Most of the professional organisations also recognise the important and fundamental value of the right, though not all to the same degree. The most protracted debate on the issue took place within the Bar and resulted in some disagreement. Thus the General Council of the Bar opposes in most cases inferences of guilt from silence (including in Northern Ireland) but is attracted to the Scottish judicial examination system which may result in adverse comment on silence.[13] For its part, the

---

4 See Jackson, C., 'Irish political opposition to the passage of criminal evidence reform at Westminster 1883–98', in O'Higgins, P. and McEldowney, J. F. (eds), *The Common Law Tradition* (Irish Academic Press, Dublin, 1990).
5 Criminal Evidence (NI) Act 1923; Criminal Justice (Evidence) Act 1924.
6 *Loc. cit.*, paras. 1.2.3., 1.2.7.
7 *Ibid.*, para. 2.2.2.
8 *Ibid.*, paras. 2.2.1 and 2.7.2.
9 *Ibid.*, p. 60.
10 *Ibid.*, p. 223.
11 *Ibid.*, p. 237.
12 *Submissions*, para. 4.4.3, p. 24, p. 29, para. 23.
13 *Submission*, paras 71–80.

Criminal Bar Association is prepared to accept only minor changes to outlaw 'ambush' defences at trial.[14]

The chapters so far seem to suggest that confessions or, in their absence, silences provide rather shaky foundations from which to mount a prosecution. The next chapter, therefore, will investigate whether forensic science can offer the courts a more reliable source of evidence.

---

14   The Law Society and CPS also express concern about this aspect of the right to silence: paras 3.26, 3.32; 10.10.4.

5

Forensic Evidence

Russell Stockdale and Clive Walker

Introduction

In the wake of a number of well-publicised criminal cases in which, on closer scrutiny, the prosecution's scientific evidence was found wanting,[1] forensic science has been variously labelled as potentially unreliable, partial and misleading. This is particularly worrying in view of the heavy reliance often placed upon it in proof of the most serious crimes.[2]

This chapter is based upon memoranda submitted by the independent forensic science consultancy, Forensic Access, to the Runciman Committee and to the House of Lords Select Committee on Science and Technology's inquiry into Forensic Science.[3] The paper puts forensic science into perspective by describing its nature and distinguishing the roles of scientists advising the police/prosecution and those appointed by

---

1 See especially *R v Maguire* [1992] 2 All ER 433; *R v McIlkenney* [1992] 2 All ER 417.
2 See HL Select Committee on Science and Technology, Forensic Science (1992–93 HL 24-1), p. 17 (hereafter cited as 'HL Select Committee'). Zander ('The Royal Commission Crown Court survey' (1992) 142 NLJ 1730) suggests its use in a third of cases surveyed and challenges in a quarter of those, but these data are dubiously drawn from the impressions of participants rather than court records. The overall usage of forensic services in criminal investigations is relatively rare (Steer, D., *Uncovering Crime*, Royal Commission on Criminal Procedure Research Study No. 7, HMSO, 1980), though this may reflect police ignorance as much as limited utility (Ramsay, M., *The Effectiveness of the Forensic Science Service*, (Home Office Research Study No. 92, 1987 ch. 2).
3 *Ibid.*

the defence. It points out how inadequate testing of forensic science evidence could lead to miscarriages of justice and highlights some underlying problems facing the defence in criminal trials. It then considers some changes to existing arrangements that have been proposed from time to time, before identifying the essential ingredients of any effective way forward.

Forensic science in perspective

While forensic science is an increasingly powerful tool for clarifying issues before the courts, there is a popular misconception that it provides an especially pure and objective form of evidence and has the capacity to give universally accepted, clear-cut answers leaving little scope for debate.[4]

Forensic scientists are regarded as expert witnesses, and they occupy a special position in court in that they may give evidence of opinion as well as fact. Dangers arise if the court, and perhaps the scientists themselves, are unclear as to which is which, their evidence being regarded as somehow infallible and the pristine truth. The main danger is that when considering any piece of scientific work, it is tempting to dwell on the analytical tests employed and the manner in which these were carried out, matters which are often unimpeachable,[5] without giving sufficient weight to the provenance of the material under test, how this was collected and presented and what inferences may safely be drawn from the results obtained.[6] The effect is rather like focusing on the making of a cake without being unduly concerned about the quality of its ingredients, what it tasted like and whether it was suitable for the specific purpose for which it had been made.

In most fields of scientific endeavour the scientist has a large measure of control over the nature and condition of the raw materials in his or her tests. By contrast, the raw materials of forensic science are the everyday things of life, and the forensic scientist has to take them as he or she finds them, and to recognise them for what they are. There can be considerable difficulties in deciding what should be looked at in the first place, and

---

4   Consider the treatment of DNA profiling, the results of which seemed to be accepted without question at first but which later came under scrutiny: Hall, A., 'DNA fingerprinting' (1990) 140 NLJ 203; Thompson, W. C. and Ford, S., 'Is DNA fingerprinting ready for the courts?' (1990) *New Scientist* 31 March, p. 38; Young, S. J, 'DNA evidence' [1991] Crim LR 264; Easteal, S., McLeod, N. and Reed, C., *DNA Profiling* (Harwood, Reading, 1991).
5   See Whitehead, P. H., 'Ten years of forensic science 1974–83' [1984] Crim LR 663.
6   See Robertson, B. and Vignaux, G.A., 'Expert evidence' (1992) 12 OJLS 392.

what inferences — matters of opinion — might safely be drawn from test results in the second. In reality, and as in every other field of professional endeavour, different forensic scientists presented with the same sets of data can and do come to different views and express different opinions based on them. Moreover, the interpretation of their results and the significance they attach to these will depend upon the quality and extent of the information they have received about the case at issue.

All this means that forensic science evidence, like any other, must be thoroughly probed and tested in order to expose weaknesses or room for reasonable doubt. These can lie hidden from the lay observer, behind an apparently unassailable facade of scientific precision and accuracy.

At this point it is necessary to look more closely at the nature of forensic science and the different demands placed upon its practitioners by the police/prosecution on the one hand and by the defence on the other.

Nature of forensic science[7]

In a nut-shell, forensic science is the systematic and painstaking identification, analysis and comparison of the physical residues of crime in order to establish what happened, when, where and how, and who might have been involved. In criminal cases its purpose is to assist the court in deciding upon the guilt or otherwise of those brought before it.

Nonetheless, forensic science has other important functions to fulfil well before any such proceedings are in view and usually starting with the police investigation. This is reflected in evidence to the Home Affairs Committee[8] in which the Home Office said that the main functions of the Forensic Science Service were:

. . . to provide resources to assist the police in the investigation and detection of crime and to assist the courts in the administration of justice.[9]

Recognition that forensic scientists' terms of reference are not confined to the trial process alone is at the root of understanding the differences

---

7   See Phillips, J. H. and Bowen, J. K., *Forensic Science and the Expert Witness* (Law Book Co., Sydney, 1985); Kind, S. S., *The Scientific Investigation of Crime* (Forensic Science Services, Harrogate, 1987); Hodkinson, T., *Expert Evidence* (Sweet & Maxwell, London, 1990), ch. 14; Aitken C. C. G., and Stoney, D. A. (eds), *The Use of Statistics in Forensic Science* (Horwood, Hemel Hempstead 1991).
8   *The Forensic Science Service* (1988–89 HC 26).
9   *Ibid.*, vol. II, at p. 1.

between the roles of scientists advising the police/prosecution and those engaged, usually at a much later stage, by the defence.

Forensic science for the police/prosecution

Traditionally, the Crown has provided forensic science resources to assist the police and the prosecution.[10] This public sector work is now carried out in two main organisations.[11] One is the Forensic Science Service (FSS), an agency created in April 1991 under the Next Steps Programme in succession to the Home Office laboratories.[12] Secondly, there are police-owned laboratories, by far the largest of which is the Metropolitan Police Forensic Science Laboratory (MPFSL).[13] The defence, on the other hand, has relied on what has been available in the private sector.

The job of the scientist advising the police/prosecution begins far from the laboratory bench. In the first instance it will involve helping to train specialist scenes of crime officers (SOCOs) and detective officers to select and recover those items which are likely to be of most use in clarifying issues for the investigating officer and, ultimately, the court. The better this training, the higher the quality of starting materials the scientist will have to work with.

In the early stages of a police inquiry, the forensic scientist is part of the investigating officer's team of specialist advisers to the extent of helping to determine whether or not a crime has been committed at all and, if so, which one and how. In a suspected murder case, for example, the scientist is probably most effective working at the investigating officer's side — at the scene looking for clues, pointing out features and material likely to be of evidential value, and generally trying to piece together precisely what has happened and, wherever possible on the information available, suggesting directions in which police inquiries might usefully proceed.

---

10   Forensic laboratories were formalised in 1931 as a common service (now see Police Act 1964, s. 41).

11   Other relevant organisations are the Laboratory of the Government Chemist (which is a Next Steps agency dealing with the analysis of drugs, documents and chemicals), the Central Research and Support Establishment (described below), the Defence Research Agency (which supercedes the Royal Armament Research and Development Establishment and tests explosives) and the Northern Ireland Office Forensic Science Laboratory.

12   See Home Affairs Committee, *loc. cit.*; The Forensic Science Service (Cm 699, 1989). The Next Steps programme is described in Prime Minister's Efficiency Unit, Improving Management in Government (1988). The FSS operates at six different sites and employs about 400 scientists.

13   The MPFSL is possibly the largest single forensic establishment in Europe, with over 300 scientists.

This means that from the outset the forensic scientist is, and arguably should remain, actively engaged in the identification and investigation of crime. The nature of this aspect of the job requires close involvement with, and deep commitment to, the investigative process. In order to make an effective contribution, the scientist cannot stand on the side-lines with the lofty detachment of a disinterested observer.

When the items — several hundred in a large, serious case — arrive at the laboratory, the scientist must decide which it would be most profitable to examine, and for what. If all items were to be examined and in all respects, a single case could turn into a lifetime's work. Selections made at this stage depend, again, on experience and on the amount and quality of the information the scientist has received about the case; these decisions can dramatically affect the quality and usefulness of the scientific evidence subsequently produced.

It is only at this point that analytical procedures begin to be applied. Tests must be chosen carefully and great care and attention paid to the manner in which they are carried out, the equipment used and so on. The results they provide must then be interpreted, but this may be far from straightforward. No two cases are ever precisely the same; they all have their own peculiarities, and it is only by investigating many cases of the same general type that the effects of these can be appreciated and a balanced conclusion arrived at.

Next the scientist will prepare a written report on the findings, selecting only the ones which are considered to be most pertinent. It would not be practicable to try to report on everything seen and found. Again, decisions as to what to include and what to omit will depend very much on the information received and the scientist's perceptions of the matters at issue.

This may be the last ever heard of the case, or, alternatively, the scientist may be called to give oral evidence. If so, then the amount and type of information he or she is able to impart will be conditioned by the questions put and by the latitude allowed in making replies.

Thus the overall quality of the scientific evidence which emerges from the prosecution's scientist will depend upon many variables. One is knowledge of the circumstances of the case and, against this background, the scientist's (and/or others') initial selection of which items to submit to the laboratory. Others involve the selection of which tests to apply to which items, the conduct of the tests themselves, the interpretation of the test results, the drawing of inferences from these interpretations in the context of the case, the selection of information to impart in the written report, and the nature of questions put to the scientist at court and the freedom allowed in framing responses.

Much of the recent criticism of FSS and other public sector forensic scientists has arisen, albeit rather late in the day, as a result of doubts as to whether and to what extent the evidence they gave was balanced. Clearly, there have been occasions when it was not. But arguably, in the generality of cases, it is perhaps too much to expect anyone actively involved as a matter of course in the identification and investigation of crime, and the hunt for the perpetrator, to present all the evidence to the entire satisfaction of both prosecuting and defending counsel alike. That would be like expecting the hound who has just caught what he believes to be the hare to set to with a will to give it the kiss of life.[14]

However intellectually independent and scientifically objective FSS and police scientists may strive to be, their 'hunting' role is inescapable. As such, they are not in a position, nor necessarily have sufficient information of the right kind, to determine whether their evidence and stance are balanced or whether they list slightly to one side.

Forensic Science for the Defence

There are three main strands comprising the role of forensic scientists engaged by the defence. These are:

(a)   to check the analytical results emerging from the police/prosecution scientist's work, and to undertake any such further tests as may be warranted;

(b)   to clarify the nature of the police/prosecution scientist's findings and the interpretation of them;

(c)   to assess and to advise on the significance of the scientific evidence overall in the light of all the circumstances.

(a)   Checking analytical results. The standard of analytical work coming from the FSS laboratories and the MPFSL generally is very high. It is rare for there to be much margin for quibbling about, for example, the reported identity and purity of a particular drug, the blood group profile of a blood stain, or the conclusion that one particular fibre is indistinguishable from another. Nonetheless, the analytical procedures employed must always be scrutinised as to their appropriateness, and the results obtained checked to see how far they support what has been reported.

---

14   See further Stockdale, R., 'Running with the hounds' (1991) 141 NLJ 772.

Unfortunately, there is a strong tendency for scientists consequently employed by the defence and who have little or no forensic science training and experience to want to repeat, willy-nilly, the primary work of the police scientists. In most cases, this is impracticable and/or uninformative for a variety of reasons. For instance, the relevant material might all have been used up; or it might have deteriorated to a point beyond which any results obtained would be meaningful; or, owing to repeated handling and testing, the integrity of the material can no longer be assured. Thus it is often more important to focus on the detailed records of analyses already carried out than slavishly to set about repeating them. This is not to say that there will not be other separate and specific tests which the defence scientist will need to carry out to assess the strength of the links the prosecution has proposed, such as investigating possible alternative and innocent sources of seemingly incriminating trace evidence.

Some cases involve protracted scientific examinations but, as matters stand and unless formal interim reports are issued, the defence will have no knowledge of, or access to, the analyses in progress. In these circumstances, it would seem to be reasonable for the defence scientist to be admitted to the examination as it proceeds. As to cases in which the police/prosecution scientist's examinations are complete, the defence scientist should have full and ready access to all the working notes and be able to request copies of these as required. Until recently, access to such papers in the FSS and MPFSL depended very much on how the police/prosecution scientist was disposed to opening his or her file. It is still the case that in at least one Scottish police laboratory, scientists are expressly forbidden to reveal their notes to the defence scientist or to discuss their findings.

The position in which the defence inevitably finds itself thus underscores the need to appoint properly trained and thoroughly experienced forensic scientists who will be completely familiar with all the procedures adopted by the FSS and MPFSL. It also emphasises the special nature and weight of the responsibility placed upon the police/prosecution's scientists by virtue of their having the first and possibly only opportunity to examine materials in their original state.

(b) Clarifying the nature of scientific evidence. A number of lawyers admit that they regard forensic science evidence very much as a closed book, dealing with it as quickly as possible and avoiding tackling it head-on. One of the reasons for this might be that scientists' reports have tended to be short on explanations and long on jargon. Another is the

almost total absence of training of lawyers in forensic science, either at university or in professional courses.[15] This 'scientific illiteracy'[16] renders lawyers (and judges) handicapped in terms of comprehending the significance and meaning of forensic evidence, as was well illustrated in the *Maguire Seven* case.[17]

Accordingly, an important part of the defence scientist's work is to ensure that all concerned on behalf of the accused fully understand what the prosecution's scientific evidence means and feel thoroughly at home with the principles behind it. In this way, counsel will be best supported and equipped to cross-examine on the evidence confidently and effectively, and thus expose any weaknesses inherent in it.

(c)   Interpretation and significance. Another essential part of the defence scientist's job is to bring a fresh eye to the interpretation of the scientific evidence and the significance laid upon it. In particular, he or she should assess its significance in the context of all the circumstances, including the results of any further tests carried out for the defence and in the light of, for example, the accused's last word on the matter which the police/prosecution scientist may not have had the opportunity to consider. Depending upon those findings, the defence scientist too may be required to give oral evidence, or, at least, to advise counsel while he or she tackles what the prosecution's scientist has to say.

The overall quality of the advice and/or evidence which emerges from the defence scientist will depend upon the extent to which he or she is qualified and experienced in the field, the knowledge he or she has of the case at issue and, against this background, his or her checking of the prosecution's analytical procedures; clarifying the extent and nature of the police scientist's findings and the interpretations which have been placed on these; and assessment and advice as to the significance of the scientific evidence as he or she sees it in the light of all the circumstances.

Forensic science and miscarriages of justice

Several recent miscarriages of justice have occurred because scientific evidence adduced at trial was not properly tested. Enduring confidence in verdicts which rely heavily upon forensic science can only be achieved if the evidence, and the procedures and results which lie behind it, are

---

15 Current proposals make no reference to this deficiency: Law Society, *Policies for Completing the Academic Stage of Legal Education for Solicitors* (1992).
16 Memorandum of the Forensic Science Society to the HL Committee, *loc. cit.*, p. 67.
17 See *Interim Report on the Maguire Case* (1989–90 HC 556).

thoroughly scrutinised, rigorously checked, properly clarified and carefully balanced. Clearly, the proper time for all of this arises before the verdict is reached and not in a piecemeal fashion afterwards. Equally clearly, the only way in which effective testing can be achieved is by ensuring a proper balance of forensic science skills, expertise and resources available to the police/prosecution and the defence.

As matters stand, the defence are at a significant disadvantage. This is because it is the police/prosecution which takes the initiative in the collection of evidence, which could lead to unsuspected contamination and significant omissions. In addition, there are serious doubts about the quality and competency of some independent forensic scientists and the adequacy of the funding for the needs of the defence.

Contamination and omissions

The collection of the materials which will eventually be tested in forensic laboratories is primarily a matter for the discretion of the police.[18] Thus, the obvious dangers arise that non-scientists will blunder about and thereby contaminate evidence, or that they will fail to appreciate the value of such evidence as is available and will fail to forward it to the laboratory.

To some extent, the dangers have been decreased in recent years because of the changing profile of SOCOs who perform the task. In the first place, the post has been civilianised in many forces, allowing the appointment of individuals with specialised knowledge.[19] Secondly, their training was significantly improved in 1990 when a new and more substantial course was inaugurated at the National Training Centre for Scientific Support to Crime Investigation in Durham. Nevertheless, the raising of the quality of SOCOs by no means solves all the problems, since they attend only a minority of crimes and arrive at selected sites only after other police officers have visited.[20] Thus, training should be increased throughout the police service to ensure that patrol officers are fully aware of forensic science principles and practices and act in accordance with them.

Quality and competency

Concerns about the quality and competency of forensic science personnel apply to the profession in general. Additional problems arise from the operations of public or private sector scientists, respectively.

---

18   Serious Crime Units in the MPFSL and NIFSL allow their scientists to work alongside police collectors of evidence. In FSS laboratories, scientists have attended major crime scenes as a matter of course for many years.
19   See Ramsay, *op. cit.*, p. 32.
20   See Sargant, T. and Hill, P., *Criminal Trials* (Fabian Society, London, 1986), p. 18.

Among the general concerns are the levels of education and training of entrants into the profession. It is generally accepted that a good quality first degree in science is a prerequisite for scientists wishing to train to investigate cases and eventually to give evidence at court. In view of the diversity of case-work material, it is useful for laboratories to have a good mix of scientists with both first and higher degrees in a broad range of relevant scientific disciplines. However, first degrees are not enough. Though post-graduate courses in forensic science are useful insofar as they give potential forensic scientists a flavour of the job, they are no substitute for the necessary long professional apprenticeship which all newcomers to the profession need to undergo before they can properly offer themselves to the courts as forensic scientists. The primary source of relevant training is total immersion in the case-work of the FSS and police laboratories, day in and day out, year in and year out: forensic scientists cannot be bought off university shelves.

Existing vocational qualifications and recognitions are far from satisfactory,[21] so alternatives are currently under review. A Steering Committee, comprising the FSS and MPFSL, and independent scientists, is considering whether there is scope to introduce National Vocational Qualifications (NVQs) into forensic science. While these might be appropriate for technicians and assistants, it is difficult to see that they would be relevant at the professional, court-going level.

Can people of the necessarily high calibre be recruited and retained by forensic science? Traditionally, forensic science has been an attractive field and the FSS able to recruit its share of good quality science graduates, albeit with some difficulty in the mid-1980s. However, the establishment of scientists in the FSS is now reported to be of the order of 400 compared with 480 in 1987. It is difficult to be convinced that such a reduction could possibly be due to increased efficiency or that the quality of service has not diminished. As for retention, it would not be surprising in the current economic climate if there was less wastage than hitherto.

Even if the requisite personnel is available, professional standards should demand rigorous staff development and training. In the past, in-service education and training in the FSS have appeared to be adequate, but whether or not the present 'small team structure' of the service will adequately expose trainees to sufficient depth in any

---

21   The Forensic Science Society offers Diplomas on Document Examination and Scenes of Crime Examination. It also compiles (as does the Law Society) a register of experts, but makes no inquiry into their competence.

particular subject remains to be seen. Moreover, there are worrying signs that individual laboratories within the FSS may be extending the range of services they offer without ensuring that the necessary skills and experience are in place. Furthermore, in the light of recent criticisms concerning, *inter alia*, less than full disclosure by forensic scientists,[22] some attention needs to given to clear direction and instruction in their legal responsibilities to the courts.

A feature of a healthy profession is that there is encouragement of research and technical development. In the past British research in forensic science, centred mainly at the Central Research and Support Establishment (CRSE) of the FSS, enjoyed an unassailable prime position. With the introduction of agency status, the CRSE has been run down to the extent that, save for a rump of DNA-orientated projects, little research work is being undertaken there or anywhere else in the service. Moreover, a once thriving Information Division within CRSE, catering for the needs of research and operational scientists alike, has now apparently been substantially reduced. It is difficult to see how even the most basic and modest requirements of a scientific organisation could be expected to be met by such paltry investment.

All this is very worrying. It is essential that forensic scientists continue to keep a close watch on developments in a variety of scientific fields and that they have the means to 'adopt, adapt and improve' these to their own ends as appropriate. To do this, they need an organisation within the FSS, like CRSE, sufficiently separate from day-to-day case-work to focus on research and development, yet sufficiently close to it to be able to test new ideas under operational conditions and with the support and interest of the primary case-workers.

Other essential CRSE functions include providing a source of unimpeachable material standards for reference purposes, against which quality in routine case-work procedures can be assessed and assured (this is nothing more than a normal day- to-day requirement in any analytically based scientific operation), and for trouble-shooting when potential anomalies arise in the course of case-work.

While there is probably some scope for limited 'blue skies' research in forensic science, this could not even be contemplated without the support and direction afforded by a dedicated research resource such as CRSE. The history of collaborative projects, of which there have been many, with non-forensic science organisations such as universities and commercial bodies, is dismal. This is because there have been seemingly

---

22 See ch. 6.

insurmountable problems of defining and communicating the requirements in the first place, and controlling and coordinating the progress of
the work in the second place. As to international collaboration, and
despite a regular FSS commitment to research programmes coordinated
by Interpol, nothing of any note has emerged.

Turning towards particular concerns about scientists working in the
public sector, the FSS and MPFSL laboratories are very well equipped,
and procedures for handling and testing materials are well-defined and
carefully controlled and monitored. However, a number of unpalatable
developments traceable to the conferment in 1991 of agency status on the
FSS may be looming.[23]

As already mentioned, one problem is that a number of the most
experienced FSS scientists have recently been lost from the laboratory
bench, either through early retirement programmes or to become
managers of one complexion or another. While some restructuring of the
service was perhaps desirable and necessary in its pursuit of a new
'leanness and fitness' in preparation for agency status, many man-years of
skill and experience were lost to it. The consequence of this is that the
experience of case-working, court reporting scientists is now lower than
was previously the case. Moreover, young scientists are apparently being
encouraged to take on broader ranges of evidence types at a time when in
every other field of scientific endeavour scientists are necessarily becoming more specialised. Several laboratories have been on unlimited
overtime and at least one has been attempting to recall former members
of staff in order to cope with its backlog of police work. This indicates
that perhaps the pruning went too far and the service is now under-
manned. Against this background it is extraordinary that it should now
actively be seeking to extend its activities to defence work.

Another problem already rehearsed is that the effective demise of
CRSE means that there is no mechanism by which new scientific
developments and technologies can be recognised, tested and introduced
into the day-to-day practice of forensic science. This means that British
forensic science, which once led the world, is likely to fall increasingly
behind.

Lastly, there is the real danger that cost implications are restricting the
extent to which police employ FSS scientists, seek assistance from them
at scenes of crime or are prepared to submit items for examination,
thereby compromising the scope of scientific investigations and the safety

---

23 Agency status was approved by the Home Affairs Committee, *loc. cit.*, para. 101.

of the inferences drawn from these.[24] It cannot be be viewed as satisfactory that an ability to pay has replaced the criterion of seriousness of the case[25] as the determining factor in the reference from the police to the FSS. Nevertheless, the trend seems to be towards in-house police scientists,[26] and Forensic Access has itself been approached by a number of police forces with a view to providing them with scene of crime cover and/or exhibit screening services. Moreover, some police Scientific Support Managers have confided that they see the provision of in-house forensic science expertise as very much a part of their function which they are keen to develop. Some of these are forensic scientists by previous training and experience, while others are not. It follows that some will be better qualified than others to make scientific judgments and to screen items safely and effectively. Having said that, there is an important underlying principle here that the greater the number of 'sieves and gates' in the flow of exhibits and the information which accompanies them, the less confident one can be that the scientific interpretations which finally emerge properly take account of all the circumstances. There are also more pragmatic reasons to be wary of the proliferation of police laboratories in terms of the efficiency and capabilities of small scientific units.[27]

Forensic science is used in only in a very small proportion of police investigations (between 1 and 2 per cent), although it has the potential to be used in many more. While there is a balance to be struck here, perhaps the time has come for the police and the courts to reassess the extent to which it should be employed, particularly in the light of increasing calls for corroboration evidence. It is time too for a critical reappraisal to be undertaken as to whether the FSS (and the MPFSL) continues to be sufficiently resourced for the task at hand.

Other laboratories to whom some police forces are turning on cost grounds for forensic science services, such as those in industry, are in the main poorly equipped and their scientists lack the necessary skills and experience to do the job properly. This last feature is particularly worrying and is sowing the seeds of future miscarriages of justice.

---

24 Between April to September 1991, the FSS suffered a 13 per cent drop in case referral by the police, and about one-half of police forces have expressed criticisms of the FSS on cost grounds: HL Committee, *loc. cit.*, pp. 58, 181, 182. Before 1989, the Home Affairs Committee, *loc. cit.*, had reported increasing case-loads because of the growth in reported crime, new police powers, new forensic techniques and the demands of the CPS.

25 See Ramsay, M., *op. cit.*, ch. 2.

26 See for example Chief Constable of West Yorkshire, Annual Report 1990 (1991), p. 36.

27 See Home Office, *Memoranda to the Royal Commission* (1991), Annex E, para. 5.

By contrast to the FSS and the MPFSL, the very few independent firms properly qualified to comment for the defence on the majority of forensic science evidence are short of equipment and resources. This is a reflection of the uncertain and poor remuneration for the large majority of their work which is funded by legal aid. This barely pays for scientists' time, let alone necessary overheads, and it leaves nothing for essential investment in equipment, research, and library and reference materials.

So-called defence experts are a mixed bag. While the best might be genuinely familiar with the materials they contract to examine, very few of them can properly claim anywhere near sufficient or appropriate training and experience to be able to assess the significance of these in the circumstances of the case at issue.[28] Moreover, a worrying number are ready to advance opinions in fields of expertise well outside their own. This leads, at considerable public expense, to advice which is unhelpful at best and misleading at worst. Such 'cowboys' are no match for the calibre, training and experience of the scientists who routinely give evidence for the prosecution, but the chances are that the lawyer will not always recognise this fact until it is much too late to do anything about it.

With the advent of agency status, the FSS now undertakes some work for the defence. However, whether it is properly placed or trusted by defence lawyers to do so is another matter. The Home Affairs Committee found that most lawyers viewed the FSS as too close to the police, especially because of its practice, until recently, of disclosing defence examination reports to the prosecution.[29] Between April 1992 and February 1993, only 167 (about $\frac{1}{2}$ per cent) of FSS customers were defence related,[30] the figure is growing very slightly but is not expected to amount to a significant part of the business in the near future.[31] Whether the FSS's response to pressing police needs should in any event be diluted by outside commissions is open to debate. Nonetheless, agency status does mean that independent practitioners can now make use of the service's specialised equipment which, in the main, is peculiar to forensic science.

Funding

Access by the defence to properly qualified, experienced forensic scientists is further hampered by inadequate funding. In most criminal

---

28 See JUSTICE, *A Public Defender* (London, 1987), p. 10.
29 *Loc. cit.*, para. 80.
30 Information supplied by FSS, April 1993. See also Home Office, *loc. cit.*
31 See also FSS, Annual Report for 1991–92.

cases, the cost of the defence is met from public funds administered by local legal aid authorities and the Crown Courts.

In the worst cases, legal aid authorities may withhold funds altogether on the grounds that, for example, the scientific evidence is, in their (lay) view, unassailable and that any fresh investigation of it would be unwarranted. Pre-judgments of this kind contribute further to the manifest unfairness of the current system, and they induce miscarriages of justice.

Even when funds are forthcoming, the defence may be required to instruct a 'local expert'. But there is only a handful of properly qualified, experienced forensic scientists practising independently in this country. This means that unless there just happens to be one in the appropriate area, the advice the defence receives could be inadequate, incompetent, or both. Indeed, some legal aid boards go so far as to recommend experts themselves. In reality, these are often inappropriately qualified for the job in hand, and this also highlights the common danger of relying on lists of experts compiled and administered by non-scientists. Whatever legal aid boards assume or wish to pretend is the case, proper forensic scientists are thin on the ground and, more often than not, there is no sound advice to be had 'locally'.

As to cost implications, the early instruction of a competent forensic scientist for the defence can lead to substantial savings of public money. This is because in cases where the strengths and soundness of the prosecution's scientific evidence can be authoritatively confirmed, the accused may be persuaded that it is in his or her best interests to plead. Alternatively, where the evidence is exposed as weak, flawed or misunderstood, the case may be withdrawn altogether. Forensic Access has been instrumental in both these sorts of outcome.

Further difficulties result from the scandalously slow and arbitrary system of payment from legal aid funds. In simple contractual terms, instructing solicitors are responsible for meeting experts' fees and costs, but they are often not in a position to settle unless and until they themselves are placed in funds by the relevant Crown Court. This takes many months, so independent consultancies can be placed under threat of financial collapse while they wait for up to a year or more for bills, which may total tens of thousands of pounds, to be processed and paid. Moreover, experts' bills are subject to taxation by the Crown Court which means that, even where detailed estimates have been approved in advance, there are constant uncertainties not only as to when but also to what extent these will be met.

The consequences of nonsensical arrangements such as these are serious in the extreme[32] and have already persuaded some of the handful of properly qualified independent forensic scientists to refuse further legal aid work in favour of more lucrative business elsewhere. They also help to ensure that scientists in the FSS and the MPFSL are discouraged from entering the independent sector.

Suggested Remedies

In recent times, a number of suggestions have been made for improving the reliability of forensic science evidence. Some have pressed for reforms of the FSS which, it is claimed, would lead to a greater measure of impartiality, while others have concentrated on new organisations and/or frameworks to strengthen the position of the defence. These ideas have included:

(a)   a move towards a system of corroboration such as exists in Scotland;

(b)   the creation of a single organisation to serve the needs of both the police/prosecution and the defence, but which is independent of both;

(c)   the setting up of a separate, single organisation mirroring the FSS/MPFSL, but serving the defence alone;

(d)   a system of regulation and accreditation of all forensic scientists, methodologies and laboratories;

(e)   a fundamental change in the criminal justice system from an adversarial to an inquisitorial process, and the appointment of experts by the court or by some sort of *juge d'instruction*.

(a)   The Scottish system of corroboration. Scots law requires each case to be examined by two forensic scientists[33] who then produce a joint report on their findings. On the face of it, this would seem an ideal approach, since every aspect of the case is corroborated as a matter of course. But in practice, it appears to make no difference to the overall quality and balance of the work produced by the police laboratories there. This is probably because both scientists in the case approach their examinations from the same point of view, having the same information at their

---

32   The same complaints are, of course, often made by solicitors dependent on legal aid payments. See Law Society, *Response to the Legal Aid Efficiency Scrutiny* (London, 1986), p. 10.

33   It is a general requirement that the essential facts to establish a case against the accused be based on evidence derived from more than one source. See Sheehan, A. V., *Criminal Procedure* (Sweet & Maxwell, London, 1990), para. 2.03.

disposal and responding to it in very much the same way and at the same time.

In this regard it is interesting to recall the case against John Preece.[34] Dr Alan Clift's work was publicly discredited even though it had been properly corroborated by another forensic scientist because the case was to be heard by a Scottish court.

All in all, the corroboration of scientific opinion as demanded by the Scottish legal system seems to provide nothing more than a gloss. Moreover, in contrast to practice in England and Wales, it appears very difficult for Scottish defence lawyers to make acceptable and practicable arrangements for their scientists to examine relevant items and to discuss these with the police scientists who first looked at them. The consequence of this is that the work of the Scottish police laboratories cannot be properly tested.

(b)   A single organisation. Perhaps partly in recognition of the imbalance between forensic science resources available to the police/prosecution and the defence, and the pressing need to reinforce public perceptions of its impartiality, the resources of the FSS are now available to the defence on a customer-contractor basis. While superficially it might be argued that a blend of commitment to police/prosecution and defence work by the FSS could lead to more balanced and impartial scientific evidence, fundamental problems remain. The FSS continues to regard the police as its primary customer. The transition to executive agency status, which took place in the spring of 1991, is unlikely materially to cool the relationship which has always existed between them.

Owing to their unique, first claim to most evidential material, the FSS and MPFSL bear a heavy responsibility to ensure that their handling and testing of evidence is carried out in the most appropriate, accurate and up-to-date way possible, and that a uniformly excellent service is provided to police forces across the country. Central to this task is a high level of cooperation and exchange of research and case-work information between the scientists in all the laboratories in the network. Against this background, it is difficult to see how one scientist from one FSS laboratory could effectively test and probe the findings, and in particular the professional opinions, of a colleague at another. A number of senior FSS scientists have confided that, in their view, such arrangements and

---

34 See [1981] Crim LR 783; PCA, Fourth Report (1983–84 HC 191). Preece was convicted in 1973 of rape and murder on the basis of semen, hair and fibre analysis. His conviction was quashed in 1981.

expectations will lead to schisms in the service if the job is rigorously carried through, or a rubber stamping exercise if it is not.

Looking at the other side of the coin, now that the FSS has opened its doors to a potentially broader range of work, be it criminal or otherwise, there must be an attendant danger that its response to immediate police needs could be weakened by an increased volume of non-police work. Some police forces would surely view such a dilution as disturbing. In particular, it may be noted that agency status has not been extended to the Northern Ireland Forensic Science Laboratory (NIFSL), which naturally has only one police force as its customer, namely the Royal Ulster Constabulary (RUC). The NIFSL has remarked that it views agency status as risky to its relationship with the police.[35] By the same token, the police can now shop around for scientific assistance, and may be encouraged to do so by the greater expense and lower priority they incur by employing the FSS. But justice could well suffer from such a development, because the police are likely to have to approach a number of different sources to cover the range of evidence types they encounter, so that the cohesion and therefore the force of conclusions emerging about these might be diminished. In addition, the freedom of choice now enjoyed by the police encourages the use of laboratories which might be cheaper than the FSS, but which recent experience has shown are not up to the job.

As to the MPFSL, in evidence to the Home Affairs Committee,[36] the Metropolitan Police referred to the unique character of 'a single laboratory [the MPFSL] and a single customer'. Although there were certain indications at one stage that the MPFSL might have traversed some way down the same road as the FSS,[37] it is even more doubtful that it could ever be seen by the defence as a preferred source of advice or that such arrangements would sit comfortably with the needs of the Metropolitan Police.

Aside from difficulties arising from structural arrangments, another, but rather less tangible, factor concerns some FSS (and MPFSL) scientists' approach to their work. A number still fail to acknowledge the need for independent scientific scrutiny of it, even when they have seen

---

35 See HL Committee, *loc. cit.*, p. 50. The Chief Constable has revealed that police officers are formally part of the NIFSL's Serious Crime Unit: Annual Report 1991 (1992), p. 38. The NIFSL rarely acts for the defence, and there are few alternatives within Northern Ireland: SACHR, 17th Report (1992–93 HC 54) Ch. 6, para. 14, p. 275.

36 *Loc. cit.*, vol. II, p. 129.

37 MPFSL stated policy is now to the opposite effect.

the complexion of their own evidence altered as a result of proper intervention by the scientist engaged by the defence. Regrettably, a small number appear to regard themselves as occupying the high moral ground, from which vantage point defence work *per se* appears to be as offensive as it is unnecessary.

Comparisons have been drawn between the roles of forensic scientists and medical experts, such as forensic pathologists, who routinely advise the police one day and the defence the next. Such comparisons are fatally flawed. Unlike forensic scientists, medical experts rarely play any part at all in searching for, and providing evidence about, the identity of the perpetrators of crime. Rather, they are principally concerned with, for example, the nature of injuries and how and when these might have been caused. Against this background, it is difficult to see that, so far as disinterestedness is concerned, their roles have much in common.[38]

(c) A separate single organisation for the defence. It has been variously suggested that one (or more) university department(s) could provide the basis of a national organisation for the defence. However attractive such a proposal might seem at first blush, it must be remembered that with one or two exceptions, there are no properly trained and experienced forensic scientists in university departments. Arguably, the FSS laboratories and MPFSL are the only credible sources of training in forensic science, because it is only at these establishments that newcomers to the profession can acquire the necessary experience of case-work in sufficient volume and variety. Only two universities offer MSc courses in forensic science (King's College London and Strathclyde). While students coming from these might be better informed in theoretical terms than other new graduates, they still need just as much training in day-to-day case-work as anybody else fresh from university.

Leaving aside available expertise, it has also been suggested that universities are the natural home for defence forensic science, because they tend to be well blessed with a range of equipment and instrumentation. But this is not a telling point because, as already indicated, the scope for retesting evidential materials is often limited, and even where the right sort of equipment exists, it often lacks essential modifications. Furthermore, in the current entrepreneurial climate, it is not necessary to be part of a university to have access to all its scientific instruments.

In any event, be it in a university or otherwise, centralising forensic

---

38 There are also differences in terms of professional regulation, though these may be narrowed by the suggestions *infra*.

science expertise for the defence in a single organisation is to be avoided at all costs. Such a development would lead to narrowing of horizons, introspection and complacency as well as politicking, rivalry and polarisation so far as its relations with the FSS/MPFSL were concerned. Indeed, in evidence to the Home Affairs Committee, the Home Office expressed concern 'if there was any suggestion of centralising defence work . . . since this could inhibit the development of defence facilities'.[39] A public defender system[40] based on salaried employees would also be vulnerable to underfunding. At least with individual applications for legal aid the courts can undermine a government policy of stringency, and have effectively done so in recent years.

(d)   A system of regulation and accreditation. In evidence to the Home Affairs Committee,[41] the Home Office was not persuaded by the case for formal regulation of the forensic science profession.[42] While admitting to varying standards among defence scientists, it doubted that the problem justified any new measures to deal with it. Nonetheless, FSS and MPFSL scientists continue privately to express concern about poor standards and incompetence displayed by some defence scientists who visit their laboratories to examine their work. On the defence side, there is a long history of incompetence and charlatanism; indeed, one of the aims in setting up Forensic Access was to improve the quality of mainstream forensic science advice available to the defence.

At present there is no regulation of the forensic science profession. This means that anyone with any sort of scientific background, or just plain brass neck, can advertise his or her services to police or defence as a forensic scientist. The advice that is given in these circumstances is usually unhelpful at best, and dangerously misleading at worst. In the interests of both prosecution and defence, it is time that forensic science was closed to dabblers.

So far as its own scientists were concerned, the Home Office was satisfied with its efforts to ensure that they met a high standard. But, since 1989 far-reaching changes in the organisation and structure of the FSS

---

39   *Loc. cit.*, vol. II, p. 195.
40   Sargant, T. and Hill, P., *op. cit.*, p. 17.
41   *Loc. cit.*, vol. II, p. 194. The Committee itself, *loc. cit.*, para. 84, was not convinced, though largely because of the then very limited number of independent forensic services.
42   Some official accreditation already exists. By the Criminal Justice (Scotland) Act 1980, s. 26, scientists approved by the Scottish Secretary can present evidence by certificate, and about 30 forensic pathologists are listed by the Home Office: see Home Affairs Committee, *loc. cit.*, vol. II, p. 181.

have resulted in the loss from the laboratory bench of significant numbers of its most experienced scientists. This has consequently precipitated an increased reliance on relatively inexperienced staff, and at the same time the encouragement of staff to tackle broader ranges of evidence types when the pace of scientific development means that, in other fields, scientists are becoming ever more specialised. In addition, FSS scientists are now exposed to, and deeply conscious of, commercial pressures for the first time. In the light of all of this, it could be argued that the basis for the Home Office special pleading has disappeared.

In consequence, there is a pressing need for all forensic scientists to be covered by a statutorily constituted and empowered governing council,[43] perhaps like the General Medical Council[44] or the Law Society.[45] This council would be responsible for formulating, implementing and maintaining arrangements for the effective regulation of the forensic science profession as a whole. In this way, the defence (and the prosecution) could be more sure of instructing a scientist who was up to the task.

It is essential that accreditation should cover all aspects of the work, beginning with the individual scientists and extending to the ways in which they work and the analytical tests they carry out.[46] Accreditation and regulation should be entirely independent of the FSS, or of any government department or university.

So far as the scientists are concerned, each should be certified in specific fields of expertise on the grounds of qualifications and experience. This should be undertaken by peer review under the auspices of a properly constituted and empowered governing council drawn partly from relevant professional bodies, including the Royal Society of Chemistry and the Institute of Biology, and partly from practitioners who have the respect of the profession as a whole. Thereafter, the council should be required to monitor and to regulate the scientists' work against a code of conduct and competence standards, all centred upon individual professionalism.

As to the scientists' work, there are already quality management systems available, especially those recognised by the National Measurement Accreditation Service (NAMAS)[47] and British Standard 5750,

---

43   The Forensic Science Society cannot readily perform this function as membership is
     based on interest rather than qualification.
44   Medical Act 1983.
45   Solicitors Act 1974.
46   On the latter, compare Sargant, T. and Hill, P., *op. cit.*, p. 27; Alldridge, P.,
     'Recognising novel scientific techniques' [1992] Crim LR 687.
47   The Service is part of the National Physics Laboratory, an arm of the DTI. See NIS46,
     Accreditation for Forensic Analysis and Examination (1992).

which cover different aspects of work from its organisation to performance of the analytical tests themselves. Differences of opinion are
emerging as to which of these two quality management systems in
particular is appropriate in different organisations. For example, ICI at
Cellmark Diagnostics have chosen BS5750 as appropriate to their DNA
profiling operations, whereas the FSS and MPFSL have applied to
NAMAS. These are issues which should be investigated on behalf of a
governing council, to whom recommendations about future requirements in the profession should then be made.

Virtually all forensic services and their main customers now accept the
need for external accreditation, and most also support the idea of a
professional body to enforce standards.[48]

(e)   Change to an inquisitorial process. For some of the reasons already
discussed, it is difficult to see how a single scientist could function
adequately and in equal measure for all parties concerned in a criminal
investigation and subsequent trial, whether the legal framework was
inquisitorial or adversarial. The multifaceted role to be fulfilled would not
sit comfortably with the level of involvement and commitment needed at
each stage of the work, and seems to run the risk of requiring such
impartiality as to render the scientist's contributions largely ineffective.

Over and above these difficulties, there is a number of concerns
seemingly inherent in an inquisitorial system relying on the appointment
of experts by the court.[49] For instance, as a court appointee, there might
be a tendency for the expert's findings, and any opinions offered,
automatically to be regarded as stamped with the court's seal of approval.
In the possible absence of a ready means of challenging scientific
evidence, the expert might well be encouraged to go beyond the proper
limits of his or her expertise. The court itself, or the *juge d'instruction*,
might be tempted to look more favourably on experts it knew were likely
to endorse its own views, and an 'old boy network', such as some French
defence lawyers complain about, could easily develop. In any event, it is
difficult to see that the court would be in a position effectively to question
any expert in order properly to test his or her evidence.

All in all, the adversarial system appears to offer the best scope for
properly testing and challenging scientific evidence, but only provided

---

48   See HL Committee, *loc. cit.* However, the FSS rejects the concept of an independent
     governing body, *ibid.* p. 15.
49   Compare Sargant, T. and Hill, P., *op. cit.*, p. 28; Howard, M. N., 'The neutral expert:
     a plausible threat to justice?' [1991] Crim LR 98; Spencer, J. R., 'The neutral expert:
     an implausible bogey' [1991] Crim LR 106.

that the defence has effective access to scientists of a similar standing to those called for the prosecution.

Conclusion

The central problem with forensic science evidence is that, for the most part, it is not being properly probed and tested at trial. There have been misconceptions about its nature and an imbalance of forensic science skills and expertise available to the prosecution and defence.

The following are essential ingredients in securing an effective way forward:

(a) The profession of forensic science should be rigorously monitored and regulated by a properly constituted governing council with a full set of teeth and the necessary statutory powers to use them.

(b) Adequate funding should be provided as a matter of course to enable the defence properly to scrutinise scientific evidence in every case in which it is presented and/or available.

(c) Arrangements for payment of experts' fees should be radically altered to bring them into line with normal commercial practice in order to attract appropriately qualified and experienced forensic scientists into defence work, and to retain them.

(d) Greater priority should be accorded to the training of lawyers and police officers in forensic science so that its relevance and meaning can more readily be appreciated.

The implementation of these measures would promote healthy growth in independent forensic science and would thereby help to enrich and stimulate both the public and private sectors. They would ensure that scientific evidence was properly tested and balanced at trial and was therefore more likely to be sustainable thereafter.

EDITORS' COMMENTS

Given that forensic evidence is available in only 1:200 cases[1] and that resources do not stretch to its analysis and use in all possible cases, the hope that science may provide an antidote to the police construction of criminality, especially through interrogation, seems forlorn. Even when it is available, the foregoing chapter highlights the dangers of placing

---

1   Police Service, *Submission to the Royal Commission* (1991), para. 1.1.19.

faith in the infallibility of scientists, just as it has proven mistaken to believe in the total honesty of all constables. The fond belief that the Police and Criminal Evidence Act 1984 has remedied all ills is even less well-founded in regard to forensic, as compared to police, practices.[2] The Act has extended police discretion to obtain physical evidence in several important respects[3] but does little to impose regulation even upon the police. It is wholly silent on the subjects of forensic scientists and expert witnesses. Thus there remain problems, especially about the standards employed in analysis and the soundness of the interpretation of results, with the grave danger that the jury will be seduced by the purity of the science without fully considering the impurity of its application. As well as the notorious cases giving rise to the foundation of the Runciman Commission, alleged examples of an over-eagerness to draw inferences from forensic evidence include in recent times the cases of Patrick McLaughlin in 1985[4] and Gilbert MacNamee in 1987.[5] Other defects already rehearsed concern the relationship between police and forensic laboratories and the failure to offer matching resources to the defence through legal aid, thereby fostering inequality between defence and prosecution, as recognised in *R* v *Ward*.[6] The remedies suggested to the Runciman Commission reflect several of the five ideas canvassed in the foregoing chapter. In particular, a new defence-orientated forensic service is advanced by the Bar Council,[7] having long attracted the support of JUSTICE as part of its campaign for a public defender.[8] However, the bulk of opinion seems to favour a better regulated range of forensic facilities operated by more proficient personnel, both in the public and private sectors, with more generous legal aid for the latter.[9] Regulations, which

---

2   Standards demanded elsewhere are little better: *California* v *Trombetta* 467 US 479 (1984); *Arizona* v *Youngblood* 488 US 51 (1988).

3   See ss. 8, 9, 18, 32, 54, and 61–63. The powers to search for property are in general rather better regulated than the powers to take bodily samples, which may reflect the general failure in English common law to recognise a right to privacy: *Malone* v *MPC (No. 2)* [1979] Ch 344.

4   [1988] 3 All ER 431; (1986) *The Times*, 26 November, pp. 1, 20. His fingerprints were detected on a bin-liner in which bombs had been wrapped. The owners of other prints were not charged. See Woffinden, B., 'The influence of justice' (1990) *Counsel*, May, p. 14.

5   See *The Times*, 28 October 1987 pp. 1, 3; *R* v *Ellis* (1991) *The Times*, 31 October, pp. 1, 3. His prints were taken from electrical equipment found in bombs. He admitted working as an electrician in Dundalk.

6   (1992) 96 Cr App R 1.

7   *Submission*, para. 16.2.

8   Op. cit., para. 55.

9   See *Submissions* of Amnesty International, para. 4.6; CPS, para. 12.3.24; Home Office, p. 8; Law Society, paras. 4.31, 4.35, 4.37, 4.38; Liberty, p. 63; Police Service, p. 149.

could cover issues such as testing which destroys samples, defence presence during tests and access to equipment and records, the storage and retention of records and samples, might be set by a code of practice under the Police and Criminal Evidence Act, the compliance with which would then have a direct bearing on admissibility.[10] On the whole, this stance seems most in keeping with the ethos of an adversarial system of justice.

Despite the overwhelming support for a stronger and more regulated range of forensic services, three difficulties may persist. First, there is the ever present problem of funding. The Police and Criminal Evidence Act was implemented during a decade of unprecedented growth in police budgets, which allowed for new facilities and training without unduly prejudicing other priorities. By contrast, forensic services would need to be expanded, not simply redeployed, and at a time of public spending retrenchment. Secondly, the proper extent of the reforms in the forensic area, as opposed to their direction, remains largely unconsidered. For example, it might be asked why fingerprints are currently collected and analysed by the police without reference in the vast majority of cases to scientists or independent laboratories. The answer seems in the main to be historical; fingerprinting was developed two or three decades before the establishment of formal laboratories.[11] It is true that the process does not involve any experimentation, but it may be subject to mistakes of implementation or interpretation at the stage of obtaining the print, typology and matching, and then inferences drawn from its presence.[12] Another forensic service which is likewise commonly used but alarmingly unregulated concerns the work of interpreters. Thus, forensic science should be defined in wide terms if the quality of justice is to be improved. The third and final problem concerns how forensic evidence is handled and the particular danger that tests adverse to the contentions of the prosecution will be disregarded and suppressed. That danger forms the focus of the next chapter.

Postscript

The House of Lords Select Committee on Science and Technology has now reported on 'Forensic Science'.[13] Though working from the

---

10 See s. 66(11).
11 See *R* v *Castleton* (1910) 3 Cr App R 74.
12 See Campbell, D., 'Fingerprints' [1985] Crim LR 175; Kind, S. S., *The Scientific Investigation of Crime* (Forensic Science Services, Harrogate, 1987).
13 (1992–93) HL 24.

blinkered premise that forensic science primarily suffers from an 'image problem',[14] it concurs with many of the recommendations put forward in chapter 5, but also adds some rather unpalatable ideas of its own. Its principal conclusions are as follows:

(a)   that the development of NVQs is to be welcomed;[15]

(b)   that a new centre for forensic research be established in the light of commercial pressures on the FSS;[16]

(c)   that laboratories should make public their quality assessment trials;[17]

(d)   that NAMAS standard setting should extend to sampling processes;[18]

(e)   that forensic scientists should be individually registered with a Board fostered by the Home Office on proof of competence;[19]

(f)   that the law on DNA techniques and the application of the hearsay rules to the work of junior staff be clarified;[20]

(g)   that experts be encouraged to engage in pre-trial conferences and reviews and be allowed to make statements after their examination;[21]

(h)   that lawyers should receive training in forensic science.[22]

The Committee members were unable to reach any firm conclusion as to whether the MPFSL should be merged with the FSS[23] but were hostile to the proliferation of further police laboratories.[24]

14   *Ibid.*, para. 1.33.
15   *Ibid.*, para. 2.36.
16   *Ibid.*, para. 2.48, 2.51.
17   *Ibid.*, para. 3.13.
18   *Ibid.*, para. 3.34.
19   *Ibid.*, para. 3.52 to 3.61.
10   *Ibid.*, para. 5.5, 5.10.
21   *Ibid.*, para. 5.18, 5.20, 5.31.
22   *Ibid.*, para. 5.33.
23   *Ibid.*, para. 4.26.
24   *Ibid.*, para. 4.13.

6

Prosecution Disclosure: Principle, Practice and Justice[1]

Patrick O'Connor

Introduction

For in criminal cases, the State has in the police, an agency for the discovery of evidence, superior to anything which even the wealthiest defendant could employ.[2]

This imbalance of resources, and the prosecution's consequent control over information, has contributed significantly to the majority of recent miscarriage of justice cases. Belated recognition of this problem emerged in the last judgment in the *Birmingham Six* case:[3]

A disadvantage of the adversarial system may be that the parties are not evenly matched in resources . . . But the inequality of resources is ameliorated by the obligation on the part of the prosecution to make available all material which may prove helpful to the defence.

The problem is compounded by the timing of deployment of those resources. The police, unsupervised, have a virtual monopoly over the

---

1 An earlier version of this chapter first appeared as an article in [1992] Crim LR 464 and is reproduced by permission.
2 Report of the Departmental Committee on Evidence of Identification in Criminal Cases (1975–76 HC 338) ('Devlin Report'), para. 1.17.
3 *R v McIlkenny and others* (1991) 93 Cr App R 287, at p. 312.

immediate investigation and collection of information. The defence under our current system play a reactive role. There may not even be an arrest or a charge for weeks or months after the crime. Even then the defence lawyers will not know the case they have to meet until the service upon them of the prosecution witness statements, after further delays of some months, when the police investigation has finished. The trail of any independent witnesses will long have grown cold. Forlorn advertisements in little-read local newspapers often attest to this hopeless task.

We have learned painfully that there is no satisfactory substitute for the consideration of all the relevant evidence by one tribunal of fact; and it is the jury who have the constitutional task of deciding a citizen's guilt or innocence in our system. The prosecution's duty of disclosure plays a vital role in safeguarding the integrity of our criminal trials.

The intention of this chapter is to discover the origins and development of the duty of disclosure in English law, now set out in the Attorney-General's Guidelines; to examine some of the defects in current policies and practices; and to recommend certain clarifications and improvements.

Before the Guidelines

The Devlin Report[4] in 1976 found that 'Until 30 years ago, no authority existed for the proposition that there was any duty at all'. This would seem to be borne out by two 1958 cases, in which trial judges ordered only in the most tentative of terms the disclosure of particular material to the defence.[5] The only other distant precedent was in 1930, when the Court of Appeal had criticised the non-disclosure of an earlier inconsistent description of an identification witness.[6]

The reference in the Devlin Report to '30 years ago' was to the 1946 decision in *R* v *Bryant and Dickson*.[7] The Court of Appeal had then held that there was no actual duty to serve an unused witness statement on the defence. On the facts, there was infertile ground for any defence complaint in that case. The witness was well known to the co-accused; they had been invited by the Crown shortly after committal to take a statement from him; he had attended the trial but the defence decided not to call, or even take a statement from, him. Plainly, on those facts, the defence had every opportunity to call the witness.

---

4   *Loc. cit.*, para. 5.1.
5   *R* v *Hall* (1958) 43 Cr App R 29; and *R* v *Xinaris*, *ibid.*, at p. 30.
6   *R* v *Clarke* (1930) 22 Cr App R 58.
7   (1946) 31 Cr App R 146.

The other so-called leading case was *Dallison* v *Caffery*.[8] In this civil action for damages for false imprisonment and malicious prosecution, the Court of Appeal had to consider the significance of the failure to disclose statements supporting the plaintiff's alibi at the time of his committal for trial. Did this failure amount to prima facie evidence of 'lack of honest belief' in the plaintiff's guilt? The Court of Appeal unanimously answered 'No'. In fact the statements were handed over immediately after committal.

Unfortunately the Court went further and commented *obiter* and generally upon the duty of disclosure. The waters were thereby successfully muddied for ensuing decades. Lord Denning MR contended:[9]

> . . . [the prosecutor] must either call that witness himself or make his statement available to the defence. It would be highly reprehensible to conceal from the court the evidence which such a witness could give.

Diplock LJ held that actual service of the statement was 'more than necessary propriety' and suggested that the only duty was to 'make the witness available'.[10] The third Judge (Dankwerts LJ) did not participate in this debate, probably since it was irrelevant to the decision on the appeal.

It is difficult to understand how our system can have operated under such a confusion of policy. Successive editors of *Archbold's Criminal Pleading* have attempted to soften the regime, by recommending that 'an inflexible approach to these circumstances can work injustice'.[11]

Meanwhile, the system occasionally showed signs of creaking. In 1947, Walter Rowlands was convicted and executed for a murder. A Home Office inquiry conducted by Jolly KC had confirmed his guilt, just before the execution. However, the police had withheld evidence supporting Rowlands's alibi. On 6 December 1951, the Home Secretary, Maxwell Fife, conceded Rowlands's innocence in the House of Commons, saying:[12]

> I certainly agree . . . that it is the practice at the Bar of England, as I understand it, that prosecuting counsel must make known to the defence any evidence which is relevant to the matter.

---

8 [1965] 1 QB 348.
9 *Ibid.*, at p. 369B.
10 *Ibid.*, at p. 376C.
11 41st ed., para. 4–178.
12 HC Debs, vol. 494, col. 2554.

This was an expedient over-statement of the safeguards against non-disclosure; the memory of a wrongly executed man deserved greater frankness.

In *Baksh*[13] the Privy Council quashed a conviction because of non-disclosure of near contemporaneous witness statements which were inconsistent with later testimony. In *Hassan and Kotaish*[14] convictions were quashed on account of the failure to disclose the complainant's previous convictions.

The Devlin Report (above) examined the conviction in 1969 of Laszlo Virag and found that the non-disclosure of a significant fingerprint of a third party had contributed to the wrongful conviction.[15] It commented that 'A duty of disclosure is not discharged by frankness in cross-examination if the point happens to be raised'.

In 1974, the defence in *Cooper and McMahon* (the 'Luton Post Office murder' case)[16] were first served with over 800 witness statements by order of the Court of Appeal only after a first appeal had failed. They had been in the possession of the Crown for over five years and proved important to the men's later release.

Summary convictions were quashed in *R v Leyland Justices, ex parte Hawthorn*[17] after the police failed to notify the defence of the existence of two witnesses to the accident in question. This had 'prevented the tribunal from giving the defendant a fair trial'.

In 1975–76, before the introduction of the 'Guidelines', the three trials took place which probably count as the darkest hours of British criminal justice.

At the trial of the *Birmingham Six*, one of the twin pillars of the Crown case was the assertion by their expert, Dr Skuse, that his Greiss test was 'specific' for nitroglycerine (i.e. proved positive only in its presence). He was '99 per cent certain' of this assertion. In fact one of his colleagues from the same laboratory, Dr Bamford, had obtained positive results with the same test that same night from the hands of two salesmen on the Belfast ferry. These were dismissed as irrelevant by that scientist, as having arisen from their contact with an adhesive tape they used for wrapping their samples. This information remained undisclosed at trial and even at the unsuccessful 1987 appeal. Nevertheless, it would have

---

13   [1958] AC 157.
14   (1968) 52 Cr App R 291.
15   *Loc. cit.*, at paras 1.20, 3.108.
16   (1975) 65 Cr App R 215; (1978) 68 Cr App R 18.
17   (1979) 68 Cr App R 269.

destroyed the credibility of Dr Skuse's basic premise, and it did form part of the basis for the quashing of the convictions in 1991.[18]

The convictions of the *Guildford Four* depended entirely upon alleged confessions by each accused. The convictions were quashed, with the consent of the Crown, on the basis of police documents, which undermined the officers' evidence that certain interviews were contemporaneously recorded. Typed versions of some interviews, with amendments inconsistent with the manuscript notes used at trial, had come to light. Detention records contradicted the police version of the timing and duration of interviews. In the view of the Court of Appeal, these latter 'might on their own, let alone in conjunction with these other matters, have made a grave difference to the outcome [of the trial]'. Further questions of non-disclosure have been raised in this case, for example, relating to the alibi of Gerard Conlon. These remain to be investigated by the next stages of the May Inquiry and by the prosecutions of some of the officers concerned.

The *Maguire Seven* were condemned entirely upon the results of Thin Layer Chromatology ('TLC') tests for the presence of nitroglycerine on hand-swabs. The trial proceeded without it ever emerging that each allegedly positive swab had been subjected to a further and different test which proved negative. These alternative results were recorded in the same notebook as, and within a few pages of, the 'positives'. Similarly, certain experiments were carried out by the Royal Armaments Research and Development Establishment (RARDE) scientists during the original trial, and in response to issues there arising, which were never mentioned or revealed to the defence. The Interim Report of the May Inquiry[19] points to a nine-month period leading up to the trial, during which defence requests for copies of the scientists' records, even of positive tests, were either ignored or refused.

The convictions were ultimately quashed, in part on the basis of information published in a scientific journal in 1982,[20] subsequently confirmed by the May Inquiry's own independent research.[21] Authors of the 1982 article included a statement from one of the Crown's witnesses at the original trial. This contradicted his own trial evidence as to the significance of traces allegedly found under fingernails. It seems not to

---

18 Other important material was unearthed during the appeals, such as the so-called 'Reade Schedule', which served to undermine the integrity of the alleged confessions.
19 1990–91 HC No. 556, at paras 12.1–4.
20 Twibell, J. D., Smalldon, K. W., Higgs, D. G., 'Transfer of nitroglycerine to hands during contact with commercial explosives' (1982) 27 *Journal of Forensic Sciences* 783.
21 *Loc. cit.*, at para. 9.5.

have occurred to anyone that something might have to be done with regard to these prisoners. Even more shocking is the footnote to the 1982 article, which reveals that the actual research was carried out in 1977. This was the year of the Maguires' first unsuccessful appeal; they all had much of their sentences to serve; Guiseppe Conlon was still alive. Perhaps there is no more moving reminder of the power that goes with the control of information. It can be a matter of life and death.

The Royal Commission on Criminal Procedure

The immediate occasion for the introduction of the current Guidelines was the disturbing state of affairs revealed by the Philips Commission, charged with examining criminal procedure.[22] The disclosure policies and practices of different prosecuting authorities were investigated. Appendix 28 sets out the detailed policies of three: the DPP, the Metropolitan Police Solicitors, and the Greater Manchester Police Solicitors. The Commission concluded that 'there are considerable variations in matters of detail'.[23]

One clear example will suffice — the disclosure of previous criminal convictions of prosecution witnesses. In 1955, the Court of Appeal had held in *Collister and Warhurst*[24] that 'It is [the prosecution's] duty to disclose to the defence actual convictions of crime standing on the record of the prosecutor'. By contrast, the DPP's policy was stated to be:

[Such records] are not normally disclosed unless counsel so advises. Sometimes this will be done during the trial, on a counsel to counsel basis. The tendency however is not to disclose unless the previous conviction, e.g. for perjury, is clearly relevant and it is also apparent that the evidence of the witness will be challenged.

The Manchester policy was very similar, with the added sting that 'It is not [the] practice actively to enquire whether or not a witness has convictions without special reason'. The Metropolitan Police policy was more satisfactory in this respect and expressly referred to the *Collister* authority (above).

It is remarkable that so recently, on such an important topic and in the face of such clear judicial ruling, there should have been such

22   Cmnd 8092, 1981.
23   *Ibid.*, para. 15.
24   (1955) 39 Cr App R 100, at p. 104.

discrepancies. The chances of many a fair trial must have been substantially affected by the likelihood of trial location and prosecuting authority. The relevance in law of a witness's previous convictions may not be so much in the nature of the actual offence, as the DPP and Manchester seemed to think; credibility may be far more damaged by the attitude of the witness to that earlier accusation, for example if there has been a 'not guilty' plea, and evidence given by that witness on oath, which must have been rejected. How many witnesses with unsavoury histories of dishonesty have been treated by all concerned as of impeccable background at trials before 1982?

On other important aspects of the duty of disclosure, the DPP told the Commission that 'Within the office . . . there is no laid-down policy, but the practice with minor variations, is along the following lines . . .'. There then followed a litany of 'usually . . . may . . . sometimes . . . might . . . normally . . . tendency'. It is disturbing, therefore, that in 1976 an Attorney-General under pressure yet again misled the House of Commons. In response to the Devlin Report on Identification Evidence, the House was told:[25]

> Where proceedings are instituted, the Director will, subject to the requirement of the public interest, continue his practice of making available to the defence any material likely to assist the defence.

The Attorney-General's Guidelines

In order for the first time to establish some consistent policy and practice, the Guidelines were issued in December 1981.[26] They are set out in the Appendix to this chapter.

In terms of their status, the Guidelines probably constitute only internal instructions to CPS lawyers and prosecution counsel. They significantly lack the status of either primary or delegated legislation. The Attorney-General has every right to issue instructions to his staff, but not to make or even declare law. The Guidelines themselves do not purport to do either. Neither Parliament nor the courts have actually considered whether the contents of the Guidelines are adequate or compatible with an objective view of fairness to the defence. Nevertheless, the Court of

---

25 HC Debs, vol. 912, col. 289 w.a. 27 May 1976.
26 (1982) 74 Cr App R 302. In August 1992, the DPP issued the 'Guinness Advice' on disclosure to the police; the Advice is not intended to replace or supplement the 1981 Guidelines, but its contents remained confidential until December 1992, following a request for access by the editors. The contents are appended to this chapter.

Appeal has been prepared to quash convictions because of breaches of the Guidelines. This has been a desirable, though makeshift, resource. The Court of Appeal's stance arose in response to the radical argument, advanced by the Crown in the first Guinness trial, *Saunders and Others*, that the Guidelines 'did not have the force of law'.[27] With the agile mind of an administrative lawyer, the trial judge, Henry J, answered with a sort of 'legitimate expectation' argument:[28]

> . . . it seems to me that any defendant must be entitled to approach his trial on the basis that the prosecution will have complied with the . . . guidelines and those accordingly are the ground rules which govern his trial.

He continued by pointing out correctly that the Court of Appeal had held that breach of the Guidelines could constitute a 'material irregularity' within s. 2(1)(c) of the Criminal Appeal Act 1968. However welcome, these are rather abstruse ways of conferring authority upon one of the basic foundations for a fair trial.

In the absence of statutory authority, a particular problem is caused by the conflict between the requirements of the Guidelines, which we shall examine below, and the pre-existing case-law, where the leading precedents of *Bryant and Dickson* and *Dallison* v *Caffery* bear no relation to the former. For example, Henry J in *Saunders*[29] suggests that the Guidelines had resolved the conflict between Lords Denning and Diplock in *Dallison* in favour of the former. Similarly, the 1991 first edition of *Blackstone's Criminal Practice* suggested that the Guidelines:[30]

> . . . have rendered the common law on disclosure somewhat otiose in that the Guidelines extend beyond what the authorities strictly require.

On the other hand, the Court of Appeal in *Lawson*[31] stated 'it must be remembered that an inflexible application of *Bryant and Dickson* can lead to injustice'. Such an exhortation would not of course be necessary at all, if that case had indeed been overtaken by the Guidelines. The reality is that the two leading cases do conflict within and between themselves and

---

27 Unreported, Central Criminal Court, 29 August 1989, transcript. See also (1990) *The Times*, 8 February; (1991) *The Independent* 17 May.
28 *Ibid.*, at p. 7F.
29 *Ibid.*, at p. 5.
30 At para. D11.19.
31 (1989) 90 Cr App R 107, at p. 114.

are wholly inconsistent with the higher standards of the Guidelines. The only way to ensure clarity is to resolve by legislation the anomalies of their contents and their status. Thereby, after full debate, Parliament will authoritatively and conclusively set the standards.

Turning to the contents of the Guidelines, the broad presumption in favour of disclosure is established by para. 2, which provides that 'all unused materials should normally . . . be made available to the defence solicitor'. By para. 9, 'Any doubt as to whether the balance is in favour of, or against, disclosure should always be resolved in favour of disclosure.'

A clear policy as to the timing of disclosure is set out as follows:

2. In all cases which are due to be committed for trial . . . 3(a) If it will not delay the committal, disclosure should be made as soon as possible before the date fixed . . . (b) [otherwise] . . . it should be done at or as soon as possible after committal.

The importance of timing is, of course, that the defence should have the best practicable opportunity to absorb, assess and use the material. The decisions as to mode of committal, and which witnesses to call or to cross-examine, may each be affected thereby. This policy is often ignored; disclosure is commonplace in the weeks before trial or on the first day of the trial itself. Low priorities and lack of resources are often the reasons.

The subject-matter of disclosure is described by para. 2, which enjoins the service of 'all unused material . . . if it has some bearing on the offence(s) charged and the surrounding circumstances of the case'. The definition of 'unused material' in para. 1 is extremely wide and inclusive, so that the specified categories are mere examples: 'All witness statements and documents . . . not included in the committal bundles'.

The breadth of this definition cannot be criticised. However, its true implications have yet to be appreciated fully by prosecutors. The recent ruling of Henry J in *Saunders and Others* gives full weight to the plain intention of the Attorney-General. As he commented, 'it is hard to imagine wider words than that . . .'.[32] In that case, the defence were held entitled to see all preparatory notes and memoranda which led to the making of witness statements. The rationale was that since the defence have the right to cross-examine on prior inconsistent statements:[33]

---

32 *Loc. cit.*, at p. 6D.
33 *Ibid.*, at p. 4F. See also *Berry* v *R* [1992] 3 WLR 153.

. . . so the defence should, as a general rule, in normal circumstances, be given the right to see information that would enable the right to be exercised, i.e. to give the right meaning.

An important further observation was that the only area in which the Crown has any business making its own assessment 'of the utility of the disclosure to the defence's legitimate case' is where there may be a question of sensitivity, such as national security or the identity of informants.[34]

A faithful observation of the full definition of 'unused material' and of this judgment would provide earlier and deeper access for the defence to much relevant material. Before committal, copies of all police officers' notebooks should be provided. Whether later used as memory refreshing documents or not, they are plainly material preparatory to their witness statements. Persistent obstructions to acquiring access to observation logs should now evaporate. It is still common to have to ask prosecution counsel at trial for a copy of the 'Crime Report', an important first record of much detailed early information; it sometimes then takes days for it to be recovered. Copies of photofits, artists' impressions from all witnesses, notes of oral descriptions and car registration numbers should all be served, before committal and without request.

The present shortcomings in the extent of disclosure practices may be illustrated in two ways. First, there is often an alarming discrepancy between the documents disclosed upon discovery in civil litigation against the police, and those which come to light for the purposes of earlier criminals trials arising out of the same incident. There is a whole range of 'internal' police records, which are often highly revealing precisely because the officers concerned do not expect them to see the light of day. One such is an 'Injury on Duty' Form, which speaks for itself, and is completed as a matter of routine in any such case. Rarely does this emerge at a criminal trial, unless specifically requested. In this author's own experience, the forms often tell a remarkably different story from the same officer's witness statement in police assault cases. They should be disclosed as a matter of routine.

The second example concerns police witness statements. In large scale disturbances of public order, police officers can quite legitimately make several witness statements for the purposes of different proceedings. These are rarely provided to the defence in criminal trials. Yet once, through the chance that this author's instructing solicitor represented

---

34   *Ibid.*, at p. 7C.

more than one alleged participant, the opportunity to compare such statements had dramatic consequences. The police officer had put himself in two places at once and offered diametrically contradictory accounts of events. The trial judge stopped the case and referred the papers for investigation. Meanwhile, the police paid out over £20,000 in damages to the accused.

As well as the inherent limitations in the duties to disclose, para. 6(i)-(iv) of the Guidelines insert express discretions not to disclose in certain situations. Each encourages the adoption of a dangerously subjective and vague approach by prosecutors.

It may be helpful to examine para. 6(i) in detail:

> There are grounds for fearing that disclosing a statement might lead to an attempt being made to persuade a witness to make a statement retracting his original one, to change his story, not to appear at court or otherwise to intimidate him.

Upon whom is placed the task of assessing such grounds? Do there have to be reasonable grounds or is it entirely subjective? In what serious criminal case with civilian witnesses is it not possible to assert that there 'might' be such an attempt? Since this exception relates to 'unused material', is it not nonsense to posit an accused seeking to persuade such a witness not to attend court? The witness is not to be called anyway. Why are the defence treated as if they are the sole source of threats to the integrity of a witness's evidence?

The exception in para. 6(ii) has created particular problems. A statement may be withheld if it 'is believed to be wholly or partly untrue and might be of use in cross-examination if the witness should be called by the defence'. Of course, by the time the Crown knows if the defence are to call the witness, it is too late. Effective cross-examination does not entirely depend upon taking the other side by surprise. The extra tactical advantage to the Crown of surprise is at the risk of the jury not hearing valuable evidence, if the defence happen not to know of the witness anyway. A dangerous cat-and-mouse game by prosecutors is encouraged. The interests of a fair trial may be better advanced by the defence making an informed decision not to call a dubious witness, rather than falling into a calculated trap to the tactical advantage of the Crown.

In *Lawson* (above), the Crown withheld service of a witness statement favourable to the defence, despite specific requests. The defence were unaware of the witness's address and mistakenly thought that she would be hostile to the accused anyway. Just after conviction, prosecution counsel communicated the true state of affairs to the defence. The Court of Appeal quashed the conviction because of this non-disclosure. Prosecution counsel sought to rely upon the exception in para. 6(ii) of the Guidelines, but the Court held 'That this was in this case an error of judgment and a wrong exercise of discretion, the Court has no doubt'.

The Court was even more explicit recently in *Phillipson*.[35] The Crown had held back incriminating documents, until cross-examination of the accused. The Court said that the opportunity given to the accused by service to trim her evidence was no excuse for non-disclosure:[36]

> . . . an accused needs to know in advance the case which will be made against him, if he is to have a proper opportunity of giving his answer to that case to the best of his ability. The accused is also entitled, when he decides whether or not to go into the witness box . . . to know what the case is which he has to meet. It is better in the interests of justice that an accused is not induced, by thinking that he is safe if he does so, to exaggerate, or to embroider, or to lie . . . so to do might be to ambush the accused. It is not in our view fair for the prosecution to have resort to such a device.

In *Sansom*[37] the Court of Appeal again had occasion to quash a conviction for a very similar 'material irregularity'. The fundamental problem is that the Guidelines themselves encourage such forensic conduct (and the exceptions in paras 6(iii) and (iv) can be subjected to the same criticisms). The only saving grace is that the Guidelines provide that the name and address of the relevant witness should 'normally' be supplied to the defence.

Sensitivities over informants and national security are the subject of para. 6(v). Even here there is a presumption in favour of disclosure.[38] Furthermore, perhaps the most significant development in the *Ward* case is that the Crown can no longer, without informing the defence of the issue or obtaining a favourable ruling from the court, withhold material on the ground of its sensitivity or possible immunity.[39] In the event of a conflict with the requirements of a fair trial, no evidence may have to be offered.

---

35   (1989) 91 Cr App R 226.
36   *Ibid.*, at p. 235.
37   (1991) 92 Cr App R 115.
38   But note the exception created by the Interception of Communications Act 1985, s. 9, in response to which the Court of Appeal called for supplementary guidelines: *Re Preston and Others* (1992) 95 Cr App R 355.
39   (1992) 96 Cr App R 1 at pp. 56–57.

Even when materials fall within the provisions for disclosure, it might be asked what powers do our courts of first instance have to order disclosure, or even effectively to supervise the compliance by the Crown with its duties. When this question is raised many judges wring their hands, unable to devise a procedure for intervention. Certainly none is provided by the Guidelines. Unfortunately, in many courts the position is even worse; the 'well-intentioned Good Chap' test of the propriety of the Crown's position still prevails.

Normally, in practice, as soon as the Crown knows that the defence are aware of its possession of some material, it is disclosed. If the court is ever put in a position to rule upon some particular material, the Crown does of course comply. Faced with defiance, the court has a common-law power to order a stay or to quash the indictment for abuse of process. Yet these sanctions are worthless where there is material of which the defence are completely unaware, so that nobody is in a position to challenge the non-disclosure before the court. A further problem arises where the defence think that the Crown or the police have some material of a general type but may be unable to specify precisely what it is. There appears to be no mechanism for the court to investigate the query. The court simply relies upon assurances of greater or lesser clarity from the Crown. Yet another quandary arises when the court is faced with assurances from Crown counsel that the 'unused material' has been inspected carefully by counsel personally, and that there is nothing falling within the duty to disclose. Questioned further, counsel may then reveal that there is something that should normally be disclosed but that, in his or her view, it falls within one of the exceptions. What does the court do? There seems to be no mechanism for the court to investigate further, in particular by inspecting the material so that it can form its own view on the issue.

There seems to be a need for clear enforcement procedures, to enable the defence to challenge the Crown's judgment and the court to adjudicate thereupon. As will be suggested later, we can learn much from the procedures for discovery in civil litigation. Indeed, how can we contemplate weaker safeguards in the criminal arena than those in the civil forum?

Next, the responsibilities purportedly imposed by the Guidelines are also unsatisfactory. The Guidelines are addressed only to lawyers. However, the deliberate or erroneous suppression of information is equally damaging whether perpetrated by lawyers, witnesses or investigating police officers. Indeed, the last two categories have the capacity to inflict the most harm, since their suppression of information may never reach the stage of assessment by a professional who is aware of the criteria and their importance.

The extent of the Guidelines' duties has been considered by the courts on a number of occasions. In *Knightsbridge Crown Court, ex parte Goonatileke,*[40] the store detective in a shop-lifting case completely misled the court about his previous character; this conduct was held to have been a denial of natural justice vitiating the proceedings, and the conviction was quashed on judicial review. In *Liverpool Crown Court, ex parte Roberts,*[41] a conviction was similarly quashed after a prior oral statement by a police officer, inconsistent with his evidence, came to light. 'The total apparatus of prosecution had failed to carry out its duty to bring before the court all the material evidence.' In *Kingston Justices, ex parte Khanna,*[42] a summary conviction was quashed, even though based upon a plea of guilty, because the officer presenting the facts to the justices had failed to inform anyone of a calibration check which vitiated the breathalyser test. In *Bolton Justices, ex parte Scally,*[43] the Divisional Court set aside summary convictions, because the prosecuting police force bore responsibility for failing to ensure the integrity of the blood sampling kits, which in fact were contaminated with alcohol in the form of ethanol in the swabs, even though no fraud or dishonesty was involved in the non-disclosure.

The Court of Appeal had to consider the boundaries of the relevant duty in the recent *Maguire Seven* appeal judgment.[44] It held that the duty applied to prosecution expert scientific witnesses, so that a breach constituted a 'material irregularity' within s. 2(1) of the Criminal Appeal Act 1968.[45] The same point was reiterated in the appeal of Judith Ward.[46] Of course, few, if any, scientists are aware of such duties under the rules of criminal procedure. Indeed, those working within some laboratories used by the prosecution, where they may be employed by the Ministry of Defence, often labour under a regime of secrecy, reinforced by their contracts of employment and pension provisions, which are wholly alien to any concept of openness or fairness to third parties.

Disputes about whether the person responsible for not passing on the relevant document is or is not part of the 'prosecution team' for the

---

40   [1986] 1 QB 1.
41   [1986] Crim LR 62.
42   [1986] RTR 364.
43   [1991] 2 WLR 239.
44   [1992] 2 All ER 433.
45   However, the material irregularity was not sufficient to render the convictions unsafe, a point criticised in the Second Report on the Maguire Case (1992–93 HC 296), para. 8.7.
46   *Loc. cit.* The judgment of the Court of Appeal also highlighted several shortcomings in the Crown Court (Advance Notice of Expert Evidence) Rules 1987, SI No. 716.

purposes of the Guidelines, are not very helpful to remedying the harm to the integrity of any particular trial. This author suggests, however, that the prime responsibility must be placed upon prosecution counsel, who should be provided in every single case with any undisclosed material, so that a professional decision can be made about it. He or she must make positive inquiry, through the CPS, of the officer in charge of the case, as to the existence of any other such material. A system of clear, accountable, professional responsibility should be established as a matter of unswerving practice.

Material Relevant to Credit

Though our courts limit the extent to which the credit of witnesses may be challenged on collateral matters, going purely to their credit, the effect of such a successful attack can be decisive. A witness, apparently unimpeachable on the facts of the particular case, may legitimately be destroyed by some 'skeleton in the cupboard'. Yet the defence right to test a witness in this way may be undermined if the vital background information is monopolised and suppressed by the other side. The reasoning in *Saunders* (above) applies here; disclosure is necessary to give meaning to the right.

Unfortunately, the decision in *Collister and Warhurst* (above) limited the police obligations in this respect. Though holding that previous convictions of witnesses had to be disclosed, the Court also held that:[47]

> The police are not to be expected to examine the records or see whether possibly there exists anywhere in the country any matter which might affect the character of the witness.

There, the witness had been adjudged bankrupt and had in those proceedings admitted to dishonesty.

Witness credit becomes of great importance with police officers. In two *West Midlands Serious Crime Squad* appeals against conviction, the Court of Appeal quashed the convictions in reliance upon material that adversely affected the credibility of certain officers who had been prosecution witnesses. In *Edwards*,[48] the Court relied upon an internal disciplinary finding against one officer and acquittals at two trials at which several police officers had given prosecution evidence. In

---

47 *Loc. cit.*, at p. 104.
48 [1991] 1 WLR 207.

Cheetham,[49] the Court relied upon internal disciplinary convictions against two officers, reflecting gravely upon their honesty. Such disciplinary charges have to be proven beyond reasonable doubt. The nature of the charges may themselves be serious enough. The real sting, however, may lie in any plea of not guilty to the charges entered by the officer and any evidence given in his or her own defence. The latter must have been rejected with certainty as false by the tribunal. Any later court evidence from such an officer, if called at all by the Crown, would have to be treated with the greatest caution by whatever tribunal of fact; *provided* they are made aware of the background.

The importance of the sort of 'credit' material above means that the fairness of the hearing should not be left to the arbitrary chance that defence solicitors may pick up the information by rumour or by other indirect means. Police forces must all maintain efficient, probably computerised, disciplinary records for personnel (and possible insurance) reasons. They ought to be readily accessible to senior supervising officers. Their contents should be divulged to prosecution counsel and then to the defence in any criminal trial, if they so damage the credibility of the officer as in *Cheetham*. Their relevance and disclosability should not depend upon whether the hearing is to be before the Court of Appeal or the Crown Court; release after a successful appeal, and after perhaps years in custody, is not to be regarded as a satisfactory alternative to a just acquittal at trial.

Similar considerations apply with increasing frequency to successful claims for damages against police forces arising out of tortious misconduct by police officers. If heard before a judge alone, the reasoned judgment may explicitly both reject the sworn evidence of named police officers and find them responsible for battery, false imprisonment or malicious prosecution. If before a jury, any verdicts and awards of damages for the civilian plaintiff will, by necessary implication, reflect extremely badly upon the conduct and sworn evidence of named officers. On one occasion the Court of Appeal has quashed a criminal conviction for exactly these reasons, and indeed Crown counsel stated that the Commissioner's policy was that such officers should not be called as witnesses of truth again at criminal trials.[50] At the moment, however, nobody knows (except by sheer chance) if this policy is adhered to in London or elsewhere in the country. Nevertheless, the outcome of such

---

49   30 July 1991, Court of Appeal, *per* Lane LCJ.
50   *R v Steadman-Thompson* (31 May 1986) (Court of Appeal) *per* Lawton LJ, discussed in *LAG Bulletin*, November 1986, p. 146.

civil proceedings should be treated with sufficient seriousness by all police forces, so that their outcomes should be systematically logged, and as readily accessible as disciplinary records, under the scheme suggested above.

Post-conviction Material

We have seen from the tragic death of Guiseppe Conlon, the need for mechanisms to make any post-trial fresh information available to those most affected. The same lesson is learned from the double wrongful conviction of Adolf Beck, which led to the setting up of the criminal appeal system in 1907.[51] The prison authorities during his first sentence recorded that he was not circumcised, which fact alone would have immediately excluded him from being the person alleged at his trial. Unfortunately for him, this did not emerge until he had been released, and then again convicted on the same false basis.

Clear channels of communication must be established for such information, which could best be achieved by those who may in future be charged with reviewing alleged miscarriages of justice.

Proposals

The disastrously chequered history of the rules on disclosure, bring home the extent of the power that the Crown wields in controlling information. The whole country must have been moved by the tragedy of the recent case of *Stefan Kiszko*,[52] a miscarriage of justice entirely attributable to the suppression of information. The Crown must be regarded, and must regard itself, as the trustee of information, not its monopoly owner. The only question for debate should be the terms of that trusteeship. It is plain that there is no innate or consistent perception amongst prosecution lawyers, witnesses or police officers, which can be relied upon to fulfil this trusteeship, without external control by Parliament and effective supervision by the courts of first instance. Neither of these safeguards are provided by our current system.

Legislation would in principle bring home the seriousness of these duties and oblige the prosecution to devote sufficient attention and resources to the question. The quality of justice before our criminal courts depends upon it. Even those who examine these matters with the

---

51 See Watson, E. R., *The Trial of Adolf Beck* (Hodge, London, 1924).
52 (1978) 68 Cr App R 62; (1992) *The Times*, 18 February, p. 5; 19 February, p. 3.

eyes of an accountant would appreciate that the expense of these more rigorous routines for our prosecution services is dwarfed by the cost to them, the Government and society as a whole of the many recent miscarriages of justice engendered by the problem. Thus, legislation is needed:

(a)   to foster a 'culture of disclosure' and an awareness of the responsibilities of the trusteeship of information;
(b)   so that Parliament can lay down considered standards;
(c)   so that we can escape from the baleful influence of the prevailing, confusing case law;
(d)   so that the current uncertainty about the status of the rules can be clarified; and
(e)   so that our courts of first instance may have clear jurisdiction to investigate and supervise compliance.

Turning to the details of the rules to be enacted, the current definition of 'unused material' seems to be acceptable, provided that its full implications are appreciated and observed, unlike at present. All the current exceptions that provide for tactical advantage to the Crown (i.e. paras 6(i)–(iv) should be abolished, for the reasons given above.

Next, it is unacceptable that the current Guidelines apply only to offences tried on indictment. Those offences triable only summarily can have equally shattering consequences for people's lives in terms of opprobrium and sentence. The judicial review cases cited above illustrate that non-disclosure can occur and taint summary trials to the same extent. Indeed, there may be greater risk because of the more cursory attention and supervision affecting these cases. The very fact that summary trials are at the moment excluded from the Guidelines may itself encourage a more lax approach. Any new scheme should expressly include summary trials.

Enforcement should be along the lines of the following scheme, which owes much to our civil procedure. As a matter of unswerving routine, the officer in charge of the case and the CPS must provide to prosecution counsel the file of any 'unused material'. Subject to counsel's advice, that file should normally be supplied to the defence before committal. If counsel advises that there is some material which should normally be disclosed but which falls within some exception to the duty, a list of such material should be prepared, describing each item in broad terms. That list should then be served on the defence and on the court, together with an account of the justification for the non-service of the material. If the defence can satisfy the court, *prima facie*, that there may be some further undisclosed material than that admitted by the Crown, then the court should investigate with evidence on oath from the parties, normally including the officer in charge of the case. If the defence can show *prima facie* that the claimed exception may not apply to the relevant material, the court should investigate by inspecting the material itself, and if necessary hearing live evidence, and then should adjudicate.

The duty of disclosure is too fundamental to be treated other than systematically, professionally and with a full appreciation of the gross imbalance of resources between the parties to criminal trials. Blind trust has been discredited. Trusteeship, with verification, should now be tried.

Appendix

Attorney-General's Guidelines (1981)

Disclosure of information to the defence in cases to be tried on indictment

The following guidelines were issued in December 1981 from the Attorney-General's Chambers.

1.   For the purposes of these Guidelines the term 'unused material' is used to include the following:—

(i)   All witness statements and documents which are not included in the committal bundles served on the defence.

(ii)   The statements of any witnesses who are to be called to give evidence at committal and (if not in the bundle) any documents referred to therein.

(iii)   The unedited version(s) of any edited statements or composite statement included in the committal bundles.

2.   In all cases which are due to be committed for trial, all unused material should normally (i.e. subject to the discretionary exceptions mentioned in paragraph 6) be made available to the defence solicitor if it has some bearing on the offence(s) charged and the surrounding circumstances of the case.

3.(a)   If it will not delay the committal, disclosure should be made as soon as possible before the date fixed. This is particularly important — and might even justify delay — if the material might have some influence upon the course of the committal proceedings or the charges upon which the justices might decide to commit.

(b)   If however it would or might cause delay and is unlikely to influence the committal, it should be done at or as soon as possible after committal.

4.   If the unused material does not exceed about 50 pages, disclosure should be by way of provision of a copy — either by post, by hand, or via the police.

5.   If the unused material exceeds about 50 pages or is unsuitable for copying, the defence solicitor should be given an opportunity to inspect it at a convenient police station or, alternatively, at the prosecuting solicitor's office, having first taken care to remove any material of the type mentioned in paragraph 6. If, having inspected it, the solicitor wishes to have a copy of any part of the material, this request should be complied with.

6.   There is a discretion not to make disclosure — at least until counsel has considered and advised on the matter — in the following circumstances:

(i)   There are grounds for fearing that disclosing a statement might lead to an attempt being made to persuade a witness to make a statement retracting his original one, to change his story, not to appear at court or otherwise to intimidate him.

(ii)   The statement (e.g. from a relative or close friend of the accused) is believed to be wholly or partially untrue and might be of use in cross-examination if the witness should be called by the defence.

(iii)   The statement is favourable to the prosecution and believed to be substantially true but there are grounds for fearing that the witness, due to feelings of loyalty or fear, might give the defence solicitor a quite different, and false, story favourable to the defendant. If called as a defence witness upon the basis of this second account, the statement to the police can be of use in cross-examination.

(iv)   The statement is quite neutral or negative and there is no reason to doubt its truthfulness — e.g. 'I saw nothing of the fight' or 'He was not at home that afternoon.' There are however grounds to believe that the witness might change his story and give evidence for the defence — e.g. purporting to give an account of the fight, or an alibi. Here again, the statement can properly be withheld for use in cross-examination.

(N.B. In cases (i) to (iv) the name and address of the witness should normally be supplied.)

(v)   The statement is, to a greater or lesser extent, 'sensitive' and for this reason it is not in the public interest to disclose it. Examples of statements containing sensitive material are as follows:

(a)   It deals with matters of national security; or it is by, or discloses the identity of, a member of the Security Services who would be of no further use to those Services once his identity became known.

(b)   It is by, or discloses the identity of, an informant and there are reasons for fearing that disclosure of his identity would put him or his family in danger.

(c)   It is by, or discloses the identity of, a witness who might be in danger of assault or intimidation if his identity became known.

(d)   It contains details which, if they became known, might facilitate the commission of other offences or alert someone not in custody that he was a suspect; or it discloses some unusual form of surveillance or method of detecting crime.

(e)   It is supplied only on condition that the contents will not be disclosed, at least until a subpoena has been served upon the supplier — e.g. a bank official.

(f)   It relates to other offences by, or serious allegations against, someone who is not an accused, or discloses previous convictions or other matter prejudicial to him.

(g)   It contains details of private delicacy to the maker and/or might create risk of domestic strife.

7.   If there is doubt as to whether unused material comes within any of the categories in paragraph 6, such material should be submitted to counsel for advice either before or after committal.

8.   In deciding whether or not statements containing sensitive material should be disclosed, a balance should be struck between the degree of sensitivity and the extent to which the information might assist the defence.

If, to take one extreme, the information is or may be true and would go some way towards establishing the innocence of the accused (or cast some significant doubt upon his guilt or upon some material part of the evidence on which the Crown is relying) there must either be full disclosure or, if the sensitivity is too great to permit this, recourse to the alternative steps set out in paragraph 13.

If, to take the other extreme, the material supports the case for the prosecution or is neutral or for other reasons is clearly of no use to the defence, there is a discretion to withhold not merely the statement containing the sensitive material, but also the name and address of the maker.

9.   Any doubt as to whether the balance is in favour of, or against, disclosure should always be resolved in favour of disclosure.

10.   No unused material which might be said to come within the discretionary exceptions in paragraph 6 should be disclosed to the defence until (a) the investigating officer has been asked whether he has

any objections, and (b) it has been the subject of advice by counsel and that advice has been considered by the prosecuting solicitor. Should it be considered that any material is so exceptionally sensitive that it should not be shown to counsel, the Director of Public Prosecutions should be consulted.

11.   In all cases counsel should be fully informed as to what unused material has already been disclosed. If some has been withheld in pursuance of paragraph 10, he should be informed of any police views, his instructions should deal — both generally and in particular — with the question of 'balance' and he should be asked to advise in writing.

12.   If the sensitive material relates to the identity of an informant, counsel's attention should be directed to the following passages from the judgments of (a) Pollock CB in *Attorney-General* v *Briant* (1846) 15 MWR 169, 185 and (b) Lord Esher MR in *Marks* v *Beyfus* (1890) 25 QBD 494, 498.

(a)   '. . . the rule clearly established and acted on is this, that in a public prosecution a witness cannot be asked such questions as will disclose the informer, if he be a third person. This has been the settled rule for 50 years, and although it may seem hard in a particular case, private mischief must give way to public convenience . . . and we think the principle of the rule applies to the case where a witness is asked if he himself is the informer.'

(b)   '. . . if upon the trial of a prisoner the judge should be of opinion that the disclosure of the name of the informant is necessary or right in order to shew the prisoner's innocence, then one public policy is in conflict with another public policy, and that which says that an innocent man is not to be condemned when his innocence can be proved is the policy that must prevail.'

13.   If it is decided that there is a duty of disclosure but the information is too sensitive to permit the statement or document to be handed over in full, it will become necessary to discuss with counsel and the investigating officer whether it would be safe to make some limited form of disclosure by means which would satisfy the legitimate interests of the defence.

These means may be many and various but the following are given by way of example:

(i)   If the only sensitive part of a statement is the name and address of the maker, a copy can be supplied with these details, and any identifying particulars in the text, blanked out. This would be coupled with an undertaking to try to make the witness available for interview, if requested; and subsequently, if so desired, to arrange for his attendance at court.

(ii)   Sometimes a witness might be adequately protected if the address given was his place of work rather than his home address. This is in fact already quite a common practice with witnesses such as bank officials.

(iii)   A fresh statement can be prepared and signed, omitting the sensitive part. If this is not practicable, the sensitive part can be blanked out.

(iv)   Disclosure of all or part of a sensitive statement or document may be possible on a counsel-to-counsel basis although it must be recognised that counsel for the defence cannot give any guarantee of total confidentiality as he may feel bound to reveal the material to his instructing solicitor if he regards it as his clear and unavoidable duty to do so in the proper preparation and presentation of his case.

(v)   If the part of the statement or document which might assist the defence is factual and not in itself sensitive, the prosecution could make a formal admission in accordance with section 10 of the Criminal Justice Act 1967, assuming that they acccept the correctness of the fact.

14.   An unrepresented accused should be provided with a copy of all unused material which would normally have been served on his solicitor if he were represented. Special consideration, however, would have to be given to sensitive material and it might sometimes be desirable for counsel, if in doubt, to consult the trial judge.

15.   If, either before or during a trial, it becomes apparent that there is a clear duty to disclose some unused material but it is so sensitive that it would not be in the public interest to do so, it will probably be necessary to offer no, or no further, evidence. Should such a situation arise or seem likely to arise then, if time permits, prosecuting solicitors are advised to consult the Director of Public Prosecutions.

16.   The practice outlined above should be adopted with immediate effect in relation to all cases submitted to the prosecuting solicitor on receipt of these guidelines. It should also be adopted as regards cases already submitted, so far as is practicable.

The 'Guinness Advice' (1992)

Disclosure of unused material

1.   Police officers are reminded that the prosecution in criminal proceedings has a duty to disclose to the defence all 'unused material', being material which has some bearing upon the offence(s) charged and surrounding circumstances of the case, unless it is incapable of having

any impact upon the case in question or there are good reasons for withholding the material. The duty is set out in Guidelines issued by the Attorney-General in 1981, and considered by Mr Justice Henry in unreported rulings given in the trial of *R* v *Saunders and Others*.

2.   The Attorney-General's Guidelines of 1981, the case of *R* v *Saunders and Others*, and some recent judgments of the Court of Appeal have considered the prosecution's duty to disclose material to the defence in cases to be tried upon indictment. Common law authorities and best practice require the prosecution to observe a similar duty to disclose material in cases to be tried summarily.

3.   For these purposes, 'the prosecution' includes not only the Crown Prosecution Service (CPS), but also police officers, forensic scientists and others who have some responsibility for criminal proceedings. All those parties are obliged to make full and proper disclosure, so that the CPS, on whom the duty finally rests, can decide what disclosure to the defence may be required. The CPS cannot properly discharge that duty unless it either has a copy of all the potentially disclosable material, or is at least aware of that material. The duty of disclosure inevitably raises an obligation on all parties to preserve potentially disclosable material.

4.   It may be that the law in relation to the prosecution's duty of disclosure will be revised or restated in the foreseeable, but not immediate, future. In the meantime, however, it may assist police forces to have some general advice on this topic.

5.   The prosecution is required to provide to the defence copies of, or to reveal the existence of, material which may assist the defence, save in certain exceptional circumstances. It must be for the CPS to determine whether such circumstances exist in any particular case. Since there is presently no general obligation upon the defence to disclose what (if any) defence will be raised at trial, it can be difficult to assess what may assist the defence. In the course of any enquiry, therefore, police officers should maintain a schedule of all material coming into their possession and should copy that schedule to the CPS with the case papers. 'Material' in this context means not only documents, but also articles and information (see paragraph 9 below).

6.   Wherever possible, every item should be individually listed in the schedule. In exceptional cases, where there are many similar documents or other items, it may be appropriate to describe groups of material by identifiable generic categories.

7.   Officers need not necessarily maintain a schedule from the start of every investigation, but should at the outset consider whether or not to do so. In making that decision they should have regard to the nature and

seriousness of the matter under investigation and the likelihood of a schedule being required, either for committal proceedings or for summary trial when the obligation of disclosure is most relevant. A schedule should be prepared and submitted when a Full File is required in accordance with the Manual of Guidance for the preparation, processing and submission of files. In cases where no schedule has been maintained from the start, but is subsequently required, officers will need to prepare a schedule retrospectively for submission to the CPS.

8. The general rule must be to preserve documents and other material which come into existence during a criminal investigation, unless they are plainly of no interest or value to either the prosecution or defence: for example, a note of a witness's date of birth which is subsequently formally recorded on a statement form. It is impossible to list every category of material which should be retained and included in the schedule for the CPS, but the following should be included, even if any particular item has already been disclosed to the defence:

(a)   interview notes and audio or video tape-recordings of interviews with actual or potential witnesses, suspects or defendants;

(b)   draft witness statements, including those prepared or amended by witnesses or their advisers;

(c)   statements taken from all potential witnesses during the investigation, whether or not they assist the prosecution case, and any exhibits referred to in such statements;

(d)   correspondence or other notes relating to the contents of witness statements;

(e)   any documents or other material containing a description of the alleged criminal by a potential witness;

(f)   crime reports;

(g)   custody records and associated documents relating to the defendant's detention in police custody;

(h)   any documentary or other record of communications to or from medical witnesses or forensic scientists;

(i)   any material casting any doubt upon the reliability or consistency of any potential witness in the proceedings;

(j)   any material casting any doubt upon the reliability of any confession;

(k)   any other material or information which the police officer fairly and reasonably considers ought to be considered in turn by the CPS.

Similarly, all material falling within categories (a) to (k) above which is held on computer should be included in the schedule.

9. For the purpose of this advice, 'material' includes information

relevant to the topic of disclosure which comes to the knowledge of a police officer. Where that information is received orally rather than in a written form, and is not to be found elsewhere in the schedule in written form, then the police officer should make a written record of that information and include the record in the schedule to the CPS.

10.   A duty is inevitably placed upon police officers to preserve any possibly relevant material which is in their possession, and to seek to ensure that such material retained by others is also preserved; and then to inform the CPS of all that material. If in doubt, the officer should seek to preserve the material and include it in the schedule for notification to the CPS.

11.   Police officers need only include with their initial report to the CPS copies of such material as they think appropriate to forward at that stage, in accordance with normal practice. The schedule should be forwarded when available and, in any event, when a Full File is submitted in accordance with the Manual of Guidance.

12.   It is for the CPS, in consultation where appropriate with the police, to determine ultimately whether material must be disclosed to the defence. Disclosure will normally be made unless there is good reason not to do so. One of the grounds for non-disclosure is that the material contains 'sensitive' information as described in the Attorney-General's Guidelines. Police officers should not be deterred from informing the CPS of the existence of such material for fear that it will automatically be disclosed to the defence. On the contrary, it is essential that the CPS is informed of *all* material; but at the same time, if an officer believes that some material is sensitive and should not be disclosed to the defence, this should specifically be drawn to the attention of the CPS at the earliest opportunity.

13.   The CPS will always seek to ensure that sensitive material is given due and proper protection. It must be remembered, however, that the reason for its sensitivity may not be apparent from the face of the material and the CPS will therefore often be dependent upon police officers in drawing its attention to such material. Factors such as those referred to in paragraph 6(v) of the Attorney-General's Guidelines should be specifically drawn to the attention of the CPS.

14.   The obligation on the prosecution of disclosure of unused material to the defence is a continuing one, as emphasised by recent decisions of the Court of Appeal. The obligation upon police officers will not end with the submission of a schedule to the CPS. If additional material becomes available to the officer at any subsequent stage the CPS should be advised of it and the schedule up-dated and kept up-to-date until the prosecution is concluded.

15. The duty of disclosure is a fundamental component of the prosecution process. As the courts have made clear in recent cases, failure to observe that duty may lead to the premature termination of proceedings, or to successful appeals against conviction.

EDITORS' COMMENTS

The disclosure of unused prosecution materials is bound to impose burdens on the criminal justice system in terms of time and money. First, the CPS will have to assemble and copy the documentation; then the defence lawyers will have to scrutinise it. Some agencies in their submissions to the Royal Commission have baulked at this prospect of the rules on paper becoming stronger and more enforceable, and are seeking to have them trimmed. In particular, the Police Service expresses unhappiness about the existing rules of disclosure, especially as interpreted in *Saunders*, fearing that they could compromise police intelligence sources.[1] Others have yet to recognise that even the present Guidelines demand that *all* unused materials be disclosed, and therefore imagine that there may be an interpretative problem for the prosecution of deciding what is 'relevant' material in absence of pleadings in a criminal case when they are not sure what defences might be raised.[2] Even the Attorney-General's Evidence expresses concerns that fuller disclosure may be used to create a plausible defence, may make witnesses reluctant to pass on information to the police and will again entail resource costs. In response, it must be firmly established that an adversarial system demands the fullest disclosure — it is up to the defence to have conduct of the material and to use it as it thinks fit. Indeed, the US Supreme Court has likewise recognised the danger of the suppression of unfavourable prosecution evidence and has therefore recognised constitutional duties to disclose. Such a duty in federal cases was imposed in *Jencks* v *US* in respect of prior statements of witnesses.[3] This duty, with some modifications, is now contained in the 'Jencks' Act.[4] Next, the Court decided that it would be a violation of due process for the prosecution to fail to disclose evidence in its possession that testimony

---

1 *Submission*, para. 2.3.2, p. 133. Such fears probably account for the failure to replicate the Attorney-General's Guidelines in Northern Ireland, though they are considered: *R v McAllister* [1985] 9 NIJB.
2 See Lawton, Sir F., 'What follows the Judith Ward case?' (1992) 136 Sol Jo 616.
3 353 US 657 (1957). See notes at (1959) 11 Stan L Rev 257; (1979) 54 NYUL Rev 801.
4 18 USCA, s. 3500. See note at (1958) 67 Yale LJ 674; (1960) 38 Texas L Rev 595; Traynor, R. J., 'Ground lost and found in criminal discovery' (1964) 39 NYUL Rev 228.

given on its behalf was perjured.[5] Eventually, however, the Court developed a wider duty to disclose any evidence sufficient to create 'a reasonable doubt that did not otherwise exist' as to the guilt of the accused.[6]

The question thus arises as to how best to secure full disclosure, and various relevant submissions have been made to the Royal Commission. Perhaps the most authoritative is the Attorney-General's 'Evidence', which wholly concentrates on the subject. It is accepted that the current practices are not sufficiently precise.[7] Solutions advanced include written pleadings, discovery against the prosecution, automatic disclosure of witness statements and a code of practice.[8] It may be commented that these proposals still envisage less than total, automatic disclosure, so much discretion, and therefore the chance to cover up, is left with police and prosecution.

A further point rightly canvassed in the submission is that prosecution disclosure is in turn dependent on candour by the police to the prosecution. The Home Office has made progress on the standard of files compiled by the police,[9] but ensuring quality is different from ensuring candour. Accordingly, there must be statutory rules governing how the police deal with unused materials. This point is taken up by the CPS, which calls for a certificate of disclosure signed by the police.[10] The Law Society proposes even tighter procedures, to the effect that the police maintain an investigation log for each case and disclose all papers in it to the CPS.[11] The Criminal Bar Association takes the Law Society's useful model one step further with the idea that specified officers in police and prosecution service, plus prosecution counsel should certify that there has been full disclosure, the named individual thus taking responsibility for ensuring enforcement.

A duty to disclose by the prosecution is of limited utility if the investigators have closed their eyes to all avenues of exploration

---

5   *Alcorta* v *Texas* 355 US 28 (1957); *Nagua* v *Illinois* 360 US 264 (1959); *Miller* v *Pate* 386 US 1 (1967).

6   *US* v *Agurs* 427 US 97 (1976). See also: *Brady* v *Maryland* 373 US 82 (1963); *Giles* v *Maryland* 386 US 66 (1967); *US* v *Bagley* 473 US 39 (1985); *Pennsylvania* v *Ritchie* 480 US 39 (1987).

7   Para. 7.1.

8   Para. 7.8.

9   See Home Office Circular 34/1992, Working Group on Pre-trial Issues. A *Police Manual of Guidance* regulates the preparation of files and their submission to the CPS. The manual advises that investigative files be vetted and signed by a supervisory officer.

10 *Submission*, ch. 11. It might be suggested that failure to comply be made a police disciplinary offence.

11 Paras 3.8, 3.10.

promising to the accused. This dilemma raises the fundamental issue of whether an adversarial system is the best that can be designed to discover the truth, or whether an inquisitorial system might be preferable. The conduct of trials in this country under the adversarial model will be taken up in the next chapter; the attractions of inquisitorial systems will be left until later.

7

Trial Procedures

John Jackson

Introduction

In its report, *Miscarriages of Justice*, in 1989, the organisation JUSTICE commented that there have been five common threads running through most of the allegations of injustice over the years: wrongful identification, false confession, perjury by a co-accused and/or other witnesses, police misconduct in the form of concocting confessions that were never made or planting incriminating evidence, and bad trial tactics.[1] These faults raise questions about the way in which present trial procedures in England and Wales treat dubious kinds of evidence such as identification evidence and confession evidence. They equally raise questions about the adversary nature of trial procedures.

The issue of adversarial trial tactics emphasises the fact that the contested trial is not a court-directed inquiry into an accused's guilt but a party-directed attempt by the prosecution to demonstrate the accused's guilt as charged and then by the defence to undermine the prosecution case. To protect the accused effectively, this procedure requires not only that the prosecution bear a heavy burden of proof but also that the defence are able to operate in an approximate position of 'equality of arms' so that they have an equal opportunity to present evidence and

---

1 *Miscarriages of Justice* (London, 1989), p. 4.

contradict evidence produced by the prosecution.[2] Yet, as the Court of Appeal recognised in the *Birmingham Six* and Judith Ward appeals, a disadvantage of the adversarial nature of criminal proceedings may be that the parties are not evenly matched in resources.[3] Nowhere is this clearer than in summary trials, where legal aid may be restricted in certain kinds of cases, with wide inconsistencies between courts,[4] and where there is no right to disclosure when defendants face purely summary charges.[5] Recently the Divisional Court even denied defendants the right to have a friend help with the conduct of a case, though its decision was reversed on appeal.[6]

Another defect in the adversarial system is that the pre-trial stage of the criminal process is left largely unregulated by the criminal courts. Unlike inquisitorial systems, which represent a continuous process of proof, with perhaps a number of phases of investigation supervised and conducted by judicial figures in serious cases,[7] the adversarial system focuses on one particular event — the contested trial. This means that there is little direct supervision of police conduct, so police misconduct can easily skew evidence presented at trial. It also means that there is no independent assessment of the evidence in the vast majority of cases where the accused plead guilty.[8]

Since recent miscarriages raise questions about the nature of adversarial trial procedures, rather than just about the way the courts handle particular kinds of unreliable evidence, it is not surprising that the entire adversarial system has come under scrutiny[9] and that it has been

2   The European Commission and Court of Human Rights have recognised the principle of equality of arms as endemic in the notion of a fair trial under Art. 6 of the Convention; see Jacobs, F., *The European Convention on Human Rights* (Oxford University Press, Oxford, 1980), pp. 109–11.

3   *R* v *McIlkenny and others* [1992] 2 All ER 417; *R* v *Ward* (1992) 96 Cr App R 1.

4   See Young, J., Moloney, T. and Sanders, A., *In the Interests of Justice?* (Legal Aid Board, 1992); Wall, D. and Wood, A., *The Grant and Refusal of Legal Aid in the Magistrates' Courts* (ESRC, forthcoming).

5   Criminal legal aid is governed by the Legal Aid Act 1988, ss. 21 and 22. Disclosure is required in summary cases only where the offences charged are triable either way, see Magistrates' Courts (Advance Information) Rules (SI 1985 No. 601). It may be available in summary only cases where courts have adopted pre-trial review procedures, which many have. See Mulcahy, A., Brownlee, I. and Walker, C., *Pre-Trial Reviews in the Magistrates' Courts* (1993, 33 Home Office Research Bulletin, 10).

6   *R* v *Leicester City Justices, ex parte Barrow* [1991] 2 QB 260.

7   For description of the French system which is commonly characterised as an inquisitorial system, see ch. 11; Vogler, R., *France: A Guide to the French Criminal Justice System* (Prisoners Abroad, London, 1989).

8   90 per cent of cases in the magistrates' court and 60 per cent of cases in the Crown Court result in a guilty plea, see Zander, M., *A Matter of Justice* (Oxford University Press, Oxford, 1989), p. 188.

9   See McEwan, J., *Evidence and the Adversarial Process* (Basil Blackwell, Oxford, 1992).

suggested that judges should take a more active investigative role in the conduct of cases, both before and during the trial itself.[10] But before this possibility is considered, it is proposed to examine in more detail the respects in which present trial procedures may contribute to injustice, dealing in turn with the mode of trial, the treatment of evidence, the role of the defence and the role of the judge.

Mode of Trial

Over the years, Parliament has gradually eroded the ability of defendants to elect for trial by jury. In 1976, the James Committee[11] recommended that a number of offences be transferred to the sole jurisdiction of magistrates, and s. 15 of the Criminal Law Act 1977 responded by making certain offences triable either way, such as various public order offences, and drink-driving offences purely summary. Only spirited opposition in the House of Lords prevented the classification of thefts under £20 becoming summary offences only. Despite these changes, pressures for further restrictions on jury trial continued largely on grounds of cost and delay, so the Criminal Justice Act 1988, ss. 37 and 39, made the offences of taking a motor vehicle, driving while disqualified and common assault purely summary.[12]

As more serious offences are reclassified as summary, it becomes imperative that defendants in the magistrates' courts receive a fair trial. But there are increasing doubts about its achievement. As already mentioned, defendants can be refused legal aid and disclosure is not required in summary cases. There are also doubts about the fairness of the system which appoints magistrates. The local advisory committees which advise the Lord Chancellor on the appointment of lay magistrates are shrouded in secrecy. There is a clear over-representation of middle-class persons and an under-representation of women and members of ethnic minorities.[13] One study has concluded that advisory committees operate racist criteria in selecting magistrates, such as 'being assimilated into the English way of life' as a criterion of suitability for the selection

---

10 The Royal Commission on Criminal Justice has to consider within its terms of reference the possibility of the courts having 'an investigative role both before and during the trial'.
11 Interdepartmental Committee on the Distribution of Criminal Business between the Crown Court and the Magistrates' Court (Cmnd 6323, HMSO, London, 1975).
12 For discussion see Emmins, C. J. and Scanlan, G., *Criminal Justice Act 1988* (Blackstone Press, London, 1988), pp. 84–8.
13 For discussion see Crane, J. W., *Local Justice* (T & T Clark, Edinburgh, 1989), pp. 43–66.

of black magistrates.[14] Another barrier to representativeness apart from the selection procedures is the demands of the job, which require persons to 'have time to carry out the full range of magisterial duties'.[15]

Questions about the representativeness of magistrates raise questions about their independence and impartiality. These doubts are fuelled by concerns about the traditional close ties between the magistracy and the police, and about the ability of magistrates to avoid becoming case-hardened.[16] Research has shown that magistrates have a tendency to accept police evidence too readily, although the research concluded that most convictions were in accord with the weight of the evidence.[17]

It is not surprising that persons who want to plead not guilty see the Crown Court as offering a better chance of acquittal. The Crown Court offers clear advantages over trial by magistrates. First of all, almost all accused are granted legal aid in the Crown Court. Secondly, defendants are granted disclosure of the prosecution case at committal hearings, as well as the chance to have the case dismissed. However, the value of committal proceedings has diminished over the years. Most committals are now in paper form only, and submissions of no case to answer are rarely acceded to. The prosecution has also increasingly resorted to the policy of avoiding committal proceedings in particular cases by seeking voluntary bills of indictment which send cases directly to the Crown Court.[18]

The most important advantage claimed for process in the Crown Court is, of course, the jury. One advantage of jury trial is that jurors are not privy to inadmissible evidence which may prejudice any tribunal of fact. Another is that the principle of random selection appears to be a better foundation for impartiality and independence than the principle of selection by unaccountable advisory committees appointed by the Lord Chancellor. However, the principle of random selection is not fully adhered to, and there arguably have to be mechanisms to prevent unfairness to vulnerable accused. In reality, however, the Government has in recent years taken a number of steps which have, on the one hand, increased the opportunities for the prosecution to influence the

---

14 King, M. and May, C., *Black Magistrates* (Cobden Trust, London, 1985).
15 Lord Chancellor's Department, 'The qualities looked for in a Justice of the Peace', (1988) *The Magistrate*, p. 78.
16 Enright, S. and Morton, J., *Taking Liberties* (Weidenfeld and Nicolson, London, 1990), pp. 96–9.
17 Vennard, J., *Contested Trials in Magistrates' Courts* (HMSO, London, 1982).
18 A recent *Practice Direction* [1990] 1 WLR 1633 seeks to restrict the use of this procedure, see (1991) 155 *Justice of the Peace*, 83–85. But see also Criminal Justice Act 1987, ss. 7–11.

composition of the jury but have, on the other hand, decreased the opportunities for the defence to do so. In 1978 and 1980, the Attorney-General issued guidelines which permit the prosecution to make checks regarding the suitability of jurors in certain cases involving national security and terrorism.[19] The prosecution are also given a wide brief to carry out criminal record checks on jurors in any case. A further step taken in the Criminal Justice Act 1988, s. 118, was to abolish the defence right of peremptory challenge on the ground that it enabled the accused to rig juries in their favour. Although the Government later followed this up with a *Practice Direction* restricting the prosecution's corresponding right to stand by jurors,[20] the abolition of the peremptory challenge has made it particularly difficult for the defence to challenge jurors whom they think are unsuitable. There are other methods of challenge, such as a challenge to the array (an objection to the whole panel of jurors) and a challenge for cause, but these are difficult to mount successfully as they require reasons to be given.[21] As the courts discourage the questioning of jurors, it is very difficult to show that a particular juror would be biased. The abolition of the peremptory challenge has also prevented accused persons from ethnic minorities ensuring that members of their community are represented on the jury. There was a period during the 1970s and 1980s when some judges were prepared to stand by jurors to ensure a multi-racial jury in racially sensitive cases, but the Court of Appeal has since held that the power of the judge to stand by jurors is limited to removing jurors who are not competent to serve on a jury.[22]

Research suggests that ethnic minorities are under-represented on British juries.[23] It does not necessarily follow that accused persons from ethnic minorities are at greater risk of wrongful conviction. Research has also found that it is difficult to predict verdicts on the basis of general characteristics such as age, sex, race or social class.[24] But very little is known about the actual behaviour of juries, because researchers are forbidden by the Contempt of Court Act 1981, s. 8, to investigate jury deliberations. In any event, it has been argued that bias may intrude into the courtroom in a more subtle way than by overt racial or class

19 See *Note* [1980] 2 All ER 457 and *Note* [1980] 3 All ER 785.
20 [1988] 3 All ER 1086.
21 See Buxton., R, 'Challenging and discharging jurors', [1990] Crim LR 225.
22 *R v Ford* (1989) 89 Cr App R 278. See Enright, S., 'Multi-racial juries', (1991) 141 NLJ 992.
23 Baldwin, J. and McConville, M., *Jury Trials* (Clarendon Press, Oxford, 1979), pp. 97–8.
24 Sealy, A. P. and Cornish, W. R., 'Jurors and their verdicts' (1973) 36 MLR 496; Baldwin J. and McConvillle M., *op. cit.*, pp. 99–105.

prejudice.[25] Until more is known about jury behaviour, it would be wrong to underestimate the effect of excluding members of an accused's community from the jury, since there then may be no one on the jury who is able to understand and explain the accused's actions.

The Treatment of Evidence

It has been argued that various features of the contested trial can be viewed against the background of a concern to protect the innocent.[26] Examples include the presumption of innocence, the burden of proof on the prosecution, the standard of proof beyond reasonable doubt, the rules relating to similar facts, character, corroboration, restrictions on cross-examination of the accused and the rules on confessions. The effect of recent legislation, however, has been to dilute the principle that the prosecution must prove the accused's guilt beyond reasonable doubt. One example is the provision in s. 74 of the Police and Criminal Evidence Act 1984 (PACE) which provides that the conviction of a person other than the accused for an offence shall be proof of commission unless the contrary is proved. The impact of this on an accused can be clearly seen in conspiracy cases, where the conviction of a co-conspirator is strictly evidence only of the conspiracy but may also point to the participation of the accused.[27]

Another problem with existing rules is that they are not always effective in protecting accused persons from certain kinds of unreliable evidence. Neither Parliament nor the courts have been prepared to adopt a consistent approach towards unreliable evidence. In particular, the common law has not in general favoured corroboration as a means of protecting accused persons. It has viewed certain categories of witness, such as accomplices, complainants in sexual cases and children, with sufficient suspicion as to warrant a warning from the judge that it is dangerous to act on the witness's evidence in the absence of corroboration; but corroboration as such is not required in these situations, with the result that the jury has been free to ignore the warning it has been

---

25 See, for example, Hans, V. P. and Vidmar, N., *Judging the Jury* (Plenum, New York, 1986), pp. 136–42.

26 Galligan, D. J., 'More scepticism about scepticism' (1988) 8 OJLS 249; Zuckerman, A. S. S., *The Principles of Criminal Evidence* (Clarendon, Oxford, 1989).

27 The courts have softened the rigours of this provision by exercising their discretion under s. 78 of PACE to exclude evidence of third-party convictions in certain cases. See *R* v *O'Connor* (1987) 85 Cr App R 298. Compare *R* v *Lunnon* (1988) 88 Cr App R 71.

given.[28] A number of miscarriages of justice have arisen from what one commentator has called 'prison grasses', and it is arguable that this evidence should not be enough on its own to secure a conviction.[29] Nevertheless, the courts have not been inclined to extend the categories of witness in respect of whom a corroboration warning should be given, and have preferred judges to give more general warnings to the jury to treat certain witnesses with caution.[30]

So far as types of unreliable evidence are concerned, such as identification and confession evidence, there is again no consistent approach. In 1976, the Devlin Committee recommended that, in the absence of any supporting evidence, visual identification evidence should not be allowed to go to a jury unless there were 'exceptional circumstances' which reduced the risk of mis-identification.[31] Parliament did not act on these recommendations, but shortly after the publication of the report the Court of Appeal laid down specific guidelines, known as the *Turnbull* guidelines, governing the way in which a judge should direct a jury when the evidence against an accused rests substantially on identification evidence based on personal impression.[32] The guidelines followed the Devlin recommendations in a number of respects, but the Court criticised the 'exceptional circumstances' formulation on the ground that it was likely to lead to a build up of case law. The Court instead expounded a quality test: a judge should withdraw cases altogether where the quality of the evidence is poor and there is no supporting evidence; the judge should otherwise give a detailed warning to the jury of the special need for caution before acting on such evidence. Certain decisions since *Turnbull* have confined the impact of the guidelines to 'fleeting glimpse' sightings.[33] Another problem is that since apparently good quality identifications can also be mistaken, the guidelines give no guidance on how to decide whether or not identifications are mistaken in

---

28 Section 34 of the Criminal Justice Act 1988 abolished the need for corroboration warnings in respect of children. For criticism of these warnings see Dennis, I. H., 'Corroboration requirements reconsidered' [1984] Crim LR 316; Zuckerman, A. A. S., 'Miscarriage of justice and judicial responsibility' [1991] Crim LR 492.

29 Woffinden, B., *Miscarriages of Justice* (Hodder and Stoughton, London, 1989), p. 487. For the use of supergrasses in Northern Ireland, see Hogan, G. and Walker, C., *Political Violence and the Law in Ireland* (Manchester University Press, 1989), pp. 123–6.

30 *R v Beck* [1982] 1 WLR 461; *R v Spencer* [1987] AC 128.

31 Report to the Secretary of State for the Home Department of the Departmental Committee on Evidence of Identification in Criminal Cases, HC Paper No. 338 (HMSO, London, 1976), paras 4.61–4.65.

32 *R v Turnbull* [1977] QB 224.

33 See, for example, *R v Curry*; *R v Keeble* [1983] Crim LR 737.

a particular case.[34] JUSTICE has concluded that the guidelines have not proved as effective in preventing miscarriages of justice as the Court of Appeal had hoped.[35]

Warnings are also now required under s. 77 of PACE in circumstances where the case against a mentally handicapped person depends wholly or substantially on a confession and the confession has been made in the absence of an independent person (a person not a police officer). It is hard to see what additional protection the section offers. Judges are always required to put the defence case fairly and adequately, and if confessions made by mentally handicapped persons are challenged by the defence, the judge would be under a duty to warn the jury to proceed with caution in any event. Such confessions may also be excluded under other provisions in PACE.

The traditional response to unreliable confessions has been by way of an admissibility test requiring confessions to be excluded in certain circumstances, and by way of a residual common-law discretion to exclude unreliable confessions. Section 76 of PACE has replaced the old voluntariness test (under which confessions had to be excluded if they were obtained as a result of threats or inducements exercised by a person in authority) with a new test which requires confessions to be excluded where they have been obtained by oppression or by anything said or done likely to render them unreliable. At first sight this test goes to the very issue of preventing the admission of unreliable confessions, but the test is not one of actual unreliability, as the courts have tended to interpret the provision as requiring that something is said or done in the course of questioning which is out of the ordinary, such as a failure to comply with the rule that an independent person be present during interviews with juveniles, mentally disordered and mentally handicapped persons.[36] The discretion to exclude unreliable confessions does enable the courts to take into account other factors such as the state of mind of the suspect, but one of the difficulties with it is that judges need to be able to recognise unreliable confessions for this discretion to work effectively. Experts now claim that there are two types of false confession — the 'coerced compliant' confession and the 'coerced internalised' confession.[37] The

---

34 Dennis, *op. cit.*, n. 28, above; Jackson, J. D., 'The insufficiency of identification evidence based on personal impression' [1986] Crim LR 203.

35 *Op. cit.*, n. 1, para. 3.11.

36 See *R* v *Goldenberg* (1988) 88 Cr App R 285; *R* v *Crampton* [1991] Crim LR 277.

37 See Pattenden, R., 'Should confessions be corroborated?' (1991) 107 LQR 319; Gudjonsson, G. H., *The Psychology of Interrogations, Confessions and Testimony* (John Wiley, Chichester, 1992).

former is usually the result of forceful or persistent questioning, while the latter are the result of a belief on the part of the suspect of actual commission of the crime. But the restrictive rules on expert evidence, which prevent experts testifying about the likelihood of a person making a false confession unless the person is suffering from a recognised mental illness or is educationally subnormal, mean that the courts may not be able to identify false confessions in particular cases.[38]

An added danger with confessions is that they may have been concocted by the police. The revelations of police misconduct in the *Birmingham Six* case and the *Tottenham Three* cases, and the disbanding of the Serious Crimes Squad in the West Midlands have aroused fears that the police routinely manufacture admissions as a short-cut to convictions. One problem at trial is that the accused are discouraged from alleging concoction because the effect of such allegations is to open up the accused to cross-examination on their criminal records.[39] The courts have excluded confessions in a number of cases where there have been breaches of the duty to record interviews contemporaneously.[40] They have also recognised that the presence of a solicitor, which is provided for under s. 58 of PACE, can have the effect of helping to authenticate a police account,[41] although they have not always been prepared to exclude confessions after wrongful denial of access to legal advice.[42] It is questionable whether the PACE rules are sufficient to safeguard against the risk of unreliable or concocted confessions. The wrongful convictions in the *Tottenham Three* cases,[43] which arose in spite of the operation of PACE rules at the time, have fuelled demands for confessions to be corroborated before the accused can be convicted on the basis of them.

Another concern in recent years has been the way that the courts handle forensic evidence, which is becoming increasingly important in serious criminal cases.[44] One question which will be dealt with later concerns the ability of the defence to challenge evidence adduced on behalf of the prosecution. A more immediate point concerns the control that the courts exercise over such evidence. There has been particular

---

38   *Ibid.*, pp. 326–7. The decision of the Court of Appeal quashing the convictions of the *Tottenham Three* suggests that courts should take a more relaxed view of the admission of expert evidence, see *R* v *Silcott and others* (1991) *The Times*, 9 December.

39   See *R* v *Britzman* [1983] 1 All ER 369.

40   See *R* v *Doolan* [1988] Crim LR 747; *R* v *Delaney* (1988) 88 Cr App R 338; *R* v *Keenan* [1989] 3 All ER 598; *R* v *Canale* [1990] 2 All ER 187.

41   *R* v *Dunn* (1990) 91 Cr App R 237.

42   *R* v *Alladice* (1988) 87 Cr App R 380; *R* v *Dunford* (1990) 91 Cr App R 150.

43   *The Times*, 9 December 1991.

44   See ch. 5.

concern recently about the quality of the techniques adopted by the scientific community. In the inquiry into the case of the *Maguire Seven*, Sir John May found that tests which at the time of the trial were said to be almost foolproof methods of detecting nitroglycerine proved on later reflection to be defective.[45] DNA profiling is the latest technique to be hailed as the solution for identifying suspects and is being increasingly employed in criminal investigations.[46] But experience in the United States suggests that although there is general acceptance of the molecular and genetic principles involved in DNA analysis, the application of the technology to sample populations can be problematic. There is also a need for quality assurance to ensure that the samples match and to calculate the statistical probabilities of the match being random.[47] Unlike the US courts, however, which require scientific techniques to have general acceptance in the relevant field,[48] the UK courts have no established procedure for ensuring the reliability of novel scientific evidence.

Further doubts about potentially unreliable evidence arise out of the recent changes in s. 23 of the Criminal Justice Act 1988, which provide for the admissibility of first-hand documentary evidence in criminal cases.[49] This concession has increased the ability of the prosecution to submit dubious documentary evidence against the defence. First-hand documentary evidence is now admissible if the maker is dead, ill, outside the UK and cannot be brought back, cannot be found despite all reasonable steps taken, or if the statement is made to a police officer and the maker does not give oral evidence through fear or because of being kept out of the way. Although this represents a diluted version of what the Government originally wanted, it still opens the door to conviction upon written, as opposed to oral, evidence. It is true that s. 26 requires the leave of the court to be given if the document has been prepared for the purpose of pending or contemplated criminal proceedings or a criminal investigation, and much will depend on whether judges apply this section in a manner which is fair to the accused.[50] A recent Privy

---

45 Return to an Address of the Honourable House of Commons dated 12 July 1990 for the Inquiry into the Circumstances Surrounding the Convictions arising out of the Bomb Attacks in Guildford and Woolwich in 1974, HC Paper No. 556 (HMSO, London, 1990).

46 See Walker, C. and Cram, I., 'DNA profiling and the law' [1990] Crim LR 479.

47 Sufian, J., 'DNA in the courtroom', February 1991, *Legal Action* 7.

48 *Frye* v *United States* 293 F 2d 1013 (DC Cir 1923).

49 For comment see Birch, D. J., 'The Criminal Justice Act 1988: documentary evidence' [1989] Crim LR 15.

50 See *R* v *Cole* [1990] 2 All ER 108; *R* v *Price* [1991] Crim LR 707.

Council case suggests that there is nothing inherently unfair in an accused being convicted on the sole evidence of a sworn deposition statement.[51] In this case a witness had identified the three co-accused as the murderers of the deceased at a preliminary inquiry and was himself murdered before trial. However, statements made to the police are different from depositions taken at an oral preliminary hearing because they give the defence no opportunity to cross-examine the maker; we shall have to wait to see how far down the road the courts will be prepared to admit them.

Another aspect of unfairness in these provisions is that the admission of documentary hearsay has the effect of favouring the prosecution at the expense of the defence.[52] The defence are less able to adduce written statements, with the result that they may only be able to rely on oral hearsay statements. These continue to be largely inadmissible, as illustrated in *R* v *Blastland*[53] where the accused who was charged with murder, was unable to adduce a series of admissions made by a third party.

So far, attention has focused on how trial procedures deal with unreliable evidence. Another question is how trial procedures deal with evidence which may not in itself be unreliable but which has been obtained in consequence of a breach of pre-trial procedure. The English courts have traditionally been reluctant to exercise any exclusionary jurisdiction in respect of this kind of defect, on the ground that their role at the criminal trial is to ensure a fair trial for the accused and not to punish the police.[54] The wording of s. 78 of PACE seemed to follow this approach by giving the courts a statutory discretion to exclude evidence but limiting it to evidence which would have such an adverse effect on the fairness of the proceedings that it would not be proper to admit it. But the courts have rather surprisingly interpreted this section as permitting them to exercise a stricter control over pre-trial process than might have been expected. In one decision the Lord Chief Justice indicated that proceedings may become unfair where there has been an abuse of process because evidence has been obtained in deliberate breach of procedure laid down in an official code of procedure.[55] This suggests that the courts are giving a wide meaning to 'proceedings', taking the view that proceedings up to trial are part of the overall criminal process because there is an intimate connection between what happens in the investigatory process

---

51   *Scott* v *R* [1989] 2 All ER 305.
52   The author is indebted to Dr Alex Stein who has made this point to him.
53   [1986] AC 41.
54   *R* v *Sang* [1979] 2 All ER 1222.
55   *R* v *Quinn* [1990] Crim LR 581. See commentary of D. J. Birch.

and what happens at trial.[56] Adopting this approach, the Court of Appeal has held that significant and substantial breaches of the codes of practice under PACE inevitably have an adverse effect on the fairness of the proceedings because Parliament has laid down the standards of fairness in the codes.[57] But the Court has not been prepared to consider that every breach has such an adverse effect on the fairness of the proceedings that justice requires exclusion, and in deciding whether to exclude or not it has consistently disclaimed any disciplinary role.[58] Some decisions which have stressed the bad faith of the police suggest, it is true, a disciplinary approach.[59] However, other decisions, which have stressed the need for a causal link between the breach and the obtaining of evidence, point more towards protecting the individual accused from unfairness, so no clear principle seems to emerge overall.[60] If the courts have a responsibility to ensure that the accused are not wrongfully convicted, it can be argued that insofar as rules such as the verballing provisions and rights such as access to legal advice assist in preventing false convictions, the exclusion of evidence obtained in breach of them can be justified, however reliable the evidence, because it illustrates the courts' commitment to protecting the innocent.[61]

The Role of the Defence

Doubts have already been cast on whether the defence are properly equipped to challenge the prosecution evidence in summary trials. Mention has been made of the lack of any duty on the prosecution to disclose their evidence to the defence when purely summary offences are charged. It is true that in recent years the prosecution have been prepared to disclose their case in the magistrates' courts in the course of pre-trial reviews, but this has sometimes occurred in the context of mutual disclosure where the defence have had to disclose their information in

---

56 See Feldman, D., 'Regulating treatment of suspects in police stations' [1990] Crim LR 452.

57 *R v Walsh* (1989) 91 Cr App R 161; *R v Keenan* [1989] 3 All ER 598; *R v Dunford* (1990) 91 Cr App R 150.

58 *R v Mason* [1987] 3 All ER 481; *R v Delaney* (1988) 88 Cr App R 338, at p. 341; *R v Keenan* [1989] 3 All ER 598, at p. 609.

59 *R v Fulling* [1987] 2 All ER 65; *R v Mason* [1987] 3 All ER 481; *R v Alladice* (1988) 87 Cr App R 380.

60 *R v Samuel* [1988] 2 All ER 135; *R v Alladice, supra*, n. 50; *R v Dunford, supra*, n. 42. See Birch, D. J., 'The pace hots up: confessions and confusions under the 1984 Act' [1989] Crim LR 95.

61 For more discussion of this point, see Jackson, J. D., 'In defence of a voluntariness doctrine for confessions: *The Queen v Johnston* Revisited' (1986) 21 *Irish Jurist* 208.

return. One commentator has said that this practice represents a challenge to traditional adversarial methods of criminal justice which would have been unthinkable a short time ago.[62] Another effect of pre-trial reviews is to facilitate pre-trial bargaining, with the danger that the prosecution evidence is accepted uncritically by defence lawyers and used as a means of putting pressure on defendants to plead.[63]

In the Crown Court, by contrast, the prosecution case is disclosed to the defence at the committal stage, and there are obligations on the prosecution to divulge unused material, although these leave much to be desired.[64] But disclosure of evidence is not always enough to mount an effective defence. The defence need also the resources to investigate the evidence disclosed, and the importance of this can be illustrated by the example of forensic evidence. During the recent past the professional competence of several forensic scientists who gave evidence in a number of cases was called into question. One was found in *Preece* v *HM Advocate*[65] to have failed to disclose to the court the fact that the dead victim in a murder case had the same group A secretor as the accused with the result that the seminal grouping result could have been due to contamination by vaginal secretion. In his first interim report into the *Maguire* case, Sir John May also raised serious questions about the independence of the forensic science services, by revealing that the forensic scientist involved in that case had failed to disclose that the tests carried out did not differentiate between nitroglycerine and another explosive substance and had also failed to disclose other tests that proved negative.[66] Since then, one of the forensic scientists giving evidence in the appeal of the *Maguire Seven* admitted that he had been 'economical with the truth' in respect of deficiencies in the evidence.[67] Most recently, the Court of Appeal rebuked two scientists for withholding information about Judith Ward.[68] Even with the best will in the world, it has been suggested that forensic scientists cannot be independent because they have been working with police information throughout the investigation and have therefore been 'running with the hounds' rather than with the hare.[69]

---

62 Baldwin. J., *Pre-trial Justice* (Basil Blackwell, Oxford, 1985), pp. 18–19.
63 McConville, M., Sanders, A. and Leng, R., *The Case for the Prosecution* (Routledge, London, 1991), pp. 168–70. The rate of case settlement and its impact is considered in Mulcahy *et al.*, *op. cit.*, n. 5.
64 See ch. 6.
65 [1981] Crim LR 783; (1983–84 HC 191).
66 *Loc. cit.*, n. 45 *supra*.
67 [1992] 2 All ER 433.
68 *Loc. cit.*, n. 3.
69 Stockdale, R., 'Running with the hounds' (1991) 141 NLJ 772 and see ch. 5.

All this would not matter if the defence could challenge forensic evidence effectively. But the options for the defence are extremely limited. The prosecution have a virtual monopoly on forensic science resources, and the defence have often to rely on the expertise of less competent scientists. Another problem is that certain legal aid authorities have refused to make the funds available to allow the prosecution evidence to be tested. These shortcomings have prompted the suggestion that the forensic science service should work for the courts and that it should undertake work requested by both the parties.[70]

In recent years the defence have increasingly been required to disclose elements of their defence, for example alibi evidence and expert reports.[71] In addition, in serious fraud cases a Crown Court judge may now order a preparatory hearing at which the defence may be required to indicate the matters on which they take issue with the prosecution and any points of law they wish to argue.[72] At trial the judge may comment and invite the jury to draw inferences from a failure to comply with this requirement, or from any departure at the trial from the case disclosed at the preliminary hearing. When judges are permitted to comment on the failure of the defence to disclose evidence, this infringes the right of silence which protects the accused from the adverse consequences of failing to answer questions. Although there has been considerable pressure for the right to be abolished ever since the Criminal Law Revision Committee recommended abolition in 1972,[73] the right is given only half-hearted recognition in present trial procedures, as judges are not required to warn juries to refrain from drawing inferences from silence, although they do have to warn them not to treat silence as corroboration in cases where a corroboration warning is necessary. Judges may also make some adverse comment about silence under the current state of the law. Some authorities have made a distinction between inviting a jury to draw an inference of guilt from an accused's belated explanation (which is not permitted) and commenting on the belatedness as a factor to be taken into account when deciding its weight (which is).[74] So far as comment on an accused's silence at the trial is concerned, it appears that judges may comment freely, although in most

---

70 Lord Scarman, 'Justice in the balance' (1991) *The Times*, 5 March. For discussion of the relative advantages and disadvantages of court-appointed experts, compare Howard, M. N., 'The neutral expert: a plausible threat to justice?' [1991] Crim LR 98, Spencer, J. R., 'The neutral expert: an implausible bogey' [1991] Crim LR 106.
71 See Criminal Justice Act 1967, s. 11, PACE, s. 81.
72 See Criminal Justice Act 1987, ss. 7–11.
73 *Evidence (General)*, Cmnd 4991 (HMSO, London, 1972), paras 28–45 and ch. 4.
74 See, for example, *R v Ryan* (1954) 59 Cr App R 144.

cases they must remind the jury that the accused is not bound to give evidence, that he can sit back and see if the prosecution have proved their case, and that while the jury have been deprived of the opportunity of hearing his story in the witness-box the one thing they must not do is to assume he is guilty because he has not gone into the witness-box.[75] In other so-called 'confession and avoidance' cases, where uncontested or clearly established facts point so strongly to guilt as to call for an explanation, stronger comment is apparently permissible.[76] Some of the remarks made by judges show that they have little enthusiasm for the right of silence.[77] The Lord Chief Justice, for example, has suggested that the fact that the accused has a right to legal advice in the police station means that greater comment should be allowed when suspects are silent in the police station.[78]

The danger in diminishing the right of silence at trial is that it focuses attention on the defence's account or lack of it rather than on the weight of the prosecution evidence. This might be justified if the defence were properly equipped to test the prosecution case first of all, but, as already seen, this is not always possible. Apart from this there is always the risk that untrained tribunals of fact may be tempted to read too much into an accused's silence unless properly warned about the dangers of doing so. Above all, the dimunition of the right of silence detracts from the classic view of the adversarial trial that the prosecution must demonstrate the accused's guilt as charged, not only to the court but also to the accused with the result that it ought not to rely on the accused's refusal to participate at trial as part of its justification.

The Role of the Judge

The traditional role of the judge in the adversarial trial is to adopt an umpireal stance, and there is a considerable literature on the dangers that arise when a judge is seen to descend into the dust of the conflict.[79] Judicial intervention is considered particularly dangerous in jury trials, because the judge may then unduly influence the jury.[80] Despite the

---

75   *R* v *Mutch* [1973] 1 All ER 178.
76   *R* v *Sparrow* [1973] 1 WLR 488.
77   See, for example, the comments of Viscount Dilhorne in *R* v *Gilbert* (1977) 66 Cr App R 237, at p. 245.
78   *R* v *Alladice* (1988) 87 Cr App R 380, at p. 385.
79   *Yuill* v *Yuill* [1945] 1 All ER 183, at p. 189, *per* Lord Greene. See Frankel, M. E., 'The search for truth: an umpireal view' (1975) 123 *University of Pennsylvania Law Review* 1031; Saltzburg, S.A., 'The unnecessarily expanding role of the American trial judge' (1978) 63 *Virginia Law Review* 1.
80   Saltzburg, *ibid.*, p. 56.

strictures against judicial intervention, the Court of Appeal has made little attempt to enforce the ideal of non-intervention. There are occasional judicial expressions of the adversarial ideal. The *locus classicus* is *Jones* v *National Coal Board*,[81] where Denning LJ said that judges should ask questions of witnesses only 'when it is necessary to clear up any point that has been overlooked or left obscure'. But the Court has sanctioned the questioning of witnesses which goes far beyond the narrow boundaries of simply clarifying evidence, and has tended to focus on whether the interventions prevented the defence from presenting their case rather than on whether they were compatible with the adversarial ideal.[82] At the stage of summing-up judges are given free rein to comment as they wish upon the strength of the evidence, provided it is ultimately clear to the jury that the facts are for them to consider.[83] It is impossible to know how much influence a judge's summing-up exerts upon a jury, but there have been a number of notable alleged miscarriages of justice where judges have made extremely damning and sometimes inaccurate observations before the jury on summation. In the *Carl Bridgewater* case, for example, the judge told the jury that they might have no hesitation 'in concluding that the farm was raided that day by a number of men, possibly four, and that they went there in two vehicles: one a light blue Cortina Estate, and probably also a Transit or Bedford type of van, and that they arrived at the farmhouse itself shortly before a quarter to four and left by about 4.40 or 4.45'.[84] In fact the state of the evidence was much less conclusive than this. Eyewitnesses were far from agreed about the number of men seen at the farm; no one saw two vehicles at or near the farm, and no one saw four men there or in the vicinity, either together or separately.[85] In this case, as in so many others, the judge was not content merely to summarise the evidence; he also commented in a manner extremely prejudicial to the defence. The judge referred to the evidence of a convicted prisoner who gave evidence against the accused as perhaps 'unusually convincing for a man of his background'.[86] Another tendency

---

81 [1947] 2 QB 55, at p. 64.

82 R v *Hamilton* [1969] Crim LR 486. Compare *R* v *Matthews and Matthews* (1983) 78 Cr App R 23; *R* v *Gunning*, unreported, 7 July 1980. For a review of the authorities, see Doran, S., 'Descent into Avernus' (1989) 139 NLJ 1147; Pattenden, R., *Judicial Discretion and Criminal Litigation* (Oxford University Press, Oxford, 1990) pp. 98–102.

83 *R* v *O'Donnell* (1917) 12 Cr App R 219; *R* v *Canny* (1945) 30 Cr App R 143. See Pattenden, *op. cit.*, pp. 180–1.

84 Foot, P., *Murder at the Farm: Who Killed Carl Bridgewater?* (Sidgwick & Jackson, London, 1986), p. 135.

85 *Ibid.*, pp. 135–6.

86 *Ibid.*, p. 164.

on the part of judges has been to speculate on the testimony without offering any evidence for what is suggested.[87] In the course of the summing up in the trial of the *Birmingham Six* case, which serves as a classic example of one-sidedness, the judge attempted to discredit the prison doctor by suggesting that he must have been covering up for his colleagues.[88] It is one thing to comment on the answers given by a witness; it is quite another to make sweeping comments on the motives for certain testimony.

A judge's role at the summing up stage of the trial ought to be restricted to directing the jury on the law and recording the events of the trial.[89] The privilege of having the last word ought not be abused by showing favour to one side or the other. Although there is a practice in certain jurisdictions which permits the parties to requisition the judge on errors of law and fact that are made on summation,[90] it is undesirable to allow argument after summation on the way in which the judge has commented on the evidence. Arguably, though, judges should be more prepared to discuss the content of their summings-up before they address the jury, perhaps even circulating copies of their proposed summations to the parties in advance.

Conclusion

Many faults can be found with present adversarial trial procedures, but they do not necessarily require whole-hearted adoption of the procedures common to inquisitorial systems. Indeed, it is ironic that at a time when English reformers are looking increasingly at other European jurisdictions, those jurisdictions are moving towards adversarial procedures.[91] It has been argued elsewhere that truth-finding is best served by a dialectic process in which prosecution and defence are able to engage in an active process of asking questions and making investigations as early as possible under the supervision of an evenhanded third party.[92] It can also be

---

87 See for example, *R v Robson* [1992] Crim LR 655.
88 Woffinden, *op. cit.*, n. 29, p. 405. See also the Appendix to this chapter.
89 See Griew, E., 'Summing up the law' [1989] Crim LR 768; Wolchover, D., 'Should judges sum up on the facts?' [1989] Crim LR 781.
90 For example, in Northern Ireland and the Republic of Ireland, see Ryan, E. and Magee, P., *The Irish Criminal Process* (Mercier Press, Dublin, 1983), pp. 362–3. English authorities recognise that prosecution counsel have a duty to make sure that the essential ingredients of a summing-up are put before a jury, see *R v McVey* [1988] Crim LR 127; *R v Lang-Hall* (1989) *The Times*, 24 March.
91 Amodio, E. and Selvaggi, E., 'An accusatorial system in a civil law country' (1989) 62 *Temple Law Review* 1211.
92 Jackson, J. D., 'Two methods of proof in criminal procedure' (1988) 51 MLR 549.

argued that the ultimate triers of fact ought to be able to enter the dialectic process at some stage during trial. Although the judge's role at summation ought to be strictly limited, there may be less concern about judges adopting a more active role during the trial by questioning witnesses or suggesting new lines of inquiry than is permitted under the adversarial ideal, provided it is open to the parties to respond to any line of investigation developed by the judge. Judicial interruptions during the examination and cross-examination of witnesses are undesirable, but there is less objection to a judge questioning a witness after examination and cross-examination, provided an opportunity is given to the parties to re-examine in the light of a witness's response. Better that judges be given the opportunity to test theories that occur to them during the trial than that they be allowed to speculate idly on theories at summing-up when they cannot be tested one way or the other.

There remains the difficulty that in jury trials it is the jury, not the judge, who are the triers of fact, and judicial intervention can cause juries to speculate about what the judge thinks of the evidence rather than what they think. In jury trials, judicial intervention arguably should be directed more towards ensuring that the jury are given a chance to ask questions, provided these are kept within permissible boundaries. The idea of appointing friends of the jury, who could assist juries in their fact-finding task, should not be ruled out.[93]

While these changes may help to elicit and evaluate relevant information during the trial, it must still be recognised that no fact-finding procedure can protect against the risk of error. Rules of evidence will therefore continue to be necessary to allocate risks of error in favour of the accused and to prevent the accused being put in danger of conviction on insufficiently reliable evidence. Lastly, if the idea of direct supervision of pre-trial procedures continues to be resisted, trial procedures can play an important part in supervising pre-trial procedures by enabling judges to exclude evidence obtained in breach of them, and this is particularly important in the case of rules that assist in the prevention of wrongful conviction.

EDITORS' COMMENTS

Mode of Trial

The assertion is made in the foregoing chapter that Crown Courts, despite all their imperfections, offer clear advantages to the accused over

---

93   *Ibid.*, pp. 566–7.

trial by magistrates.[1] It is plainly not feasible to transfer all business to Crown Courts, so how might apprehension about the standard of justice in magistrates' courts be answered?

One response might be the professionalisation of justice within that forum, on the assumption that professional justice is better justice. To a significant extent this strategy is already being implemented by way of the growing role of stipendiary magistrates in England and Wales.[2] Though their numbers have been fairly static in London, their presence in the provinces has recovered from the low ebb of 10 in 1974 and is now higher than ever.[3] The reasons for this trend are several. One is simply mechanical — that the process of appointment is now simpler and no longer depends on local petition.[4] However, the main motivation seems to reflect concerns about efficiency in the light of the growth in workload of magistrates' courts and the tendency to reclassify as summary more complex and serious cases. Such court business demands frequent and prolonged attendance at court, as well as legal expertise, factors which make life difficult for part-time amateurs. There have also been concerns about court delays and efficiency,[5] and stipendiaries are widely perceived to be quicker and cheaper than lay justices.[6] With 28,000 lay justices still operative within the system, it cannot be claimed that professionalism predominates. Nevertheless, stipendiaries are key figures in a growing number of magistrates' courts, and so their importance transcends their modest numbers. Yet does this trend improve the quality of summary justice? There are undoubted advantages in terms of speed, convenience and appropriate legal expertise. Nevertheless, it is rather less certain that professional justice is unfailingly superior to lay justice and should supplant it. After all, verdicts depend on facts as well as law, and there are many who still believe that the minds of the lay magistrates are more

---

1   There is, however, concern about the impression given by placing the accused in the dock: Sargant, T. and Hill, P., *Criminal Trials* (Fabian Research Series, 1986), p. 12; Law Society, *Submission* (1991), para. 3.79; Liberty, *Submission* (1991), p. 46. Most accused view the layout as a hindrance to their effective representation: Zander, M., 'The Royal Commission's Crown Court survey' (1992) 142 NLJ 1730.

2   For their history, see Jackson, P., 'Stipendiary magistrates and lay justice' (1946) 9 MLR 1; Milton, F., *The English Magistracy* (Oxford University Press, Oxford, 1967); Skyrme, Sir T., *History of Justices of the Peace* (Barry Rose, Chichester, 1991). Resident magistrates are, of course, the model in Northern Ireland.

3   In 1991, there were 26 provincial stipendiaries and 50 Metropolitan stipendiaries: HC Debs, vol. 200, cols 419–420w.a., 11 December 1991.

4   See now Justices of the Peace Act 1979, s. 13.

5   See *Magistrates' Courts: Report of a Scrutiny* (Home Office, London, 1989).

6   See Working Group on Pre-trial Issues (1991), para. 174. Stipendiaries were used on a temporary basis to dispense swift justice during the Miners' Strike in 1984–5: Rutherford, A. and Gibson, B., 'Special hearings' [1987] Crim LR 440.

appropriate and more accurate fact-diviners than those of lawyers. Even if that superiority in performance is dismissed as fanciful, as some would maintain, community involvement and standard setting in summary justice is nevertheless highly desirable as a social policy, and is secured to some extent by the involvement of lay justices.

An alternative strategy is to persevere with lay magistrates but at the same time to minimise the damage which this desirable social and judicial policy might, on balance, inflict on any individual defendant by removing, or at least severely curtailing, the magistrates' powers to imprison. Such a proposal has recently been advanced by Liberty.[7]

The Treatment of Evidence

As reflected in the foregoing chapter, most of the controversies in this area, and indeed many of the recent miscarriages of justice cases, have concerned confessions. If confessions offer such fallible evidence, why rely on them at all as forensic evidence, or at least why rely on them in the absence of corroboration, a warning to the jury or a formal reaffirmation of their veracity to a magistrate? Many of these restrictions have been advocated in submissions to the Royal Commission, though none is without its own drawbacks.

As might have been expected, short shrift has been given in submissions from the Police Service to the idea that confessions are dispensable, despite evidence that their importance has been exaggerated.[8] The police accept that confessions are now a less important source of incrimination in what they view as the highly regulated atmosphere engendered by the Police and Criminal Evidence Act 1984.[9] Nevertheless, the Chief Inspector of Constabulary affirmed in a recent speech that confessions remain 'a vital tool of justice',[10] and it is hard to envisage him being contradicted by the Royal Commission.

There is rather greater interest in a possible rule requiring the corroboration of confessions by independent evidence.[11] Many variants on this theme have been propounded to the Royal Commission,[12] and the

---

7 *Unequal Before the Law* (1992).
8 See McConville, M. and Baldwin, J, 'Questioning police interrogation' (1982) 132 NLJ 681; Mitchell, B., 'Confessions and police interrogation of suspects' [1983] Crim LR 596.
9 *Submission* (1991) para. 1.1.6.
10 Sir J. Woodcock, 'Why we need a revolution' (1992) 100 *Police Rev* 1932.
11 An apparent exception is in the Police and Criminal Evidence Act 1984, s. 77.
12 See Amnesty International, *Submission* (1991), para. 4.4.1; JUSTICE, *Submission* (1991), para. 2; Liberty, *Submission* (1991), p. 52. Compare Law Society, *Submission* (1991), paras 1.2, 1.97.

Fisher Inquiry into the *Confait* case also recommended 'supporting evidence' where confessions had been secured in the following circumstances:

  (a)   in breach of police rules;
  (b)   from young or mentally handicapped persons without the presence of an adult; or
  (c)   where the confession was not taped.[13]

Supporters of corroboration sometimes point to the law in Scotland, where there must be 'some independent fact incriminating the accused, altogether apart from the statements or confessions which he may have made'.[14] The accused cannot corroborate the confession by voicing it in the presence of more than one person,[15] but the corroboration rule has been progressively weakened, especially by the widening of the so-called self-corroborating confession exception, whereby the accused reveals through the confession facts which only the perpetrator of the crime could know.[16] The result is that, as in England, confessions are considered to be the best and most reliable form of evidence, while the corroboration rule is viewed as increasingly inappropriate.[17] The lesson seems to be that any attempt to impose a corroboration requirement in England would have to be clear and precise, otherwise its impact would be likely to be minimised by prosecution pressures and judicial sympathies for them.

Aside from doubts arising from the application of a corroboration rule, some doubt its inherent value. Corroboration by dubious scientific analysis of concocted or coerced confessions hardly assisted the *Birmingham Six*.[18] Additionally, the Royal Commission on Criminal Procedure feared that the refusal to convict on confessions alone would cause delay and expense,[19] as well as damage to public confidence in the judicial

---

13   (1977–78) HC 90, para. 2.26.
14   *Manuel v HMA* 1958 JC 41. Chris O'Gorman, University of Wolverhampton, provided many of the Scottish sources for this part of the commentary.
15   See *McGougan v HMA* 1991 SLT 908.
16   *Manuel v HMA, supra; Wilson v HMA* 1987 SCCR 217; *Hutchison v Valentine* 1990 SCCR 569; Brookens, D., 'Guildford: a warning' [1989] *Journal of the Law Society of Scotland* 448
17   See *Sinclair v Clark* 1962 JC 57; *Hartley v HMA* 1979 SLT 26.
18   See Home Office, *Memoranda* (1991), para. 3.117.
19   This point is emphasised by the CPS *Submission* to the present Royal Commission (1991) paras. 10.2.4, 10.2.6. A survey in September 1991 (n. = 11850) found that only 0.65 per cent of confessions are challenged in Crown Court (0.4 per cent successfully); 24 cases were discontinued; there were 11 cases where the confession was not relied on. Zander, *op. cit.*, n. 1, reports a rate of challenge of up to 10 per cent.

system.[20] Since the time of that report, account must also be taken of the positive protections in PACE, but even the most fervent supporter of PACE would have to concede that its impact is diminished in at least four situations.[21] One is where the detainee is interviewed in the absence of a solicitor, as commonly occurs. The second arises where verbal exchanges take place outside of the police station, or within the station but outside the interview room; either way, recording and supervisory arrangements envisaged by PACE do not effectively operate. The third concerns detainees under the Prevention of Terrorism Act 1989, who are by design not accorded the same protective regime as ordinary suspects.[22] Lastly, where the detainee has been detained for more than 24 hours, there exists the inherent likelihood of excessive pressures and oppression. Surely in these four situations at least it must be accepted that PACE intentionally falls short of what is necessary to ensure the reliability of confessions and so should be bolstered by a corroboration rule.[23] Furthermore, it has been suggested that all confessions should at least be subject to a warning as to reliability by the judge to the jury, though there are doubts about the impact of such warnings.[24]

Confessions in response to police interrogation are always likely to raise doubts — how can they ever be truly voluntary or reliable when the whole system of police detention and interrogation is designed to disorientate, pressurise and distress? Aside from attempting to ensure that confessions presented to court really are reliable, a further response would be to encourage the police to rely upon other sources of incriminating evidence. However, the available alternatives are also not without their detractors. The fallibility of forensic evidence has already been considered (chapter 5), and its shortcomings are exemplified by cases such as the *Birmingham Six* and *Maguire Seven*. Independent third-party witnesses equally present almost as many dangers as confessions. Insofar

---

20 Cmnd 8091 (1981), para. 4.74.
21 The Police Service, *Submission, loc. cit.* pp. 111, 217, 221, reject the exclusion of confessions which have not been corroborated or taped.
22 See ch. 9.
23 See JUSTICE, *loc. cit.*; Liberty, *loc. cit.*, p. 54. The Law Society, *loc. cit.*, paras. 1.20, 1.120 is insistent on proper recording as a condition of admissibility. The General Council of the Bar recommends that a confession only be admissible if made in the presence of a solicitor, or after advice, or if taped or corroborated: *Submission* (1992), paras. 104, 105. The Justices' Clerks' Society suggests that the confession should be recorded in the presence of a solicitor: *Submission* (1991), para. 1.4 (and see NACRO, *Submission* (1991), para. 8.
24 See Pattenden, R., 'Should confessions be corroborated?' (1991) 107 LQR 317; Liberty, *loc. cit.*, p. 54; Criminal Bar Association, *Submission* (1991); Home Office, *loc. cit.*, para. 3.110.

as the witnesses are confederates of the accused, professional informers
or cell-mates, the perils of unreliable evidence have been touched upon
in the Introduction.[25] As for genuinely independent third parties
(assuming they exist, are not ignored by the police in favour of
confessions[26] and are willing to testify), the different problems arise of
how the police select which persons to interview and then compile
statements from them. Thus, without a rival team of defence investigators to keep a check, there is always the possibility that the police will try
to construct a case from witnesses sympathetic to their analysis and will
pressure or ignore 'hostile' persons.[27] There are also scant controls
governing the taking of statements, and so all the pre-PACE dangers of
inaccurate records, pressure and verballing remain. In summary, the
message is that the avoidance of confessions and reliance instead upon
other sources of evidence may solve some problems but will highlight
several more.

The Roles of the Defence and the Judge

The fear that a judge can so influence trials as to contribute to
miscarriages has unfortunately been realised all to readily in recent
miscarriage cases.[28] The point is exemplified by the conduct of Mr Justice
Bridge (later Lord Bridge) in the *Birmingham Six* trial in Lancaster
Castle in June 1975, as documented by James Wood in the Appendix to
these comments,[29] and by the grudging attitude of the Court of Appeal in
the *Maguire* case which was criticised by the May Report.[30] Reduction of
future error is most likely to be achieved by reforms to the systems of
judicial appointment and training and by clearer delineation of the
judge's proper role (especially by limiting comments on the facts).[31]

Deficiencies in the process of the appointment of the judiciary have
long been debated. Though greater light has now been cast upon the

---

25 See also Carrington, K., et al., *Travesty!* (Pluto Press, NSW, 1991), ch. 11.
26 Sargant, T. and Hill, P, *op. cit.*, p. 4.
27 See ibid., p. 10; McConville M., et al., *The Case for the Prosecution* (Routledge,
    London, 1991).
28 Compare the conduct of Judge Thayer in the trial of Sacco and Vanzetti in
    Massachussets in 1921: Ehrmann, H. B., *The Case That Will Not Die* (W. H. Allen,
    London, 1970).
29 Compare the vindication of judicial conduct by Lord Chief Justice Taylor, 'In defence
    of the judiciary' (1992) 142 NLJ 1673.
30 Second Report (1992–93 HC 296), paras. 1.4–8.
31 See generally Pannick, D., *Judges* (Oxford University Press, Oxford, 1987); Harlow,
    C. (ed.), *Public Law and Politics* (Sweet & Maxwell, London, 1986), ch. 10; Brazier,
    R., *Constitutional Reform* (Oxford University Press, Oxford, 1991), ch. 8.

nature of the system,[32] its actual operation still appears to owe rather too much to personal connections within the Bar and an emphasis upon the skill of advocacy.[33] The result is a bench drawn from a very narrow range of experience, social class, gender and race, which is often felt to be out of touch with common reality but which is self-perpetuating.[34] The assumption that only experienced barristers can qualify as judges overestimates the talents of the Bar[35] and wastefully disregards the skills of, for example, solicitors, legal academics and the chairs of tribunals.

Substantial improvements have been secured in the training of judges (including the magistracy) since the reconstitution of the Judicial Studies Board in 1985.[36] However, two serious criticisms may be levied against the new model. The first concerns the scale of its activities. Although 2.3 per cent of judicial time is expended on training exercises,[37] there is no scope for either expansion or elaboration of the information provided within existing financial resources or the available time of the judiciary.[38] The second defect, insularity, arises from the insistence of the Board that instruction should for the main part be provided by representatives of the clientele to be instructed.[39] In other words, judges are seen as the appropriate teachers of judges, and there is hostility to the idea that other professionals within the legal system, law teachers or legal interest groups have an equally important perspective. As the Board is determined to keep its training sessions closed to the public, it is difficult to assess their effectiveness. However, their very nature gives rise to fears of inefficient and unskilled teaching methods and of the perpetuation of insular judicial misconceptions and myths.

The appointment and training of the judiciary are important issues which lie outside the effective remit of the current Royal Commission. However, the role of the judge prior to, and during, trial are matters which have been canvassed.

---

32 See Lord Chancellor's Department, *Judicial Appointments* (1986, 1990). For the magistracy, see *Today's Magistrates* (1988).
33 See Law Society, *Judicial Appointments* (London, 1991); JUSTICE, The Judiciary in England and Wales (London, 1992).
34 A word-of-mouth appointments system is also arguably discriminatory: Bindman, G., 'Appointing judges without discrimination' (1991) 141 NLJ 1692.
35 Sargant, T. and Hill, P., *op. cit.*, p. 13.
36 See Judicial Studies Board Reports 1979–82 (1983), 1983–87 (1988), 1987–91 (1992).
37 *Loc. cit.*, 1987–91, para. 31.
38 *Ibid.*, paras 29–31.
39 *Ibid.*, paras 4, 11, 11.3.

One controversy concerns the impact of pre-trial reviews (PTRs).[40] A pre-trial review is typically an informal meeting held between defence and prosecution lawyers (solicitors in the magistrates' courts/barristers in the Crown Court), presided over by a court clerk/ judge, at which a discussion takes place about issues likely to arise in cases proceeding to trial. PTRs, like the American settlement conferences to which they bear a close resemblance,[41] were initially conceived as a means of making more efficient use of court resources by facilitating advance disclosure, identifying 'weak' cases likely to collapse before or on the trial date, and serving as a forum for the discussion and clarification of contentious legal issues. Consequently, the most commonly articulated goals of PTRs are those of case streamlining (for example, by reducing the number of trial witnesses and the trial length estimate) and case settlement (by encouraging the parties to dispose of the case by means other than a contested trial).

Pre-trial reviews were first introduced into magistrates' courts in the early-1980s, primarily because of the absence of advance disclosure — the process by which, prior to the trial, the prosecution discloses to the defence such evidence as will be presented at trial. The Criminal Justice Act 1977, s. 48 had stipulated for the introduction of advance disclosure in summary trials.[42] However, these provisions were not implemented until the Magistrates' Courts (Advance Information) Rules in 1985,[43] which conferred on defendants being tried in the magistrates' courts for an offence triable either way an entitlement to advance disclosure of the prosecution evidence. In the meantime, defendants and their solicitors continued to face the difficulty of not having access to the prosecution's evidence until it was revealed during the trial itself. As a result, PTRs

---

40   See Baldwin, J., *Pre-trial Justice* (Basil Blackwell, Oxford, 1985); Mulcahy, A., Brownlee, I. and Walker, C., *Pre-Trial Reviews in the Magistrates' Courts* (1993, 33 Home Office Research Bulletin 10).

41   See Rosenberg, M., *The Pre-Trial Conference and Effective Justice* (Columbia University Press, New York 1964); Hill, S., 'Pre-trial Reviews in Magistrates' Courts in the West Midlands' (Unpublished PhD Thesis: Faculty of Law, University of Birmingham, 1986).

42   See Report of the Interdepartmental Committee on the Distribution of Court Business between the Crown Court and Magistrates' Courts (Cmnd 6323, 1975), paras. 212–230.

43   SI 1985 No. 601. As regards summary only cases, the only requirements of disclosure are found in the Code of Conduct for the Bar, para. 160(c), which states that it should be normal practice to reveal the statements of witnesses who are to be called. In most cases, this will only happen at a very late stage in the procedures, and perhaps on the trial day itself.

emerged[44] as an extra-statutory strategy whereby information could be informally exchanged between prosecution and defence well before the trial.[45]

Two factors which had a significant impact on practices in magistrates' courts were the introduction of advance disclosure in triable-either-way criminal cases in 1985 and the establishment of the Crown Prosecution Service (CPS) in May 1986.[46] The establishment of a unitary body with responsibility for the prosecution of criminal offences afforded tremendous scope for the standardisation of prosecution practices (and particularly plea negotiations — a practice which is facilitated by PTRs). Conversely, it was claimed that the introduction of advance disclosure made redundant a central aspect of PTRs.[47] Alongside these developments, dissatisfaction was voiced about PTRs in some courts. Thus, prosecution services have sometimes been reluctant to participate, complaining that PTRs favour the defence, whom they feel abuse the system. In addition, there remains the concern that even with the presence of a PTR, an unacceptably large proportion of defendants continue to enter guilty pleas immediately prior to trial, resulting in an inefficient use of court resources. On the basis of these and other difficulties, several courts which pioneered the development of the PTRs subsequently either curtailed their use or abandoned them altogether.

Despite the new climate created by these developments and, in some courts, disenchantment with the impact of PTRs, the number of magistrates' courts which continue to operate the procedure is substantial and continues to grow.[48] It may be speculated that interest has been aroused by the Le Vay Report[49] and, more generally, by pressures on court managers to achieve greater efficiency. This continued interest after the dawning of the era of advance disclosure also suggests that PTRs perform other useful functions, such as a focus for case-settlement or, in default, the identification of issues in contention and fewer cracked trials.

---

44 For the early history, see: Desbruslais, A., 'Pre-trial disclosure in the magistrates' courts' (1982) 146 JP 384; Baldwin, J., *op. cit.*; Hill, S., 'Pre-trial reviews: a study in Coventry magistrates' court (1984) 148 JP 39, at p. 58.

45 PTRs remain extra-statutory except under the Children Act 1989, s. 11(1).

46 Prosecution of Offences Act 1985.

47 See Moxon, D., (ed.), *Managing Criminal Justice* (HMSO, London, 1985), p. 105; Barnett, S.M., 'Section 48 — a viable alternative?' (1983) 147 JP 117; Baldwin, J., 'Pre-trial disclosure in magistrates' courts' (1983) 147 JP 499.

48 See Mulcahy et al., *op. cit.*

49 *Magistrates' Courts: Report of a Scrutiny* (1989). See also Home Affairs Committee, *Home Office Expenditure* (1988–89 HC 314); Justices' Clerks' Society, *Delay in the Magistrates' Courts* (1989); Home Office Research Bulletin No. 25: *MIS for Magistrates' Courts*; Working Group on Pre-Trial Issues (Home Office, 1991).

The trend towards pre-trial intervention and direction on the initiative of the court is reflected in contexts other than magistrates' courts. For instance, in civil courts[50] and Crown Courts, where the complexity of litigation can have a significant impact on its speedy and cost-effective disposition, policies of case-management have long been pursued, in a bid to ensure the best possible use of resources. Although there is no statutory system of PTRs in the Crown Court, some Crown Court centres had, in fact, evolved informal mechanisms for reviewing at least part of their case-load by the middle of the 1970s.[51] Such systems varied from centre to centre, but in the main, involved the listing of potentially lengthy or complicated cases to a preliminary date on which pleas were taken and, in some instances at least, the clarification of contested issues and the obtaining of accurate time estimates. These preliminary hearings took place before a judge, a circumstance which doubtless embued them with appropriate weight and formality. This informal practice received judicial approval in cases such as *Thorn*[52] and *Atkinson*,[53] in which the Court of Appeal demonstrated its confidence in the efficacy of PTRs to reduce time-wasting and assist the better use of judicial resources. That this confidence was also shared at that time by the Bar is evidenced by the proposal from the Criminal Bar Association in 1974 for an experimental scheme for PTRs at which, broadly speaking, the parties could identify the relevant issues and deal accurately with the question of length of trial.[54] This experimental stage was followed in 1977 by Practice Rules[55] at the Central Criminal Court which provided a formal framework for PTRs. Under the Rules, which were subsequently also promulgated by the several court circuits, counsel are expected to inform the court of such matters as anticipated pleas, the number of prosecution witnesses whose evidence will be required to be given in person, any point of law which is likely to be argued, and the probable length of the trial.[56] Hearings for

---

50 RSC Ord. 25; CCR Ord. 17.
51 *Blackstone's Criminal Practice* (Blackstone Press, London, 1993), para. D11.13; *R v Atkinson* (1977) 67 Cr App R 200, at p. 202 *per* Lord Scarman; Baldwin, J. and McConville, M., *Negotiated Justice* (Martin Robertson, London, 1977).
52 (1977) 66 Cr App R 6.
53 (1977) 67 Cr App R 200.
54 *Blackstone's Criminal Practice*, (1993), *loc. cit.*
55 Practice Rules dated 21 November 1977.
56 *Ibid.*, r. 5. The requirement to assist the court on the probable length of trial also forms part of the Bar's Written Standards for the Conduct of Professional Work (General Standard 5.11). The combination of these two requirements might be expected to concentrate counsel's mind so that reasonably accurate assessments of trial length are offered.

directions only may take place in chambers before any judge,[57] but where any orders relating to the indictment are sought, the PTR must take place in open court before the judge who is assigned to try the case.[58] In the event that an accused pleads guilty to all matters at the PTR, the judge will normally proceed to sentence, and for this reason the accused should be present in court unless it is clear that the hearing is for directions only and the court has given leave for the accused to be absent.[59]

The Court of Appeal has on several occasions and in the strongest language disapproved of PTRs in the Crown Court being used as venues for 'plea-bargaining', at least if this is seen to involve the judge.[60] However, the Court of Appeal has made it equally clear that an accused who pleads guilty may expect, by reason of that plea alone, to benefit from a reduction in sentence.[61]

Arrangements for listing cases for PTR in the Crown Court review are essentially a matter for local practice, and the Court of Appeal has recently confirmed the administrative, as opposed to statutory, nature of the procedure.[62] Cases may be so listed at the instigation of either party, or by the court of its own volition.[63] Often, court staff will send to solicitors a proforma questionnaire for listing purposes, which contains a question as to the suitability of the matter for a PTR. No systematic statistics exist to show how many or what proportion of Crown Court trials are preceded by PTRs, but it may safely be assumed that the majority are not. What is less certain is how often Crown Court listing officers are putting trials in the list 'for plea only', and how often and how far judges use these 'plea-hearings' to clarify other issues, turning them in effect into PTRs. Nor has there been any systematic study of the impact of PTRs (in this wider sense) in terms of reduction in trial length and numbers of contested trials. Despite this lack of empirical evidence, comments in the cases referred to above demonstrate a high level of confidence in the PTR system as it has emerged in the Crown Court, even to the extent of making the procedure statutory in the case of serious

---

57 *Ibid.*, r.4(a).
58 *Ibid.*, r.4(c).
59 *Ibid.*, r.4(d).
60 *Turner* [1970] 2 QB 321; *Atkinson* (1977) 67 Cr App R 200; *Pitman* (1990) *The Times*, 31 October; *Smith* [1990] Crim LR 354; *Kelly* [1990] Crim LR 204. There is some evidence, however, to suggest that this does, or did, happen in some cases: Baldwin and McConville, *op. cit.*, p. 36.
61 Thomas, D., *Principles of Sentencing* (Heinemann, London, 1979), pp. 51–2; see also Moxon, D., *op. cit.*, pp. 32, 69.
62 *Hutchinson* (1985) 82 Cr App R 51, *per* Watkins LJ at pp. 56–7.
63 Practice Rules, r.1.

frauds pursuant to s. 7 of the Criminal Justice Act 1987. However, criticisms have been directed at the administrative aspects of the system, as well as at instances where it appears that undue influence has been brought to bear on the accused to plead guilty.

The prospective gains to case disposal time and reduction of delay have made PTRs quite popular in proposals to the Royal Commission.[64] While delay and the minimisation of costs are not unrelated to the value of justice, the issue which arises in the context of this book is whether PTRs are likely to inflict injustice or unfairness on the accused. Possible benefits from PTRs may include keeping the accused better informed and thereby enhancing their confidence in the courts. A fuller exchange of information may also enhance the quality of decision-making by improving the understanding of the professionals handling the case. Conversely, the non-confrontational atmosphere of the PTR may encourage defence solicitors to weaken their guard and to feel a greater antipathy towards their defendant-clients than towards the prosecution representatives, who are their social peers. The Law Society has issued stern warnings about this danger,[65] but there is a fear that the local legal culture of cooperation (referred to in the comments to chapter 3) may prevail over the demands of an adversarial system. The danger of compromise in this way might be reduced by formality, but such structuring would probably undermine the very nature of PTRs. At least it should be recognised by the courts that plea-bargaining exists and is not necessarily unjust, so long as the accused is professionally advised and has time for reflection.[66]

Lastly, the adversarial nature of English criminal proceedings, at least once beyond the PTR, suggests that recent enthusiasm for judicial powers to examine the accused, to call witnesses, to commission scientific tests and to comment extensively on the facts (as did Bridge J in the *Birmingham Six* case) is misplaced.[67] Not only do these interventions undermine the system in theory, but they might also result in confusion in the narrative presented to jury, as well as unduly influencing a jury in awe of the judge.

---

64   See the submissions of the Bar Council, para. 169; CPS, paras. 8.3.3., 8.3.6; Justices'
      Clerks' Society, para. 2.1; Law Society, para. 3.41; Police Service, p. 171. See also
      Bredar, J., 'Moving up the day of reckoning' [1992] Crim LR 153.
65   'Pre-trial reviews in the magistrates' courts: guidance for defence solicitors' (1983) 80
      LS Gaz 2330.
66   See Bar Council Working Group, *Efficient Disposal of Business in the Crown Court*
      (1992); Law Reform Commission of Canada, Working Paper 60: *Plea Discussions and
      Agreements* (1989); Zander, *op. cit.*
67   See the Submissions by CPS, para. 7.2.14; JUSTICE, para. 19; Police Service, pp.
      181, 193.

It should be abundantly clear by now that systems of criminal justice, whether adversarial or inquisitorial, are fallible. The existence and effectiveness of appeals and post-appeal reviews are therefore considered in the next chapter.

Appendix

Extracts from the Transcript of the Trial of the Birmingham Six, Lancaster, June 1975[68]

James Wood

Though legally correct in every respect, Mr Justice Bridge brought his authority to bear upon the jury so as to ensure the outcome he clearly desired. He commenced his summing-up by reassuring the jury of the quality of the advocacy they had heard:

> All counsel have presented their cases with the utmost skill . . . no valid point has been missed on either side . . .

However, he then revealed that he had formed a clear view as to which side had been the more persuasive:

> The Judge is not an advocate for any party, or he certainly should not be. He tries in summarising the evidence to hold the scales fairly and to present a balanced picture of the evidence on both sides. . . . Some Judges tell juries that in doing that they will express no views of their own. . . . I never say that to any jury, because I think that is attributing to oneself a superhuman capacity. I do not think any of us can be so detached . . . I have naturally formed an impression of the conclusion to which the evidence leads . . . and I think, however hard a judge tries to be impartial, inevitably his presentation of the evidence is bound to be coloured by his own view.

Lest the jury should be left in any doubt as to what his view was or which side he favoured, he proceeded to tell them the reason for one of their long absences from court:

---

68   See (1975) *The Times*, 16 August, p. 1, (1976) *The Times*, 31 March, p. 9, [1980] 2 All ER 227, [1981] 3 WLR 906, [1988] 1 WLR 1, (1988) *The Times*, 29 January, p. 5, (1988) *The Times*, 22 March, p. 1, (1988) 88 Cr App R 40, (1991) *The Times*, 1 April, [1992] 2 All ER 417.

I had to hear all the evidence about the confessions, both from the police witnesses and from the defendants. . . . I decided, as you know, that the evidence was admissible.

Thereafter, the judge divided up his summation into chapters and, at the conclusion of each, chose to make comments damning of the defence contentions. A few examples will suffice to give the flavour of this approach.

First, when dealing with the conflict of scientific evidence between Dr Skuse (for the prosecution) and Dr Black (for the defence), Mr Justice Bridge commented:

> I have read the transcript of Dr Black's evidence and I discover that there is a point when I ask him a question. I said to him 'Dr Black, is this conclusion of yours based on anything other than your theorising?' and he said 'Oh, my Lord, to talk of theorising is rather unfair, is it not?' Is it? If Dr Black was not theorising, what was he doing? I am afraid that I have made my views on this issue . . . pretty plain.

Similarly, when dealing with the alleged beatings and confessions, Bridge J rehearsed the evidence which was capable of supporting the defence version of events and dismissed it. In response to Dr Harwood, the prison doctor who gave evidence of the accuseds' injuries and their probable infliction by the police, he commented:

> . . . can you believe one single word of what Dr Harwood says? There are inescapably many perjurers who have given evidence. If Dr Harwood is one of them, is he not the worst? The profession of medicine is an honourable and noble one, and doctors, I had always supposed were dedicated not only to the interests of their patients but also were men of integrity and truth. If this man has come to this court deliberately to give you false evidence, he is certainly not fit to be a member of the honourable profession upon which, by perjuring himself, he has brought terrible shame.

Of the wounds seen by the defence solicitors prior to their clients' beatings in prison, he said:

> Is it entirely coincidence that [they] all showed discolouration of the chest, scratch marks, scrawls and scrapes. Are those the sort of injuries that the police are likely to inflict — obviously visible but not one would

have thought causing any intense pain? If a man wants to inflict injuries upon himself, what more obvious place in which to do it than by scratching his chest?

Lastly, he tried to make the police conspiracy to deceive and fabricate alleged by the defence sound so outrageous as to be far-fetched:

> If the defendants are giving you honest and substantially accurate evidence, there is no escape from the fact that the police are involved in a conspiracy to commit a variety of crimes which must be unprecedented in the annals of British criminal history.

The jury were by this time no doubt well satisfied that the views of the judge were reasonable and that their duty was to absolve the police by convicting the accused. What is surprising is that it took the jury until the following day to reach the required verdict.

The woeful performance of the judiciary continued in the later proceedings connected with the *Birmingham Six*. Thus, during the appeal in March 1976, Lord Chief Justice Widgery highlighted his lack of concern for the men's plight and his lack of attention to the evidence by stating that he could not recall the origin of Walker's black eye — but he doubted whether it mattered very much. The men's injuries at the hands of the police were nothing 'beyond the ordinary'.

Next, after the Six had begun civil proceedings for assault against the police, Lord Denning struck out their action and showed again the true colours of the judiciary:

> If the six men win, it will mean that the police were guilty of perjury, that they were guilty of violence and threats, and the confessions were involuntary and were improperly admitted in evidence and that the convictions were erroneous. That would mean the Home Secretary would either have to recommend that they be pardoned or he would have to remit the case to the Court of Appeal. This is such an appalling vista that every sensible person in the land would say: It cannot be right these actions should go further.

When the case was referred back to the Court of Appeal in 1987, the judges again indicated their hostility to the accused. Lord Chief Justice Lane concluded the 168-page judgment with these words:

As has happened before in References by the Home Secretary to this Court . . . the longer this hearing has gone on the more convinced this court has become that the verdict of the jury was correct.

Even at the second, and final, reference in 1991, it was the concession of the prosecution rather than insight from the court that made the outcome certain. Thus, the court indicated at a preliminary hearing that it would not be spoiling its Christmas by looking at the papers and so securing an early release.

8

Post-Conviction Procedures

Michael Mansfield and Nicholas Taylor

The English post-appeal system, designed as a judicial 'safety net' to prevent or root out miscarriages of justice, has been an abject failure in recent years. Indeed, such have been the quantity and scale of recent mistakes that the post-appeal system itself could be regarded as the ultimate miscarriage of justice.

Role of the Home Secretary

A review by the Court of Appeal represents the wrongfully convicted person's final opportunity to secure justice. To present a case which would be credible enough to convince judges to overturn the original verdict is difficult enough. However, the restrictive attitude to petitions displayed by the Home Secretary means that very few applicants succeed even in reaching the Court of Appeal.

The basic responses available to the Home Secretary in a case where a miscarriage is alleged include the granting of a pardon (technically through the Crown) or a referral of the case back to the Court of Appeal under s. 17 of the Criminal Appeals Act 1968 (see the Appendix to this chapter). To invoke the review procedure, the prisoner must first lodge a coherent petition delineating a strong case which is likely to catch the eye of the Home Office. Filtering 700–800 petitions per year[1] obviously takes

---

1 Home Office, *Memoranda* (1991) p. 20, para. 4.44.

time, therefore the prisoner may have to wait several months for a reply. Inevitably this means that only those serving longer sentences have sufficient time and commitment to petition the Home Office, while persons serving shorter sentences have little option but to serve out their term.

From the very outset the petitioner is at a severe disadvantage through the very fact of incarceration. Without access to the outside world it will be very difficult to prepare a convincing petition. Legal aid is not available at this stage, so those prisoners without considerable private funds may have to forego even basic legal advice. In rare cases solicitors may work free of charge if they feel a serious miscarriage has occurred. Otherwise, the prisoner may attempt to enlist the support of organisations such as JUSTICE or Liberty. However, such is the current apparent epidemic of alleged miscarriages that these organisations are vastly overstretched and can apply their full attention to only a few selected cases. As a result, many petitions are ill-conceived, badly presented and do not encourage further investigation. Therefore, their authors lose the final opportunity to seek justice at the initial stage of preparing the petition.

Initiating the process of preparing and presenting the petition is the first critical stage of applying for a referral. The second stage is the Home Office's filtering and selection of those petitions which merit further investigation.[2] Somewhat alarmingly, the petition of a potentially innocent person is considered at the outset by officials in the Criminal Department of the Home Office who have no legal expertise whatsoever.[3] These officials (Higher Executive Officers) will investigate the petition on behalf of the Home Secretary, but the quality and depth of their investigation are uncertain and variable. They may ask the relevant police force to re-examine the evidence, though it is somewhat naïve to expect a police force to investigate fully its own misconduct. In such an instance it seems more likely that the police will try to shore up the case and protect themselves rather than root out any potential miscarriage. Occasionally, another police force may be called in, though, even then, group solidarity within the police may blunt the impact of fresh minds. Whatever police report is forthcoming, it is kept confidential. The petitioner is not made aware of any of its contents and will therefore be unable to respond to them and to submit further plausible representations. Thus the first, and possibly last, contact the prisoner may have with the Home Office is often

---

2   See JUSTICE, *Home Office Review of Criminal Conviction* (London, 1968), *Miscarriages of Justice* (London, 1989).

3   This omission is criticised by the *Second Report on the Maguire Case* (1992–93 HC 296), para. 12.14.

a simple, formal rejection of the petition.[4] If an innocent yet convicted person retains faith in the English judicial process, surely it is lost at this stage.

If a case is fortunate enough to have caught the eye of the Home Secretary, then he may choose to act upon it by one of two basic powers available to him. The first, and least significant, is the use of the Royal Prerogative of mercy, technically through the Crown, which will nullify, reprieve or remit the sentence (but not the conviction).[5] It is usually exercised only in minor offences where there is no right of appeal, in summary offences where the reference procedure is not available, or where the defendant has died. It has become established practice that the Home Secretary will not grant a pardon unless the petitioner can establish innocence beyond doubt; not even a reasonable doubt will suffice. Nonetheless, the high burden of proof required may be justified, in that the Home Secretary is here usurping the function of the courts and, as a principal member of the executive, should not interfere lightly with the role of the judiciary.

The most important of the Home Secretary's powers relevant to miscarriages is contained in s. 17 of the Criminal Appeals Act 1968 (see Appendix). This section is specifically designed to root out miscarriages as, in theory, it always allows a potential appeal by those who believe they have been wrongly convicted. The Home Secretary can refer the whole case to the Court of Appeal, when it is treated as a normal appeal to that Court, or the Court may offer an advisory opinion leaving any further action to the Home Secretary. The only statutory restriction on the Home Secretary's decision to refer a case is that he should only do so where 'he thinks fit'. This suggests that the discretion is practically unrestricted, but it has been commented that the overriding factor governing the exercise of the discretion is a concern to avoid even the appearance of interfering with the independence of the judiciary.[6] As a consequence, the Home Secretary will only act according to an established departmental formula, whereby the petitioner must produce new evidence or other considerations of substance which were not available at the original trial

---

4 It remains to be seen whether the judgment in *R v Parole Board, ex parte Wilson* [1992] 2 WLR 707 (mandatory disclosure of reasons for refusal of parole) will have any impact.

5 *R v Foster* [1985] QB 115. See also Rolph, C. H., *The Queen's Pardon* (Cassell, London, 1978); Smith, A. T. H., 'The prerogative of mercy, the power of pardon and criminal justice' [1983] *Public Law* 398.

6 Brandon, R., and Davies, C., *Wrongful Imprisonment* (Allen & Unwin, London, 1973), p. 167.

and could be considered properly by the Court of Appeal.[7] Additionally, the petitioner must establish very convincing grounds for showing that he or she did not commit the offence. This is a reversal of the burden of proof and as such is a formidable hurdle.

Such technicalities have enabled the Home Secretary to use s. 17 as a shield against referring several cases, despite obvious doubts about the safety of the convictions. For example, even though the jury passed a unanimous verdict at the trial of the *Maguire Seven*, the verdict was strenuously disputed for several years. However, without the availability of new evidence, the gathering of which would be virtually impossible in their position, the accused were unable to lower the Home Secretary's shield and therefore remained imprisoned.

Bearing in mind the tremendous difficulties the petitioners have in bringing their cases to the attention of the authorities, it is an invaluable resource to them that there is someone outside the prison who believes in their innocence and is prepared to nudge the authorities constantly, even in the face of adversity. Often this will be the role of the prisoner's family, but, without financial backing, their task will be great and they may attempt to engage the support of their MP or other public figures. Enlisting the assistance of public figures may be the prisoner's most potent weapon. For example, there was an inevitability about the release of the *Guildford Four* when, by late 1988, they had the endorsement of such worthies as Cardinal Basil Hume, Archbishop Runcie, two former Home Secretaries (Roy Jenkins and Merlyn Rees) and two former Law Lords (Lords Devlin and Scarman). In 1982, a House of Commons Select Committee commented that 'in practice the [Home Office] decision to act may depend upon the amount of pressure that is brought to bear on the Home Secretary by people of influence'.[8] A further decade of cases has lent considerable support to this view.

As well as public figures, journalistic interest can also prove productive. The release of Wayne and Paul Darvell in July 1992 illustrates well the power of the media. The two brothers, wrongly convicted for murder, were of below average intelligence and living in sheltered accommodation. Their conviction was convenient all round. It is in such cases that journalistic exposure is most important in keeping the case in the public eye. Only the tenacity of the BBC 'Rough Justice' programme, which

---

7   *Second Report on the Maguire Case, loc. cit.*, paras. 10.3–5. The May Inquiry largely endorsed this narrow, reactive stance (para. 10.8).

8   Home Affairs Committee, *Report on Miscarriages of Justice* (1981–82 HC 421), para. 10. See also Government Reply (Cmnd 8856, 1983); Tregilgas-Davey, M., 'Miscarriages of justice in the English legal system' (1991) 141 NLJ 668.

took up the case in 1989 and refused to accept the convenient verdict, prompted the brothers' eventual release. Hilliard summed up the current plight of the petitioner when he said that in future defence teams would do well to link up with a good investigative journalist before approaching counsel.[9]

If such a media campaign is unsuccessful, then the innocent prisoner may resort to more desperate measures to capture public attention. Ronald Barker was unable to mount such a media campaign and subsequently went on hunger-strike to draw attention to his plight. He was eventually released and claimed that it was not the result of any petition that he had written to the Home Secretary but simply 'the fuss was the key'.[10]

The recent spate of multi-accused miscarriages has created a band-wagon effect in the media, and, in such a climate, attention may be easier to secure for groups of prisoners. However, there is also the danger of what Woffinden refers to as the 'inflation of justice',[11] whereby individuals are finding attention increasingly difficult to secure. The single accused will find it much harder to build up the head of steam required to register on the scale of British justice than those with media-friendly titles such as the *Maguire Seven, Birmingham Six, Tottenham Three* and so on. Judith Ward provides ample evidence of this phenomenon. Although wrongfully convicted on similar charges and at a similar time as the *Birmingham Six* and *Guildford Four*, concern over her plight was virtually non-existent in terms of media exposure. Even in the current journalistic clamour to unearth injustice by the courts, she received very little attention until her release was imminent. As a result, it should be noted that her case was probably only recognised at all following on the coat-tails of the more notorious cases. However, it remains a fact that, 'the chances of a petition being ultimately successful might sometimes depend less on its intrinsic merits than on the amount of external support and publicity it was able to attract'.[12]

Role of the Court of Appeal[13]

To establish that a case is arguable is one thing; to prove that the verdict is unsafe and unsatisfactory in the Court of Appeal is quite another.

---

9 Hilliard, B., 'Blessed with hindsight' (1991) 141 NLJ 393.
10 Brandon and Davies, *op. cit.*, p. 175.
11 Woffinden, B.,'The inflation of justice', May 1990 *Counsel*, p. 14.
12 See Home Affairs Committee, *loc. cit.*, para. 10.
13 See O'Connor, P., 'The Court of Appeal' [1990] Crim LR 615; Boal, G., 'Last resort' (1991) 135 Sol Jo 615; Malleson, K., 'Miscarriages of justice and accessibility to the Court of Appeal' [1991] Crim LR 323.

Public confidence in the Court of Appeal as a body to prevent or root out miscarriages of justice has been substantially undermined by its handling of recent cases. The impression given is that the Court of Appeal views all persons as prima facie guilty, so acquittals represent a failure of justice.

On determining the appeal upon a reference by the Home Secretary, the House of Lords has held[14] that such a person is to be treated as if he or she were a person upon whom had been conferred by s. 1 of the Criminal Appeals Act 1968 a general right of appeal. Being a creature of statute, the Court of Appeal is limited to the powers conferred in the Criminal Appeals Act 1968 (as amended by the Criminal Justice Act 1988) and the Supreme Court Act 1981. It is limited to a power of review rather than a full appellate function.[15]

The review procedures governing miscarriages of justice are contained in only four sections of the Criminal Appeals Act 1968, namely ss. 2, 7, 17, and 23. Under s. 17, the Home Secretary will have referred the case to the Court only if there has come to light fresh information which the Court can properly and usefully consider.[16] Section 23 of the Act governs the admissibility of such evidence which may ultimately lead to the quashing of the conviction. For such evidence to be admissible, it must be reasonably explained why it was not available at the original trial.[17] Furthermore, it must be likely to be credible, subsequently interpreted to mean capable of belief in the context of the issue.[18]

In practice, the problem has been in the past, although it is changing, that the Court has been very reluctant to admit fresh evidence, still less to find it credible once admitted. It has made limited use of the broad 'unsafe or unsatisfactory' ground of appeal introduced in s. 2 of the 1968 Act: only six cases based on fresh evidence have been allowed on a 'lurking doubt'[19] during the last 20 years.[20] The Court has also rarely ordered retrials under the power enacted in 1964 under s. 7. The still more recent power to order retrials on any ground, not limited to fresh evidence, in s. 43 of the Criminal Justice Act 1988 is also sparingly used.

---

14   *R v Chard* [1983] 3 All ER 637, *per* Lord Diplock at p. 639.
15   *R v McIlkenny* [1992] 2 All ER 417.
16   Home Office evidence to the Home Affairs Committee, *loc. cit.*, para. 5.
17   A wider discretion is granted by s. 23(1), but the filter of the Home Secretary is likely to demand some fresh evidence which is then subjected to s. 23(2)(b).
18   *R v Stafford and Luvaglio* [1968] 3 All ER 752, *per* Edmund-Davies at p. 753. See Samuels, A., 'Fresh evidence in the Court of Appeal Criminal Division' [1975] Crim LR 23.
19   *R v Cooper* [1969] 1 QB 267, *per* Lord Widgery at p. 271. There were 65 referrals between 1972 and 1986: O'Connor, *op. cit.*, p. 616.
20   JUSTICE, *op. cit.*, para. 4.19.

Where the Court does receive fresh evidence, the Act is silent on the criteria to be applied in assessing its effect, and the Court itself has taken on the role of the jury and decided the guilt or innocence of an appellant.

This self-made power purportedly derives from the case of *Stafford* v *DPP*.[21] Prior to 1972, the Court of Appeal considered fresh evidence in terms of whether it would have instilled a reasonable doubt in the minds of the jury, and only if convinced on that criterion would the Court then quash the verdict under s. 2(1)(a).[22] In this way, the Court of Appeal adopted the role of a review body; it did not subvert the role of the jury and did not resolve factual disputes. However, the Court of Appeal's judgment in *Stafford* v *DPP*, endorsed by the House of Lords, apparently threw off the shackles and justified a new subjective approach by the judges through the interpretation of the words 'if they think' in s. 29(1)(a).[23] No longer was the Court of Appeal tied to reviewing the verdict given at the original trial; it was now the verdict of the Court of Appeal itself that mattered. In *Stafford* v *DPP* the verdict was not set aside because of the wealth of the new evidence but was merely 'suspended' until the Court had evaluated the new evidence. It decided that the new evidence would make no difference to the verdict, and the appeal was dismissed. In truth this was not the dismissal of the appeal, but a new verdict based on the second-hand old evidence plus the new evidence. Furthermore, the Court of Appeal's record on returning safe verdicts is itself far from inspiring.[24]

Following *Stafford* v *DPP*, fresh evidence is assessed in relation to its effect on the Court here and now, as opposed to its effect on the original jury. The Court does sometimes say, however, that it will adopt the latter approach. Contrary to the powers later contrived through *Stafford* v *DPP*, both the Tucker Report[25] and the Donovan Committee[26] had concluded that the Court of Appeal was ill-equipped to re-try cases itself and had no authority to do so. Lord Devlin[27] has long argued, and rightly so, that any jury which has convicted without having heard all the relevant and credible evidence cannot possibly be said to have produced a verdict which is safe and satisfactory. Under the *Stafford* v *DPP* interpretation of the law, the Court cannot order a new trial unless it

---

21 *Stafford* v *DPP* [1973] 3 All ER 762.
22 See *R* v *Parks* (1962) 46 Cr App R 29.
23 Compare Criminal Appeal Act 1907, s. 9; O'Connor, *op. cit.*, p. 620.
24 Consider especially *R* v *Cooper and McMahon* (1975) 61 Cr App R 215.
25 (1954) Cmd 9150, para. 30.
26 (1965) Cmnd 2755, para. 140.
27 *The Judge* (Oxford University Press, Oxford, 1981), pp. 148–76.

allows the appeal. It cannot allow the appeal unless it thinks on the evidence that the conviction is unsafe. But if it thinks that, it must follow that any jury which considered it safe to convict on the same evidence must be wrong. The only point of a new trial would thus be to give the prosecution a chance of launching a second attack. Section 7 itself suggests that the Court of Appeal is not expected to adjudicate on cases; the section states that 'where the Court of Appeal allow an appeal against conviction and it appears to the court that the interests of justice so require, they may order the appellant to be retried'. If the Court of Appeal is re-trying cases itself anyway, then what is the point of this section? Unfortunately, recent opportunities to reverse *Stafford* have not been seized. In *R* v *Callaghan and Others* in 1988, Lord Lane said:[28]

> Although the court may choose to test its views by asking itself what the original jury might have concluded the question which we in the end have to decide is whether in our judgment, in all the circumstances of the case including both the verdict of the jury at the trial upon the evidence they heard and the fresh evidence before the court, the convictions were safe and satisfactory.

Reform

The appeal system which responds to miscarriages of justice is confusing and inadequate. What has to be contemplated is a completely new structure which ensures that the hundreds of complainants post-conviction have their cases properly investigated and reviewed. The prerequisite for this is substantial funding and resources.[29] At the moment there is none until legal aid is granted upon a Home Secretary's reference, by which time a lot of groundwork and foot-slogging by a small number of unpaid, committed solicitors will have taken place. The new structure should also ensure alacrity — delay is the handmaiden of miscarriage.

A procedure which would overcome many of the ills described hitherto requires a standing commission, incorporating a secretariat and an investigative branch. This commission should be regionalised. Its powers would not depend solely on cases being referred to it by convicted persons or solicitors, but it would also be able to take action on its own

---

28   *R* v *Callaghan and Others* (1989) 88 Cr App R 40 at 47. But compare *R* v *Edwards* [1991]
     1 WLR 207.
29   See Beckman, M. and Taylor, C., 'Appellate justice unsafe and unsatisfactory?' (1989)
     139 NLJ 1523.

initiative. Its function would be to collate any fresh evidence put before it, to disclose it to all parties, and to investigate it in order to prepare a hearing in front of a lay panel of six jurors.[30] The reasons why jurors should be employed are, first, because the original verdict derives from a jury and, secondly, because judges are notoriously unreliable in judging fact — the essence of fresh evidence.

Once the matter had been put before a panel of six jurors they could either, by consent, deal with it on paper or, if one party requests, there could be an oral hearing. The object of the hearing would be to assess whether the fresh material satisfied a 'low threshold test', that is to say it must be shown to be relevant to the issues in the case and not incredible. This test would circumvent arguments about availability which are often difficult to deal with and unfair on appellants. Clearly, an accused in a retrial would have to explain why available evidence had not been called at the first trial, but that would be a matter for the second jury. If fresh material satisfied the low threshold test, the only power of the review body would be to order a retrial. There would obviously be an exception to this where a retrial would be impracticable because witnesses were dead or unavailable, or where lapse of time would make a test of memory unreal. In those circumstances the body would recommend to the Court of Appeal that the conviction be quashed, but the Court should adopt the Devlin criteria in exercising its powers.[31]

Occasionally, when deciding whether fresh material is relevant to issues in the original case, a panel might need legal advice on admissibility aside from the submissions of the two parties. The commission would therefore employ its own independent panel of lawyers — somewhat akin to *amici curiae* in the High Court — who could tender written advice which would be available to both the parties.

A further advantage of the proposed panel review lies in the nature of its investigation. In many of the well-known miscarriages there has been a paramount but unmet need to track down witnesses, to gain access to police stations, files and internal documents, to unravel the complexities of scientific tests and experiments, and to gain access to government laboratories where such tests and experiments have been carried out. The strong decision recently in the *Ward* case, where substantial non-disclosure had occurred, merely emphasises the demand for careful and detailed access by the defence/appellant to all materials which form part of the police investigation. Often several squads or forces have been

---

30   Compare the record of single, often legally trained advisers: O'Connor, *op. cit.*, p. 625.
31   Compare JUSTICE, *op. cit.*, para. 4.22.

involved and their resources far exceed those of a defence solicitor. The investigative aspect of a standing commission would require some police input in order to find its way through police procedures, but it should also employ a predominantly independent group of personnel who are not ex-police officers. Plainly, this will cost a great deal, but then so do miscarriages. In any event, justice is not to be bartered away or measured in the same way as stocks and shares.

There would have to be a provision for an appeal against a panel's decision which involves a point of law where it is adverse to an appellant and where the result is to refuse a retrial. That appeal on a point of law could follow the ordinary channels of appeal.

To balance the account, a number of new difficulties might be created by the operation of the proposed commission. One that would have to be addressed would be the situation where the review body had not quashed a conviction but had only ordered a retrial. The status of the accused on the second trial could be problematic, because the jury would be likely to know, because of publicity, that it was engaged on a retrial and, therefore, that there had been a prior conviction. This potentially prejudicial knowledge could, however, be explained to the new jury by means of a direction that that the original jury did not deal with all the available evidence and that the new evidence might cast a new light on both the credibility and substance of the old material.

Another potential complication to be faced is that there might be some cases where there were a number of different complaints which could give rise to an appeal. So, for example, an accused might have a point of law on an admissibility ruling during a trial, and/or a point of law concerning a deficiency in summing up and/or some fresh evidence. The accused should have a choice: either he or she could go straight to the Court of Appeal as at present, with points of law and fresh evidence in order to get the conviction quashed; or he or she could immediately approach the commission in order to achieve a retrial, leaving the points of law on hold. If the retrial lead to an acquittal, the points of law would become irrelevant and would not be pursued. If the retrial resulted in conviction, then any subsequent appeal from that would have to involve points of law from the second trial rather than from the first, although plainly, if the same point of admissibility had been decided mistakenly twice, it would afford a ground of appeal.

The final problem is whether there should be any limit to the number of applications relying on fresh evidence that one person could make to the standing commission. The usual floodgates argument and mutterings about one bite of the cherry seem to loom. However, there should be no limit. Provided the low threshold test was satisfied, a second jury would be well able to work out whether an accused was using or manipulating the system by holding back on evidence which could have been used in the first place. Such tactics could all be the subject of comment and cross-examination in the retrial. This resolution would also circumvent the Home Office who would no longer have a role to play. Their exclusion from the process will hardly be missed — so far as one can see, their miscarriages of justice department in the past seems to have been obsessed with traffic offenders!

One is fearful that even if the Royal Commission on Criminal Justice recommends a court of last resort or some other machinery of that kind, the Home Office combined with the Treasury will claim, as they already have, that there is no money. Another fear already expressed is that there cannot be an open-ended commitment of the kind envisaged; in other words, from the hundreds of cases received each week by organisations such as Liberty, how do you know which ones to pursue? The facts that a fair review system will be difficult to carry out or that some will abuse it should never be arguments against starting at all. If that kind of argument had won the day, basic social welfare provision in this country would have never commenced. In a sense, we are demanding the provision of basic legal welfare, which no one, irrespective of their background or circumstances, should be denied.

Appendix

Criminal Appeal Act 1968

Grounds for allowing appeal under s. 1

2.—(1)   Except as provided by this Act, the Court of Appeal shall allow an appeal against conviction if they think—

(a)   that the conviction should be set aside on the ground that under all the circumstances of the case it is unsafe or unsatisfactory;

(b)   that the judgment of the court of trial should be set aside on the ground of a wrong decision of any question of law; or

(c)   that there was a material irregularity in the course of the trial, and in any other case shall dismiss the appeal:

Provided that the Court may, notwithstanding that they are of opinion that the point raised in the appeal might be decided in favour of the appellant, dismiss the appeal if they consider that no miscarriage of justice has actually occurred.

(2)   In the case of an appeal against conviction the Court shall, if they allow the appeal, quash the conviction.

(3)   An order of the Court of Appeal quashing a conviction shall, except when under section 7 below the appellant is ordered to be retried, operate as a direction to the court of trial to enter, instead of the record of conviction, a judgment and verdict of acquittal.

Power to order retrial

7.—(1)   Where the Court of Appeal allow an appeal against conviction and it appears to the Court that the interests of justice so require, they may order the appellant to be retried.

(2)   A person shall not under this section be ordered to be retried for any offence other than—

(a)   the offence of which he was convicted at the original trial and in respect of which his appeal is allowed as mentioned in subsection (1) above;

(b)   an offence of which he could have been convicted at the original trial on an indictment for the first-mentioned offence; or

(c)   an offence charged in an alternative count of the indictment in respect of which the jury were discharged from giving a verdict in consequence of convicting him of the first-mentioned offence.

Reference by Home Secretary

17.—(1)   Where a person has been convicted on indictment, or been tried on indictment and found not guilty by reason of insanity, or been found by a jury to be under disability, and to have done the act or made the omission charged against him, the Secretary of State may, if he thinks fit, at any time either—

(a)   refer the whole case to the Court of Appeal and the case shall then be treated for all purposes as an appeal to the Court by that person; or

(b)   if he desires the assistance of the Court on any point arising in the case, refer that point to the Court for their opinion thereon, and the Court shall consider the point so referred and furnish the Secretary of State with their opinion thereon accordingly.

(2)   A reference by the Secretary of State under this section may be made by him either on an application by the person referred to in subsection (1), or without any such application.

Evidence

23.—(1)   For purposes of this Part of this Act the Court of Appeal may, if they think it necessary or expedient in the interests of justice—

(a)   order the production of any document, exhibit or other thing connected with the proceedings, the production of which appears to them necessary for the determination of the case;

(b)   order any witness who would have been a compellable witness in the proceedings from which the appeal lies to attend for examination and be examined before the Court, whether or not he was called in those proceedings; and

(c)   subject to subsection (3) below, receive the evidence, if tendered, of any witness.

(2)   Without prejudice to subsection (1) above, where evidence is tendered to the Court of Appeal thereunder the Court shall, unless they are satisfied that the evidence, if received, would not afford any ground for allowing the appeal, exercise their power of receiving it if—

(a)   it appears to them that the evidence is likely to be credible and would have been admissible in the proceedings from which the appeal lies on an issue which is the subject of the appeal; and

(b)   they are satisfied that it was not adduced in those proceedings but there is a reasonable explanation for the failure to adduce it.

(3)   Subsection (1)(c) above applies to any witness (including the appellant) who is competent but not compellable, and applies also to the appellant's husband or wife where the appellant makes an application for that purpose and the evidence of the husband or wife could not have been given in the proceedings from which the appeal lies except on such an application.

(4)   For purposes of this Part of this Act, the Court of Appeal may, if they think it necessary or expedient in the interests of justice, order the examination of any witness whose attendance might be required under subsection (1)(b) above to be conducted, in manner provided by rules of court, before any judge or officer of the Court or other person appointed by the Court for the purpose, and allow the admission of any depositions so taken as evidence before the Court.

EDITORS' COMMENTS

It takes a society which is confident in its own values and is open in its style of government to admit that mistakes may have been made during its criminal justice process. Given the nature of political society in this country, it is not surprising that the structures for addressing allegations of injustice operate in a half-hearted and secretive fashion. To pick up the baton of reform from the end of chapter 8, it would seem that attention should be paid to three areas.

There is first the issue of what count as relevant reasons for reinquiry, referral or retrial. Here, the problem is the narrowness of the grounds. For example, as has been explained in the foregoing chapter, there may be limits on the admission of evidence not previously heard if it was available but unused at the original trial. The refusal to take account of any but the most flagrant of failings in defence lawyers was raised in the Introduction.[1]

The next stage is the receptivity of the system to evidence, on any relevant grounds, that there has been a miscarriage. The authors of chapter 8 are by no means the first to suggest that the fitful scrutiny by the Home Secretary's backroom staff should be replaced by an independent and investigative tribunal.[2] Variants on this theme have been advanced, *inter alia*,[3] by the House of Commons Home Affairs Committee,[4] JUSTICE,[5] the Police Complaints Authority[6] and many submissions to the present Royal Commission.[7] A Government reply in 1983 dismissed the idea and made the empty promise that the Home Secretary and Court of Appeal would be more receptive to petitions and referrals.[8] However, the model of an independent tribunal seems to be coming back into official favour, as affirmed by the personal support given by Douglas Hurd, the ex-Home Secretary and current Foreign Secretary, in evidence to the May Inquiry[9] and by the current Home Secretary in reaction to its Second Report,[10] which also endorses the principle of independent investigative machinery in place of the Home Office.[11] There is surely an unanswerable case for avoiding the conflict of interests between justice

---

1 See *R* v *Ensor* [1989] 2 All ER 586; *R* v *Irwin* [1987] 2 All ER 1085; *R* v *Gautam* [1988] Crim LR 109; *US* v *Cronic* 466 US 648 (1984); *Strickland* v *Washington* 466 US 668 (1984); Law Society, *Submission* (1991), para. 5.21. There is equal resistance to reopening cases in Northern Ireland: SACHR, 17th Report (1992–93 HC 54), ch. 6, para. 12.

2 The Attorney-General does not conduct a thorough review of evidence in cases (such as under the Explosive Substances Act 1883) where his *fiat* is required for prosecution: *Second Report on the Maguire Case* (1992–93 HC 296), para. 9.8.

3 See also Woffinden, B., 'Independent review tribunal' (1989) 139 NLJ 1108.

4 1981–82 HC 421.

5 *Miscarriages of Justice* (London, 1989), para. 5.25.

6 Annual Report 1991 (1992–93 HC 15), para. 6.8.

7 There are variations on whether the independent body should be investigative, advisory or judicial, and therefore its relationship to the Court of Appeal. See especially Home Office, *Memoranda* (1991), paras 4.47, 4.48, 4.62, 4.67, 4.80; Law Society, *Submission* (1991), paras 5.20, 5.24, 5.31; General Council of the Bar, *Submission* (1992), para. 208; SACHR, *loc. cit.*, ch. 6, para. 12.

8 Cmnd 8856.

9 (1991) *The Times*, 3 October, p. 1.

10 (1992) *The Times*, 4 December, p. 2.

11 *Second Report on the Maguire Case, loc. cit.*, para. 12.25.

for the individual and the maintenance of general confidence in the system as may be currently experienced by the Home Secretary.[12] It seems a good bet that, whatever else it may suggest, the Royal Commission will demand changes along these lines.

Assuming it continues to have any role whatsoever in miscarriage cases,[13] the Court of Appeal would have to undergo reforms in terms of the criteria to be applied at the rehearing and in terms of its wilingness to allow retrials. Changes in the ground rules have been widely canvassed,[14] but there is much more opposition in official circles to retrials because of the fears that delay will affect the availability and powers of recall of witnesses and that testimony will be shaped by the experience of a prior cross-examination.[15] The same concerns seem rather muted when prosecutions are mounted years after the event.[16] In any event, it seems that the fundamental role of the Court of Appeal will have to be reappraised. Rather like the Home Secretary, the Court has over-concerned itself with the integrity of the system and with procedural observances; whether the right result has been achieved seems to be given a lower priority.

Moving on from issues of process, it was asserted in the Introduction to this book that miscarriages of justice may arise from the enforcement of inherently unjust laws as well as from the misapplication of just laws. A prime candidate for the label 'unjust' is the special legislation which has been passed by Parliament to combat terrorism. Its nature will now be described.

---

12 A similar conflict could arise if the Court of Appeal itself were to be rearmed (see Criminal Appeal Act 1907, s. 9, repealed in 1968) with investigative powers following the suggestion of Lord Chief Justice Taylor (*The Times*, 26 February 1992, p. 1).

13 The CPS suggestion (*Submission* (1991), paras 14.4.11, 14.4.8) is for fresh evidence cases to be tried by a new, intermediate court; a new review body is to look at allegations, so the powers of the Home Office could be abolished. See also JUSTICE, *Submission* (1991), para. 5.

14 See Home Office, *loc. cit.*, para. 4.84.

15 Compare *R* v *Saunders* (1973) 58 Cr App R 248; *R* v *Callaghan and Others* (1989) 88 Cr App R 40: Home Office, *op. cit.*, para. 4.91; CPS, *op. cit.*, ch. 14; JUSTICE, *op. cit.*, para. 4; Law Society, *op. cit.*, para. 5.31.

16 Compare *R* v *Quinn* (1990) *The Times*, 31 March; CPS, *Annual Report 1990–91*, p. 28.

9

The Prevention of Terrorism Acts

Brice Dickson

Introduction

This chapter summarises the latest version of the Prevention of Terrorism (Temporary Provisions) Act 1989 (PTA 1989), the statute which has formed the central plank in the British Government's regulatory strategy against terrorism since the mid-1970s. It seeks to demonstrate that the 1989 Act is a hotchpotch of measures which in many respects employ inappropriate concepts and embrace superfluous rules which do not strike the proper balance between protecting society against violent attacks and preserving basic civil liberties. The focus is on the operation of the Act in Great Britain; in Northern Ireland, of course, any consideration of the PTA's role cannot be isolated from the impact of related laws such as the Criminal Evidence (Northern Ireland) Order 1988 and the Northern Ireland (Emergency Provisions) Act 1991 (EPA).

The origins of the PTA 1989 are traceable to several sources: the Prevention of Violence Act 1939, the panic consequent upon the Birmingham pub bombings in 1974, the features introduced into the PTAs in 1976 and 1984, and the recommendations of the various individuals who from time to time have reviewed the legislation's operation.[1]

---

1 The PTAs of 1974 and 1976 were reviewed by Lord Shackleton (Cmnd 7328, 1978) and by Earl Jellicoe (Cmnd 8803, 1983). Sir Cyril Phillips conducted ▶

Given the number of these reviews, the need for annual renewal debates in both Houses of Parliament, and the interest shown by legal academics,[2] the literature on the pros and cons of each provision in the PTA is already extensive. Yet most of the discussion tends to dwell upon the detailed wording of the provisions, paying little attention to the philosophy underlying them. Most commentators, of course, especially Members of Parliament, are presented to all intents and purposes with a *fait accompli.* Whatever the rhetoric, the reality of party politics is that Bills and renewal orders coming before Parliament cannot fundamentally be amended during their passage. The official reviews, likewise, have all been predicated on the assumption that some kind of anti-terrorist statute is required and that the current provisions should continue to apply unless compelling reasons can be adduced for abolition.[3] In recent years people have grown fatalistic about the Act's semi-permanence, despite the word 'temporary' in its title. Indeed, the present Act does not have a fixed life-span: provided it obtains annual renewal it will endure indefinitely. During the renewal debate in the House of Commons on 24 February 1992, even the Labour Party indicated that its policy was to reform the Act rather than repeal it.[4]

The Act's short title also suggests that the primary focus of the legislation is prevention rather than cure. This is apparent in two key

---

unpublished reviews of the PTA 1984 in early 1985 and again in early 1986. In January 1987, Viscount Colville submitted a report on the Act's operation during 1986, and in December 1987 he presented to Parliament a more substantial review (Cm 264, 1987). He carried out further reviews for the years 1988 to 1992, but these too were not officially published.

2 See Bonner, D., *Emergency Powers in Peacetime* (Sweet & Maxwell, London, 1985), ch. 4 and 'Combating terrorism in the 1990s: the role of the PTA' [1989] *Public Law* 440; Dickson, B., 'The Prevention of Terrorism (Temporary Provisions) Act 1989' (1989) 40 NILQ 250; Hall, P., 'The Prevention of Terrorism Acts', in Jennings, Anthony (ed.), *Justice Under Fire: The Abuse of Civil Liberties in Northern Ireland*, 2nd ed. (Pluto Press, London, 1990), ch. 7; Scorer, C., Spencer, S. and Hewitt, P., *The New Prevention of Terrorism Act: The Case for Repeal*, 3rd ed., (NCCL, London, 1985); Walker, C., *The Prevention of Terrorism in British Law*, 2nd ed. (Manchester University Press, Manchester, 1992), *passim.* For the background to the Act purely in the context of terrorism in Ireland, see Hogan, G. and Walker, C., *Political Violence and the Law in Ireland* (Manchester University Press, Manchester, 1989), pp. 3–23.

3 For example, the terms of reference for the major review conducted by Lord Colville in 1987, *loc. cit.*, n. 1, were as follows: 'Accepting the need for legislation against terrorism, to assess the operation of the PTA 1984, with particular regard to the effectiveness of the legislation and its effect on the liberties of the subject, and to report.'

4 Mr Roy Hattersley MP said that a Labour Government would retain the proscription and financial assistance provisions but abolish the power to issue exclusion orders and introduce judicial review for detentions longer than 48 hours. Labour has voted against renewal of the PTA since 1983; in 1993 the Act was renewed by 329 votes to 202.

areas: Part II of the Act on exclusion orders and Part IV on arrest, detention and examination. Under the latter an information bank can be compiled which may be of use at a later stage in pre-empting terrorist attacks. The latest PTA also contains extensive provisions dealing with financial assistance for terrorist activities. The emphasis is on taking the lid off seemingly legitimate operations so as to unmask the reality underneath. The implication is that terrorism's lifeblood is racketeering, and if only the flow of funds could be stemmed the supply of firearms, explosives and ammunition would dry up too. The Act contains no measures concerned with the processing of alleged terrorists once they have been charged: unlike in Northern Ireland, where the EPA 1991 is in force, there are no special rules in Great Britain on bail applications, remands, confessions, the right to silence, committal proceedings, jury trial, the burden of proof or appeals.

A further general point is that there is a growing realisation that the United Kingdom's anti-terrorist legislation is in places difficult to reconcile with internationally recognised human rights standards. In relation to detentions for up to seven days, the Government has had to recognise this incompatibitlity by issuing notices of derogation under Art. 15 of the European Convention on Human Rights and Fundamental Freedoms and under Art. 4 of the UN's International Covenant on Civil and Political Rights (described later). In December 1991, the European Commission on Human Rights concluded that the notice of derogation under Art. 15 complied with all the requirements laid down in that Article.[5] However, the complaint arose from the detention of two men in Northern Ireland where political violence is far more serious than in Britain, and some of the reasons given for upholding the derogation (such as the need to maintain public confidence in the small team of Northern Ireland judiciary) may not be pertinent to the justification of extended detentions in Britain.

Other potential infringements have yet to be tested in an international forum, partly because such forums are few and far between and partly because the norms they enforce are not always exacting on account of the extensive let-out clauses the international treaties usually contain. All things considered, the opportunity to commence international human rights litigation is still limited. It is to be hoped that, as international criminal law develops further, and as non-governmental organisations increase their influence on international standard-setting and monitoring

---

5   *Brannigan and McBride* v *UK*, Appl nos 14553–4/89, report of Commission adopted 3 December 1991. The European Court's judgment is awaited.

in the human rights arena, a more effective supervisory system will in due course be established.

If such supervision is to be credible, it will have to take a stand on whether 'terrorism' is a concept which should be employed in national legislation at all. In this respect the PTA 1989 leaves much to be desired because of its efforts to give 'terrorism' a special legal status. 'Terrorism', according to s. 20(1), is violence for political ends, including any use of violence for the purpose of putting the public or a section of the public in fear. It could be argued, of course, that the use of violence by state security forces, whether in ambushing paramilitary active service units or in mistreating suspects while they are in custody, is just as much for political ends as the planting of a bomb by a paramilitary group. The PTA's definition is further to be criticised for its partiality, in both senses of that word. The acts of terrorism to which the arrest and detention provisions apply are 'acts of terrorism connected with the affairs of Northern Ireland, and acts of terrorism of any other description except acts connected solely with the affairs of the United Kingdom other than Northern Ireland'. This means that acts of violence for political ends connected with, say, Scottish or Welsh nationalism or with animal rights campaigning can never qualify as terrorism for the purposes of the PTA. It means, too, that people from Ireland may conclude that the Act is deliberately anti-Irish in its effects, a sentiment which is lent some substance by the tragic miscarriages of justice which several Irish people have experienced in English trials.

Proscription (Part I)

The anti-Irish character of the Act is further demonstrated by the provisions on proscription. These specifically outlaw the Irish Republican Army and the Irish National Liberation Army, and the Home Secretary may, with Parliament's approval, add any organisation to the proscribed list if it appears to him to be 'concerned in, or in promoting or encouraging, terrorism occurring in the United Kingdom and connected with the affairs of Northern Ireland'. Terrorist groups which are not so connected — such as the French group *Action Directe* or the Arab group *Hezbollah* — cannot be outlawed.

Proscription entails criminalising any person who belongs, or professes to belong, to the organisation concerned, or who solicits or invites support for the organisation (other than with money or other property), or who helps to arrange or manage, or who addresses, any meeting of three or more individuals knowing that the meeting is to support or further the activities of a proscribed organisation or that it is to be addressed by a person belonging or professing to belong to a proscribed organisation. A person found guilty of any of these offences can be sent to prison for up to 10 years; in Northern Ireland (where the same range of offences is governed by s. 28 of the EPA 1991) the trial will be in a Crown Court without a jury. In addition, ss. 10 and 11 of the PTA 1989, as explained further below, make it an offence to solicit or invite the contribution of money or other property for the benefit of a proscribed organisation, the making of such contributions, and involvement in an arrangement for making available such contributions or for facilitating their retention or control by or on behalf of another person. Oddly, the term 'proscribed organisation' is here extended to include those organisations outlawed under the EPA 1991 (groups such as the UDA and the UVF); this means that, while membership of these groups is not unlawful in Great Britain, a contribution to their assets is forbidden. The maximum penalty is 14 years' imprisonment and an unlimited fine,[6] the offence again being triable by a juryless 'Diplock' court in Northern Ireland.

Section 3 of the Act also makes it an offence for a person in a public place to wear any item of dress or to wear, carry or display any article in such circumstances as to arouse reasonable apprehension that he or she is a member or supporter of a proscribed organisation. This is a summary offence, with a maximum penalty of six months' imprisonment and a level 5 fine; in Northern Ireland (under s. 29 of the EPA 1991) it is still a scheduled offence and so is governed by special procedural rules.

The peculiar feature of proscription is that it punishes people for associating themselves with an idea, albeit the heinous idea of 'terrorism'. Generally speaking, and not just because of the difficulties of proof involved, the law tries to avoid regulating how people should think, but in this case the idea in question is deemed to be so obnoxious as to merit legal intervention. Thus, merely to shout 'Up the IRA', or to display a poster urging people to back the INLA, would be criminal conduct under s. 2(1)(b). Given, however, that the public order legislation in both Great Britian and Northern Ireland already criminalises the formation of military or semi-military organisations, the training or equipping of members of an association for the purpose of displaying physical force in promoting any political object, and the wearing of a uniform signifying association with any political organisation or with the promotion of any political object,[7] the need for these complementary PTA provisions is not

---

6   PTA 1989, s. 13(1).
7   Public Order Act 1936, ss. 1 and 2; Public Order (Amendment) Act (NI) 1970; Public Order (NI) Order 1987, Art. 21.

immediately apparent.[8] Nor are the provisions often invoked in practice: the Home Office's statistics reveal that not one person detained under the PTA in Great Britain has ever been charged with membership of a proscribed organisation, and only four have been charged with giving money or property for the benefit of such an organisation (only two of whom were eventually found guilty). The provisions are in place, it would seem, not so much in order to strike a real blow against terrorists but rather to reassure the general public that the law utterly condemns terrorist ideas connected with Northern Ireland.

Exclusion orders (Part II)

Exclusion orders have always been one of the most heavily criticised features of the PTA. Like the measures about proscription, they are designed solely for terrorists connected with Northern Ireland, although other 'foreign' terrorists may be refused entry into or deported from the United Kingdom under immigration laws. The main objections to exclusion orders are that they are issued by the Secretary of State and not by a court of law, that they impact most severely on persons who live in Northern Ireland and who wish to move to another part of the United Kingdom, and that there is no proper judicial procedure for reviewing the justification for the orders. Additional problems relate to the harsh penalties for breaking an order, the delays frequently encountered in notifying a person that his or her order has been revoked, and the use of orders to stifle the free expression of anti-government ideas.

The Goverment's own reviewer of the PTA has been arguing since 1986 that the Secretary of State's power to issue exclusion orders should be abolished. Lord Colville does not believe that in this case the end justifies the means or that the device does anything to enhance the United Kingdom's reputation in the outside world as a protector of human rights.[9] Although the Secretary of State supposedly considers each proposed order personally, this is hardly a safeguard when the subject of the order is not permitted to put a case against an order before it is imposed. On their face the review procedures, which have remained unchanged since the 1984 version of the Act, are difficult to reconcile with Art. 6(1) of the European Convention on Human Rights, which requires

---

8 In his major review published in 1987 (*loc. cit.* n.1, para. 13.1.7), Lord Colville said enigmatically with reference to the proscription offences: 'There now exists other legislation, such as the Public Order Act 1986, which might have precluded the necessity for this set of prohibitions; but it is too late now.'

9 1986 Report, para. 2.3.7; Cm 264, 1987, para. 11.6.1.

that in the determination of his or her civil rights — and freedom to travel within one's country surely qualifies as a civil right — a person is entitled 'to a fair and public hearing within a reasonable time by an independent and impartial tribunal established by law'. Unfortunately, arguments that exclusion breached civil rights or amounted to a criminal penalty such as to excite the procedural safeguards of Art. 6(1) were rejected in *Mooney v UK*,[10] though it is conceivable that the Commission's view might be different if the order excluding the applicant from Britain had been repeatedly renewed.

At the end of 1992, 81 persons were still excluded from Great Britain or the United Kingdom; a further nine remained excluded from Northern Ireland. The very existence of such a category provides some support for those who believe that the security forces do know who some of the terrorists are but cannot charge them because they do not have enough hard evidence against them. Except for those who are excluded after having served a prison sentence, the status of 'excluded person' is close to that of a person who is interned: too dangerous to be let loose in society, but too slippery to be prosecuted in a court of law. Some of the arguments which are used to counter the reintroduction of internment in Northern Ireland are therefore applicable in this context as well. In particular, the notorious unreliability of the security forces' intelligence information should be borne in mind.

The unfairness of exclusion orders would be less troublesome if all that was involved was the loss of liberty to move from one part of the United Kingdom to another. In practice, of course, the loss can be much greater, since exclusion from an area where a person may have lived for several years can entail cessation of employment and separation from his or her family, not to mention the dangers to be faced (if excluded to Northern Ireland) of living in a society where having an exclusion order on one's head can be tantamount to advertising oneself as a suitable target for assassination by one of the paramilitary groupings. It is true that a British citizen cannot be excluded from Great Britian or from Northern Ireland if he or she is at the time ordinarily resident in that part of the kingdom, and has been throughout the previous three years,[11] but this protection is not afforded to non-British citizens, including citizens from the Republic of Ireland who may have lived for many more than three years in Great Britain or Northern Ireland. One should think also of the dangers which a society might face from persons who are excluded to its shores: in view

---

10 Appl no. 11517/85.
11 PTA 1989, ss. 5(4)(a), 6(4)(a).

of the preponderance of exclusion orders placed upon persons who are seeking to enter Great Britain from Ireland, North or South, this could be portrayed as another example of the English 'nimby' syndrome — 'not in my back yard'. The incentive not to break an exclusion order, and not to help someone else to break it, is strong, since the potential punishment is five years' imprisonment and an unlimited fine. The exclusion order itself, however, can last for only three years, unless it is specifically renewed, which makes a five-year prison term for breach of an order seem disproportionately long.

Section 4 of the Act explicitly states that the Secretary of State may exercise his exclusion order powers 'in such a way as appears to him expedient' to prevent acts of terrorism connected with the affairs of Northern Ireland. This *carte blanche* makes judicial review of the Secretary of State's decisions extremely difficult, especially as the evidence used to support the decisions is very likely to be the object of a public interest immunity certificate.[12] Furthermore, and regrettably so, the concessions in sch. 2 of the Act about the right to make representations after being served with an exclusion order (including the right to an interview with the Secretary of State's 'adviser', which in practice brings with it the right to legal representation and to legal aid) are probably enough to satisfy the as yet underdeveloped criteria for natural justice in British administrative law.

Financial assistance for terrorism (Part III)

Besides prohibiting the giving, lending or making available of money or other property, knowing or having reasonable cause to suspect that the money or other property will or may be applied in connection with acts of terrorism, s. 9 of the PTA 1989 also criminalises the soliciting or inviting of any other person to make or receive such a contribution if the first person's intention is that it will be used in the above manner or if he or she has reasonable cause to suspect that it may be so used. The prohibitions extend not just to Northern Irish terrorism but to other terrorist activity (not connected solely with the affairs of any other part of the United Kingdom), provided that that activity constitutes an offence triable within the United Kingdom.

Next, s. 11, as mentioned earlier, attempts to get at the launderers of terrorist money by making it a crime if a person 'enters into or is

---

12   See *R* v *Secretary of State for Home Affairs, ex parte Stitt* (1987) *The Times*, 3 February.

otherwise concerned in an arrangement whereby the retention or control by or on behalf of another person of terrorist funds is facilitated'. As with some — strangely not all — of the offences created by ss. 9 and 10, it is a defence under s. 11 to prove that one 'did not know and had no reasonable cause to suspect that the arrangement related to terrorist funds'. This reversal of the burden of proof is one of the more subtle legal devices for making the position of a terrorist suspect more precarious than that of a non-terrorist suspect. Proving a negative is always difficult, and proving that one did not even have reasonable cause to suspect something is well nigh impossible. The reversed burden can really only be justified if it is true either that all forms of money-laundering are easy to detect but difficult to prove, or that terrorist suspects are significantly more likely than non-terrorist suspects to have committed the crime with which they are charged. The first claim is hard to support given that, generally speaking, the law on the misuse of funds in other contexts, such as drug trafficking, does not involve a change in the burden of proof,[13] while the second claim is incapable of demonstrable proof unless and until convicted persons later confess their guilt, which is a rare occurrence.

There seems to be a consensus, however, that the PTA's strictures against financial assistance for terrorism are not as noticeable an infringement of civil libertarian norms as the provisions on exclusion and arrest. Problems of identification do not often arise in money-laundering disputes, nor are confessions likely to be questionable, since they may well be substantiated by other, documentary evidence. Nevertheless, the scope for implicating entirely innocent individuals in prosecutions for money-laundering is hardly negligible. The customer who buys a pint of beer in a public house which is rumoured to be paying money to the IRA, the client of a construction company which is presumed to be paying protection money to the UVF in order to avoid having its installations bombed or its workforce assassinated, the intelligence officer who pays money to a paramilitary informer — all of these persons could easily fall within the ambit of the Act. What will prevent them from doing so is the discretion of the Attorney-General, since by s. 19 that official's consent is required before any prosecutions can be brought under, *inter alia*, ss. 9 to 11. Prosecutorial decisions of the Attorney-General are rarely, if ever, judicially reviewed,[14] so the potential for misguided witchhunts is still very much alive.

---

13 See Drug Trafficking Offences Act 1986, s. 24.
14 Compare *Gouriet* v *UPOW* [1978] AC 435; *R* v *DPP, ex parte Langlands-Pearse* (LEXIS, 30 October 1990).

Some constraints on the Attorney-General's discretion are nevertheless imposed by s. 12. This begins by exempting from claims for breach of contract any person who, despite a restriction on disclosure contained in the contract, discloses to a police officer a suspicion or belief that any money or other property is, or is derived from, terrorist funds, or any matter on which such a suspicion or belief is based. A bank or building society manager is therefore at liberty to divulge his or her suspicions about an account-holder's terrorist connections. Secondly, s. 12(2) exonerates persons (such as police agents) who enter into prohibited arrangements with the express consent of the police, as well as persons who get cold feet immediately after entering into a prohibited arrangement and then make a disclosure to the police 'on [their] own initiative'. Furthermore, a person has a defence to a prosecution if he or she can prove an intention to disclose to the police a suspicion or belief and a reasonable excuse for failing to do so. Presumably this might exempt some individuals who, under duress, pay protection money to a paramilitary group hoping, at a later stage, when the coast is clear, to report the matter to the police.

The maximum penalty for offences contained in ss. 9 to 11, as with handling stolen goods,[15] is imprisonment for 14 years and an unlimited fine. Just as important, however, are the court's powers to order the money or property involved in the case to be forfeited under s. 13 and sch. 4. Any person who has an interest in it must first be given the opportunity to be heard by the court, which will enable payers of protection money or victims of a robbery to argue that the items should be returned to them. Proving that money which remains in an illegal fund is theirs might be difficult, but a criminal court would not apply the same complicated restitution rules as a civil court would apply in cases of breach of trust.[16]

Arrest, detention and control of entry (Part IV)

At the heart of the PTA 1989 is s. 14, which contains the main police arrest power for persons who are or have been 'concerned in the commission, preparation or instigation of acts of terrorism'. The same power (to arrest without warrant persons whom the police have reasonable grounds for suspecting) extends to persons subject to an exclusion order (who, say, attempt to enter a part of the United Kingdom

---

15 Theft Act 1968, s. 22(2).
16 The rule in *Devaynes* v *Noble, Clayton's Case* (1816) 1 Mer 529 provides that withdrawals out of a trust account are presumed to be made in the same order as payments in.

from which they are barred) and to persons suspected of PTA offences such as membership of, or support for, a proscribed organisation or the financial assistance offences in ss. 9 to 11. Terrorism is not *per se* a crime, but a person can be arrested for suspected involvement in terrorism and can then be questioned about all sorts of matters loosely connected with terrorism. Moreover, an arrest under the PTA 1989 is valid even if the arresting officer has no personal knowledge of the grounds for suspecting the person to be arrested but simply acts on the instructions of a superior.[17]

At no time does the detainee have to be told that he or she is suspected of having committed a particular offence. Article 5(2) of the European Convention on Human Rights requires each person who is arrested to be told forthwith the reasons for the arrest, but it is a matter of great regret that in *Fox, Campbell and Hartley* v *United Kingdom*[18] the European Court of Human Rights decided that this Article was not inconsistent with the provisions on arrest in the PTA. The Court said that in the three cases before it it would have become obvious to the applicants during the course of their interrogation what offences they were suspected of having committed and that this was adequate notification for the purposes of Art. 5(2).

Persons arrested under s. 14 can be held in police custody for up to seven days without being brought before a magistrate. In England and Wales they must be treated in accordance with most of the provisions of the Codes of Practice issued under the Police and Criminal Evidence Act 1984 (PACE), but in Northern Ireland the less protective provisions of the non-statutory 'Guide to the Emergency Powers' apply.[19] In particular, there has been no tape-recording of interviews (save for recent experiments in Britain) nor disclosure of custody records, and detainees in Northern Ireland, unlike their counterparts in England and Wales, do not have the right to have a solicitor present while they are being interviewed by the police. In both jurisdictions the grounds for delaying access to a solicitor and notification of the arrest to a friend or relative are wider than for non-terrorist suspects.[20] Next, under PACE a detainee must appear before magistrates after a maximum of 36 hours, who may

---

17 See *Brady* v *Chief Constable, RUC* [1991] 2 NIJB 22; A Barrister, 'Reasonable suspicion and planned arrests' (1992) 43 NILQ 66.

18 Series A, vol. 182, (1991) 13 EHRR 157.

19 Under s. 61 of the EPA 1991 the Secretary of State is under a duty to make a code of practice for PTA detainees in Northern Ireland; at the time of writing no such code has appeared. For differences between the Code and the Guide, see Walker, *op. cit.*, ch. 8.

20 PACE, s. 58(13)(c); EPA, s. 45.

give permission to continue the detention for a further period of up to 36 hours; further extensions are allowed but the total detention time under PACE must not exceed four days. PACE allows extensions to be granted only in strictly limited circumstances in connection with specified serious arrestable offences. PTA detainees, by contrast, can be held by the police for two full days, and then the Secretary of State may extend the detention by a period or periods not exceeding five days in all. The detainee must be told as soon as practicable that an application for an extension has been made, and when, but not the reasons for it nor the period of extension requested. The grounds on which the Secretary of State can prolong the detention are nowhere specified, though during the Parliamentary debates on the 1989 Act the Home Secretary said that he authorised prolonged detention only when there was an intention on the part of the police to develop their suspicion to the point where they had evidence to justify charges or to consider applying for exclusion.[21]

This week-long executive power of detention was, of course, struck down by the European Court of Human Rights in *Brogan and Others* v *United Kingdom*[22] as being in breach of Art. 5(3) of the European Convention on Human Rights, and the Government has chosen to derogate from that Convention in response. Certainly by all civilised norms the power to detain under s. 14 is draconian, even if in England and Wales (by contrast with Northern Ireland) it is exercised comparatively rarely, as shown in Table 9.1.[23]

Table 9.1 also indicates that, whether or not detentions are extended, the percentage of PTA detainees who are charged with an offence or excluded from the jurisdiction is remarkably low. It can also be seen that, while more than six times as many people are detained under the PTA in Northern Ireland as in Great Britain, in each jurisdiction three-quarters of the detainees are released without any further legal action being taken against them. In Great Britain only 14 per cent have been charged with an offence of any description. According to the Home Office, two-thirds of the persons charged with offences under the PTA were charged with failing to cooperate with an examination at a port,

---

21 HC Debs, vol. 146, col. 67, 30 January 1989, Mr Hurd.
22 Series A, vol. 145B, (1989) 11 EHRR 117; see Finnie, W., 'Anti-terrorist legislation and the European Convention on Human Rights' (1989) 52 MLR 703 and Livingstone, S., 'A week is a long time in detention' (1989) 40 NILQ 288.
23 In Great Britain in 1990, authority was given for persons to be detained for the maximum period of seven days in 13 cases (out of 193 detentions), In 1991 and 1992 only nine detainees had a total length of extension greater than two days. In Northern Ireland as many as 571 extensions were granted in 1991 (out of 1,680 detentions).

while about 40 per cent of the persons charged with other offences were charged with offences involving explosives. Altogether, of the 257 persons charged, 175 (68 per cent) were found guilty.[24]

Table 9.1[25] — Detentions under the PTA and action taken thereafter, 1984–91

Year	Persons detained		Extensions granted[26]		Persons excluded etc.[27]		Persons charged with PTA offences		Persons charged with other offences		Persons not excluded or charged	
	GB	NI	GB	NI[28]	GB	NI	GB	NI	GB	NI	GB	NI
1984	203	908	41	533	14	—	14	—	17	258	158	650
1985	266	938	94	557	20	—	15	5	38	242	193	691
1986	202	1,309	57	484	16	—	13	8	23	350	150	951
1987	225	1,459	51	451	24	1	9	1	16	342	176	1,115
1988	186	1,717	25	542	16	1	10	8	11	364	149	1,344
1989	181	1,583	36	530	12	1	8	33	13	394	148	1,155
1990	193	1,549	35	460	16	—	6	31	22	368	149	1,150
1991	153	1,680	30	440	11	—	4	37	3	387	135	1,256
1992	160	n/a	17	n/a	3	n/a	8	n/a	30	n/a	119	n/a
Total	1,769	11,143	386	3,997	132	3	87	123	173	2,705	1,377	8,312
% of total			23%	37%	8%	<1%	5%	<1%	9%	24%	78%	75%

Though the *Brogan* case produced no concessions, the Colville Report[29] did prompt changes in that the 1989 version of the PTA now subjects the exercise of the Act's detention powers to internal police supervision in accordance with sch. 3. This provides that detentions must be reviewed as soon as practicable after the beginning of the detention and subsequently at intervals of not more than 12 hours. The detention

---

24 See *Home Office Statistical Bulletin*, Issue 5/93 (25 February 1993), Tables 5 and 6.
25 The sources are the quarterly statistics on the operation of the PTAs issued by the Home Office and the Northern Ireland Information Service.
26 Since the PTA of 1984, it has been possible for more than one extension per person to be authorised, provided the total periods do not exceed five days.
27 These are persons issued with an exclusion order under the PTA, or deported or removed under the Immigration Act 1971.
28 The figures in this column are numbers of extensions rather than persons affected by them. For example, in 1990, 405 persons were subjected to extended detention. Thus, the percentage is somewhat exaggerated.
29 *Loc. cit.*, paras 5.3.2, 5.3.4.

cannot continue after review unless the review officer authorises it, although para. 3(1)(b) makes it clear that the period of detention can still be extended by the Home Secretary. As the sch. 3 reviews are conducted by police officers, albeit senior officers who have not already been directly involved in the case, they still do not satisfy the requirements of Art. 5(3) of the European Convention, which stipulates the involvement of 'officers authorised by law to exercise judicial power'.

Moving away from arrest powers to even vaguer detention and surveillance measures, s. 16 and sch. 5 confer a power to 'examine' persons entering or leaving Great Britain or Northern Ireland, a power which is being exercised more often than before.[30] Examination must not take longer than 24 hours, unless the person is formally detained.[31] As frequent travellers to and from Northern Ireland know only too well, examinations can be begun even though the examining officer has no suspicion of the person's connection with terrorism. However, they can endure beyond 12 hours only if the officer has reasonable grounds for suspecting that the person examined is or has been concerned in the commission, preparation or instigation of acts of terrorism.[32] The review procedures in sch. 3 apply in this context as well. It is a little known fact that the Act requires a person who is being examined to produce a document satisfactorily establishing his or her identity and nationality or citizenship; failure to comply with this or any other duty imposed by sch. 5 is a summary offence punishable with three months' imprisonment and a fine not exceeding level 4 (currently £1,000).[33] There is nothing in the Act to prevent the use of strip-searching at ports or airports, though it is noteworthy that where the Act says that a constable or an examining officer may use reasonable force for the purpose of exercising any of the powers conferred by the Act,[34] there is an exception concerning the power to examine persons arriving at or leaving ports or airports.

Information, proceedings and interpretation (Part V)

Section 17 enacts the search powers detailed in sch. 7 and defines the types of investigation in which they may be used. These comprise

---

30 Home Office figures show that there has been an eight-fold increase since 1984 in the number of persons examined for more than one hour at ports or airports in Great Britain in connection with Northern Irish terrorism; the annual figures are as follows: 31 (1984), 38 (1985), 40 (1986), 68 (1987), 126 (1988), 186 (1989), 249 (1990), 247 (1991), 254 (1992).
31 For examinations at ports, sch. 5, para. 6 is equivalent to s. 14.
32 Sch. 5, para. 2(4).
33 In Northern Ireland this is not a scheduled offence.
34 Section 20(2).

investigations into the handling of terrorist funds, as well as all other investigations into terrorist acts. The search powers are exercisable after a warrant has been issued by a Justice of the Peace or, in the case of 'excluded or special procedure material' such as a journalist's sources, a doctor's medical records or an accountant's files, by a circuit judge (or in Northern Ireland by a county court judge).[35] Material which is subject to legal privilege, such as communications regarding legal advice passing between a professional legal adviser and his or her client, is completely protected against compulsory disclosure provided it is not being held 'with the intention of furthering a criminal purpose' and is still in the possession of a person entitled to possession of it (which means that privileged documents which have been stolen can be seized).

In eight important respects these powers go further than those already existing under PACE in England and Wales.

(a)   The PTA allows a search warrant to be issued if the magistrate or judge is satisfied merely that a terrorist investigation is being carried out, whereas the PACE legislation requires reasonable grounds for believing that a serious arrestable offence has been committed.

(b)   Under the PTA the material in question can be anything which there are reasonable grounds for believing is likely to be of substantial value to the investigation, whereas under PACE it must be material 'likely to be relevant evidence'.

(c)   For a warrant to be issued in respect of excluded or special material, it is enough under the PTA for the police to show that it is 'not practicable' to communicate with any person entitled to grant access to the material; under PACE a judge has to be satisfied that other methods of obtaining the evidence have failed or are bound to fail.

(d)   While the PTA permits a judge to require a person to state to the best of his or her knowledge and belief where excluded or special material is, there is no comparable power under the ordinary law.

(e)   The PTA allows orders to be made in respect of material which is expected to become available within 28 days; again, there is nothing like this in the PACE legislation.

(f)   The PTA allows the seizure of excluded materials, whereas these are available under PACE only if they fall within the scope of some additional power (such as under the Theft Act 1968).

(g)   The PTA permits a police officer of at least the rank of

---

35   See *DPP* v *Channel 4 TV Co. Ltd* (1992) *The Times*, 1 September. See also *R* v *Middlesex Guildhall Crown Court, ex parte Salinger* [1993] 2 WLR 438.

superintendent to override the requirements of sch. 7 and to issue a search warrant if he or she has reasonable grounds for believing that the case is one of great emergency and that immediate action is necessary in the interests of the state.

(h) Once material has been disclosed under sch. 7, under whichever procedure, a person can be required 'to provide an explanation' of the material. Although there are provisions confirming the person's privilege against self-incrimination, no similar explanatory duty is contained in PACE; it seems to be another attempt to reverse the burden of proof in terrorist cases. Providing a false or misleading explanation or, at least in some cases,[36] no explanation at all, is an offence punishable with up to two years' imprisonment and an unlimited fine.

As far as the operation of the PTA in Northern Ireland is concerned, sch. 7, para. 8 attempts to bypass official police and court channels altogether. In connection with investigations into acts which appear to the Secretary of State to constitute offences under the financial assistance provisions of the PTA, it permits the Secretary of State to issue a search warrant or production or access order if it appears to him that the disclosure of information that would be necessary for an application to a judicial figure 'would be likely to prejudice the capability of members of the RUC in relation to the investigation of offences . . . or otherwise prejudice the safety of persons in Northern Ireland'. The intention here is to protect the police's intelligence sources, but it may be questioned whether intelligence information will be the usual basis for a desired search and whether, even if it is, judges could not be trusted to play a role in these cases, perhaps through *in camera* hearings. Moreover, if the power is so crucial, why is it confined to investigations into allegations of financial assistance to terrorism?

By s. 17(2) to (5) of the Act, once a search warrant has been applied for or an order made under sch. 7, a person can be sent to prison for five years and fined an unlimited sum if he or she, without reasonable excuse or lawful authority, and knowing or having reasonable cause to suspect that an investigation is taking place, makes any disclosure or performs any concealment which he or she knows or suspects is likely to prejudice the investigation. There is no exception for solicitors who make a disclosure for the purpose of seeking a client's instructions or providing the client

---

36 Para. 6(4) of sch. 7 criminalises only false or misleading statements, but paras 7(5) and 8(5) of sch. 7 also appear to penalise outright refusals to provide an explanation. In Northern Ireland the offence is a scheduled one.

with advice.[37] Section 18 complements this offence by criminalising a failure to disclose information to the police (or, in Northern Ireland, to the army) which may be of assistance in preventing the commission of a terrorist act or in securing the arrest or trial of a terrorist. Strangely, s. 18 is confined to cases of Northern Irish terrorism. Since 1984 (up to the end of 1990) only 23 persons in Great Britain have been charged with the withholding offence and only 10 of them were found guilty. In Northern Ireland 100 persons were so charged. Two reviewers of the PTA, Lords Shackleton and Colville, have each recommended that s. 18 should be dropped from the Act, primarily because it does not add anything significant to the existing weaponry against terrorism. This seems particularly true in Northern Ireland, where s. 5(1) of the Criminal Law Act (Northern Ireland) 1967 already makes it an offence to fail to give information about any arrestable offence, whether a 'terrorist' one or not.

Conclusion

It is apparent from the features of the PTA highlighted in this chapter that it is a piece of legislation which in several respects inherently compromises generally accepted standards of fairness. While most would concede that terrorist activities should be countered by effective laws, it is arguable that the PTA goes too far in undermining basic principles of justice. Much of it appears to be in force for political reasons — because something must be seen to be being done about terrorism. The inordinately wide power of arrest it confers and its powers to detain on the word of a Cabinet Minister are out of place in a liberal democracy founded on the rule of law. Its anti-Irish slant and non-compliance with the spirit of the European Convention are further regrettable dimensions. Nor does the Act contain sufficient checks and balances to control any excessive zeal on the part of its enforcers. When we recall that most of its provisions overlap with, or are very similar to, existing laws (where normal safeguards do apply) and that the proportion of PTA detainees later charged or excluded is very small, we are entitled to ask whether the

---

37 During the debate on s. 17 at the Committee stage of the 1989 Bill in the House of Commons, the Parliamentary Under-Secretary for the Home Department (Mr Douglas Hogg MP) successfully opposed an amendment which would have granted a defence to a solicitor: HC Debs, Standing Committee B, cols 500–521, 17 January 1989. Mr Hogg said that a number of solicitors in Northern Ireland are unduly sympathetic to the cause of the IRA and other terrorist organisations, a remark which caused great offence to the legal profession as whole in Northern Ireland and which some people have connected with the murder by Protestant extremists, less than a month later, of the prominent Catholic solicitor Mr Pat Finucane.

Act is necessary at all. At the very least it needs significant amendment: the sections on exclusion orders should be repealed, and every other part needs to be infused with a greater commitment to the protection of civil liberties.

EDITORS' COMMENTS

As was explained in the Introduction, there are many parts of the Prevention of Terrorism Acts which might be perceived as leading to miscarriages of justice because they deny rights without due process or proof beyond reasonable doubt. In short, the powers are '...Draconian... In combination they are unprecedented in peacetime.'[1] However, it is intended in these comments to concentrate upon those features which tend towards miscarriages in the sense of an unjustifiable conviction in a court. Two points should be stressed at the outset. First, most of the notorious Irish terrorist cases which did result in miscarriages were processed before the Prevention of Terrorism Act came into force. Nevertheless, the powers and techniques applied before the Act under vague common-law and statutory police powers were to a large extent endorsed rather than altered. Thus the Act did not represent a clean break from the past, and so problems experienced before the Act have continued in later cases. Secondly, the application of the Act varies as between Britain and Northern Ireland, with more concern arising from police practices in the latter jurisdiction, especially when account is taken also of the powers in the Northern Ireland (Emergency Provisions) Act 1991.

For present purposes, attention can be confined to the operation of ss. 14 and 15 of the Act — the special arrest and search powers.[2] The arrest powers are 'special' in several respects, and it is these unusual features which arouse the danger of injustice.

The first such danger concerns the vagueness of the criteria for the exercise of the power. Most arrests are conducted under s. 14(1)(b) — on reasonable grounds for suspecting the person 'is or has been concerned in the commission, preparation or instigation of an act of terrorism'. The result is to make it easier for the police to establish a reasonable suspicion compared to their 'normal' arrest powers under s. 24 of PACE. One difference is that there is no need to have any offence in mind. By s. 20(1), 'terrorism' means 'the use of violence for political ends'. It is true that the

---

1 HC Debs, vol. 774, col. 35, 25 November 1974, Mr Jenkins.
2 The powers and their operation are more fully described in Walker, C., *The Prevention of Terrorism in British Law*, 2nd ed. (Manchester University Press, Manchester, 1992), ch. 8.

concept is close enough to that of a crime for the European Court not to notice any difference;[3] it is also true that any form of violence will usually amount to a crime. Nevertheless, the distinction could be significant, especially when linked to the second, which is that s. 14 differs from normal powers in that the suspicions need not be precise in terms of the wrongdoing suspected. The word 'terrorism' is used to cover a multitude of sins, and no specific crime or activity need be isolated.

Linked together, the beneficial effect mooted as part of the attraction of s. 14 is that it allows an early police intervention, well before any life-threatening attack takes place. For example,[4] X, a student from Northern Ireland who claims to be on a camping holiday in the west of England, is stopped by the police for a traffic violation. The police search the vehicle. They find a list of the names and addresses of famous people living in the area as well as books about guerrilla warfare and Irish Republicanism. If X is a terrorist, then it would be difficult to invoke PACE. Possession of the suspicious materials is not an offence[5] — at worst preparatory actions have occurred — nor is there in this case any possibility of vague conspiracy charges in the absence of an association with a fellow traveller. None of these problems limits the use of s. 14 in these circumstances. Similarly, imagine that Y and Z, known Republicans living in Britain, have received visits at home by members of the IRA and have recently enrolled for an electronics course at the local college of education. Several offences might spring to a suspicious mind — membership of a proscribed organisation, the possession of firearms or explosives, or conspiracy to make bombs. Under s. 14 there is no need to decide which is the most likely — arrest first, sort out the details later.[6]

These same features which make s. 14 attractive to some cause concern to others. The intentional effect is to allow arrests on vaguer suspicions than under PACE, and this feature equally creates the increased danger that preconceptions or prejudices will mould the choice of subject for arrest in the absence of hard evidence. Once, however, the person fits the police profile or is linked with persons or groups perceived as hostile, then the danger is that the police will endeavour to vindicate their choice to their superiors, to defence lawyers and to the community. Miscarriages

---

3   See *Ireland* v *UK*, Appl no. 5310/71, Judgment of Court Ser. A, no. 25, para. 196; *Brogan* v *UK*, Appl nos 11209, 11234, 1266/84, 11386/85, Judgment of Court Ser. A, no. 145–B, para. 50.
4   Compare *R* v *McCann* (1991) 92 Cr App R 239.
5   Compare Northern Ireland (Emergency Provisions) Act 1991, ss. 30 and 31.
6   This aspect is reflected in the reasons to be given on arrest. See *R* v *Officer in charge of Police Office, Castlereagh, ex parte Lynch* [1980] NI 126.

can then arise when the apprehensive, disorientated and isolated suspect (someone like Judith Ward) obliges them with a confession, or when a forensic scientist supplies them with results that could fit the police construction of events implicating the suspect (such as Guiseppe Conlon). Most arrests under s. 14 will not result in catastrophes of this kind, since the purpose of many police anti-terrorist operations is intelligence-gathering rather than prosecution. Unfortunately, all s. 14 arrests may in the longer term create the dangers described because of the effect of s. 15, which allows the police to take fingerprints and other tests almost as a matter of course. There is no obligation to destroy the records of persons released without charge (unlike under PACE, s. 64), and so those subjected to s. 14 become branded as suspects, which may have a cumulative impact on any subsequent arrest.

The second notable and hazardous distinction between s. 14 and normal powers concerns the detention period following arrest. The Prevention of Terrorism Act allows 48 hours at the discretion of the police, extendable by up to five days on the authority of a Secretary of State. Under PACE, the police can detain for only 36 hours on their own direction, and extra periods of up to 60 hours in total must be approved by magistrates. Thus, the length of detention and the authorising authority are different in each case, with important consequences.

The maximum of seven rather than five days of detention may be put to a number of purposes. A list produced by the Home Office to guide police applications for extensions contains no fewer than 14 separate headings, including forensic testing, further investigations and checking with other records and police forces.[7] The list curiously omits the purpose of interrogation, and the Colville Report claims that it is not important because of anti-interrogation training of terrorist suspects.[8] Despite this rhetoric, there is ample evidence that one of the main rationales for extended detention is the interrogation of suspects, and this is felt to be necessary because of the dangers that their activities present, the difficulties of normal detection methods when dealing with secretive, disciplined and sophisticated groups and, indeed, the anti-interrogation training to be overcome. The reliance upon interrogation is particularly pronounced in Northern Ireland, where confessions have always provided the principal source of evidence in Diplock courts[9] and where

---

7 Home Office Circular 27/1989, para. 4.11.
8 Report of the Operation of the Prevention of Terrorism (Temporary Provisions) Act 1984 (Cm 264, 1987), para. 5.1.4.
9 Walsh, D. P. J., *The Use and Abuse of Emergency Legislation in Northern Ireland* (Cobden Trust, London, 1983).

interrogation centres have been specifically designed for that purpose.[10] Such intensive interrogation certainly occurred in the *Armagh Four* case, and there have been reports of suspects undergoing more than 30 sessions of questioning over a seven-day period.[11] The courts in Northern Ireland have stated that they do not regard such treatment as inherently oppressive,[12] even though it inevitably pressurises and confuses the detainee, making a false confession all the more likely.

As for leaving the decision to extend the detention in the hands of a politician rather than a judicial officer, this feature was at the centre of the litigation in *Brogan* v *UK*,[13] wherein detention periods under s. 14 varying from four days six hours to six days $16\frac{1}{2}$ hours were held in breach of Art. 5(3) of the European Convention. The problem was not the length of detention before charge (which is quite modest by Continental standards) but the fact that the detention was never scrutinised and approved within a reasonable period by a judicial officer. After some behind the scenes negotiations with the police and judiciary to secure judicial oversight, the Home Secretary concluded that the process was inherently unsuitable for such a resolution. Therefore, the interim response to the Court's judgment, a notice of derogation under Art. 15, was adopted as the final solution for the foreseeable future. The rectitude of this decision may be doubted.[14] It must be accepted that security considerations would require a hearing *in camera* and some of the evidence might have to be presented in the absence of the detainee. Nonetheless, such restrictions need not render the process non-justiciable or threaten public confidence in the judiciary. Such closed hearings are common in interlocutory proceedings — such as for the issuance of search warrants and interim injunctions — and the judiciary have been happy to cooperate with investigations and reviews under the Interception of Communications Act 1985 and the Security Service Act 1989. Furthermore, there would remain the advantage to the suspect in lodging the decision with a legally trained, independent mind, even if its working remains as inscrutable as that of the rather more partisan Secretary of State.

Relating extended detentions to miscarriages, the risks are that extensions are not independently scrutinised and so result in a far higher

---

10   See *R* v *Gargan* [1972] May NIJB; *R* v *Flynn and Leonard* [1972] May NIJB

11   See *R* v *Howell* [1987] 5 NIJB 10; *R* v *Mullen* [1988] 10 NIJB 36.

12   *R* v *McBrien and Harman* [1984] NI 280.

13   *Loc. cit.* The police reviews under sch. 3 are of little assistance. The police cannot be described as judicial officers, and the reviews terminate once an application to the Secretary of State has been made.

14   See further, Walker, C., 'The detention of suspected terrorists in the British Islands' (1992) 12 *Legal Studies* 178.

proportion of cases under the Prevention of Terrorism Act than under PACE.[15] Having been detained in this way, similar problems can arise to those described earlier — pressure is put on the suspect in the hope that damning admissions will make up for the wide gaps in the police's knowledge.

Most intimately connected with the fairness of detentions and interrogations under the Prevention of Terrorism Act, and the chances of miscarriages arising therefrom, are the special rules governing the treatment of the detainee. In many respects, the regime under s. 14 corresponds with that under PACE. Indeed, the provenance of the concepts of extensive written records and supervision by a senior uniformed officer lies with the Bennett Report[16] and so pre-dates PACE. In some ways, the treatment of Prevention of Terrorism Act detainees is actually superior to the requirements under PACE. Extra concessions as to diet, bedding and exercise are recommended by a Home Office circular and the Northern Ireland Office 'Guide to the Emergency Powers'.[17] In Northern Ireland, detainees are also supposed to benefit from routine inspection via viewing lenses and closed-circuit TV, as well as routine medical checks.[18] Yet there are some aspects where the s. 14 detainee is left with less protection. In England and Wales, the PACE Codes generally apply but not the requirements as to the taping of interviews, save for a two-year experiment in two police stations where the recording was confined to a retrospective summary of the interview.[19] In Northern Ireland, the PACE Codes do not apply, and instead the Northern Ireland Office issued the 'Guide to the Emergency Powers' in 1990. This diverges from the PACE equivalent in many detailed respects. Two important contrasts are that it lacks any sanction by way of disciplinary offences or invitation to the courts to exclude evidence tainted by breach of it.[20] Furthermore, taping is again not mandatory.

The absence of recording is common to both jurisdictions and deserves

---

15 33 per cent for Britsh PTA arrests, 47 per cent in Northern Ireland and under 1 per cent under PACE (up to the end of 1990).
16 Report of the Committee of Inquiry into Police Interrogation Procedures in Northern Ireland (Cmnd 7497, 1979).
17 Home Office Circular 114/1979, paras. 5–7; NIO Guide, Pt IV, para. 36.
18 NIO Guide, Pt IV.
19 See Home Office, *Memoranda* (1991), Annex 1A. It has now been announced that PACE-style taping (with just a few modifications) is to be applied to all police stations in Britain (but not Northern Ireland) for a further two year test: Home Office Circular No. 108/1992.
20 See *Moore* v *Chief Constable* [1988] NI 456. The Northern Ireland (Emergency Provisions) Act 1991, s. 61 allows for the issuance of a statutory code but none has been forthcoming (save for a draft).

special comment. The Government fears that the availability of a tape could prompt retaliation by the colleagues of a suspect who gives too much away, especially if that person is not to be prosecuted and remains at large. There is also the fear that terrorists may learn further anti-interrogation techniques or sources of police information from analysis of the tape at their leisure. Two replies might be offered. One is that the same problems presumably arise from written transcripts of interviews with terrorists who are to be prosecuted on the basis of that evidence. Such records must nevertheless be disclosed as part of the normal criminal process, so it is difficult to see how a tape could be any more dangerous, unless, of course, written statements are regularly selective. Next, there would still be great value in keeping an accurate record of those interviews which are not to be put before a court. The treatment of terrorist suspects prior to their confessions lies at the heart of most of the contested cases both in Britain and Northern Ireland, and the treatment of those who are not charged also remains a major sore, despite the efforts of the Bennett Report. A full, contemporaneous record would be of invaluable assistance to those investigating the many complaints against the police made by detainees and would not require disclosure to the complainant. Terrorist incidents produce police anger and frustration, and so terrorist suspects are deserving of the utmost protection if mistakes or misdeeds are to be avoided. Consequently, it appears bizarre that this category of prisoner is left in the most vulnerable position of all.

The same reasoning could be applied to the final divergence between PACE and terrorist detainees, namely their access to outsiders. The most important of the special rules, those relating to access to legal advice,[21] display some notable variations as between the three United Kingdom jurisdictions. All differ from the normal rules in s. 58 of PACE, in that access to a solicitor can be denied for 48 hours rather than 36 hours and any consultation which does take place may be in the presence and hearing of the police. The least generous rules in theory and practice are set out in s. 45 of the EPA 1991, which empowers refusal on the wide ground that access will interfere with the investigation[22] and also allows

---

21 On notification to family members, see PACE, s. 56(11); Northern Ireland (Emergency Provisions) Act 1991, s. 44. Refusal of notification is rare under the latter because most arrests are at home, but the power is invoked in England in order to put pressure on suspects, as in *McVeigh* v *UK*, Appl nos 8022, 8025, 8027/77, DR 25, p. 15.

22 Unlike in the English case of *R* v *Samuel* [1988] 2 All ER 135, the Northern Ireland courts do not require a high degree of proof by the police: *R* v *Harper* (1990) 4 NIJB 75; *In re Mckenna* (1992) 3 BNIL n. 54. Furthermore, enforcement of access may be made conditional upon an undertaking not to discuss the case: *R* v *Duffy* (1992) 6 BNIL n. 41. It follows that the exclusion of a confession because of the denial of access is rare, but see *R* v *Gilgunn* (1991, unreported).

denial for each 48-hour period after access. The latter restriction does not apply in England under s. 58(13) of PACE; after the initial period of refusal reasonable access should be given. The Scottish rules in the Law Reform (Miscellaneous Provisions) Act 1985, s. 35, are the closest to normal, in that the criteria refer to the need to investigate crime rather than terrorism, though there is no qualification that the crime be serious.

Many English police forces do not now deny access, even during the initial period of 48 hours. However, access to lawyers was denied in 59 per cent of cases between 1987 and 1990 in Northern Ireland. Clearly, such refusals are designed to put further pressure on the suspect in terms of isolation and confusion about how to respond to the police, in the hope that admissions will be forthcoming. The tactic is often successful, and it has been estimated that 57 per cent of confessions are made within the first three hours of detention — in other words, long before a solicitor arrives on the scene.[23] The individual's position is especially fraught because of the operation of the Criminal Evidence (Northern Ireland) Order 1988, Art. 3 of which applies to silence in the police station. The consequence may be that the detainee is pressured or induced into speaking the words suggested by the police, which may secure convictions but not necessarily the truth.

In the light of the history of the cases which prompted the Royal Commission's establishment, the lack of attention accorded to the operation of the Prevention of Terrorism Act almost beggars belief. The terms of reference devised by the Home Secretary are silent on the issue and none of the 88 interrogatories issued by the Commission itself makes reference to the Act. It follows that few of the submissions to it concentrate upon the Act, and many ignore it altogether. Several remedies could be suggested. With the advent of a comprehensive code of arrest powers in PACE (apart from Scotland), it is dubious whether arrests on the basis of 'terrorism' are either necessary in most cases or desirable in any. Similarly, now that four-day detentions have become part of the regular law, it may also be doubted whether more extensive detentions are justifiable. At the very least, it might be argued that any confession should be corroborated, and any which is made after four days should not be admisssible at all in the light of the oppressive circumstances. Other changes could include extensions being authorised by judges, the abolition of the special rules about access to lawyers, the full recording of interviews, regular medical checks, access by lay visitors in Northern

---

23   Haldane Society of Socialist Lawyers, *Upholding the Rule of Law?* (1992), p. 22.

Ireland, and a greater readiness on the part of the courts to act and penalise the police when ill-treatment is alleged.[24]

Some of the few submissions to the Royal Commission which do discuss the Act contain many similar prescriptions.[25] Of the State-sponsored groups, that of the CPS advocates the most adventurous proposal, namely that all of the PACE rules should apply to terrorist detainees, though presumably without change to the arrest powers themselves.[26] Not unexpectedly, there is greater caution from the Home Offfice and outright opposition to reform from the Police Service. The Home Office gives evidence about its experiment on taping but expresses little enthusiasm, which is hardly surprising given the very limited nature of the experiment.[27] For its part the Police Service concentates on the threat of the introduction of taping and fears that it will constrict the flow of intelligence.[28] Further police submissions on the subject, virtually all of which were presumably in favour of the *status quo* or even greater powers, were made in secret.

In the light of the way that the issue has been presented to the Royal Commission, it would be very surprising if it concentrated its firepower in that direction. Consequently, the momentum for reform remains largely in the hands of the annual reports produced by Viscount Colville. Given that he appears to be increasingly supportive of the Government and that all of his major reform proposals (such as the repeal of exclusion) have been rejected out of hand, the prospects for change appear inauspicious.

The major shortcomings in English criminal justice which can (and do) lead to miscarriages of justice have now been explained. The remainder of this book will examine whether other jurisdictions have fared any better. The chosen jurisdictions are the Republic of Ireland, which shares similar legal and policing traditions as well as a threat from paramilitary violence, and France, which in principle offers a contrasting model for criminal investigation and adjudication.

---

24 Compare *In re Gillen's Application* [1988] 1 NIJB 47; *Wheldon v Home Office* [1990] 3 WLR 465.
25 See the submissions of Amnesty International (paras 4.2.3.4, 4.4.2, 5.1.2), Committee on the Administration of Justice (pp. 1, 2, 5), Liberty (pp. 7, 20, 22).
26 Para. 3.6.10.
27 Para. 1.46 and Appendix 1A.
28 At p. 108.

10

Miscarriages of Justice in the Republic of Ireland

Dermot Walsh

Introduction

In the latter years of the 1980s the Irish legal and political establishment began to address the treatment of Irish persons in the British criminal justice system.[1] Through the machinery of the Anglo-Irish Conference the Irish Government repeatedly expressed its concern about the reliability of the convictions in cases such as the *Birmingham Six* and, generally, about an apparent bias in the British criminal justice process when dealing with Irish suspect terrorists. At one point the Irish Attorney-General even went so far as to refuse a British application for the extradition of a Fr Patrick Ryan to answer terrorist charges.[2] The refusal was explained on the ground that the Attorney-General could not be satisfied that Fr Ryan would get a fair trial in Britain. While the Irish Government's stance, albeit belated, can be supported by the experiences of Irish suspects, it would appear that the Irish Government itself has not entered the fray with clean hands. The fact of the matter is that the Irish criminal justice process has also produced a few disturbing examples of likely miscarriages of justice; some of which are contemporaneous with

---

1 A summary of the Irish Government's representations to the British Government is given at Dail Debs, vol. 402, cols 1089–1092, 1990.
2 Dail Debs, vol. 385, cols 1199–1207, 1988.

the *Birmingham Six* saga. Embarrassingly for the Irish Government, these examples reveal that, in some respects, Irish criminal procedure is even more conducive than is its British counterpart to the emergence of such cases, and is less capable of rectifying injustice once it has occurred.

Current cases

The Irish examples fall into two categories:

(a)   convictions based on mistaken identification, and
(b)   convictions based on false confessions obtained in police custody.

That mistaken identification has given rise to wrongful convictions in the past has been accepted by a committee set up by the Minister for Justice in 1989 to inquire into certain aspects of criminal procedure under the chairmanship of Judge Martin.[3] The most recent example is the *Meleady* case.[4] Although dating from 1984, the case remains controversial today. The facts were that some youths took a car at night from the driveway of the owner's home. As the car was being driven away the owner jumped onto the bonnet. He managed to hold on for a few minutes, even though the front seat passenger was trying to knock him off with an umbrella. Subsequently, at the request of the police, the owner attended a sitting of the District Court where he identified Joseph Meleady and Bernard Grogan as the persons responsible. Both were convicted of taking and driving away a car without the owner's consent. A retrial was ordered on appeal,[5] but they were convicted again and this verdict was upheld on appeal. The conviction, however, was based solely on an identification, which in turn was based on what the owner could see at night looking through the windscreen of a moving car while lying on its bonnet and being subjected to attempts to force him off.[6]

Meleady and Grogan always protested their innocence. Initially they were supported only by local opinion in their own neighbourhood, and

---

3   Report of Committee to Inquire into Certain Aspects of Criminal Procedure (Dublin, 1990), pp. 9–10.
4   (1984, unreported). For a summary of the facts, see Dail Debs, vol. 396, col. 1202, 1990.
5   A retrial was ordered because at the appeal hearing a third youth, Paul McDonnell, gave evidence that he, and not Meleady and Grogan, was in the car on the relevant night. Subsequently, McDonnell was charged and convicted of perjury.
6   It is permissible to convict solely on the basis of identification evidence. However, the judge is obliged to deliver a strongly worded warning to the jury on the dangers of convicting on the basis of identification alone: *People* v *Casey (No. 2)* [1963] IR 33, at p. 39.

by a few senior politicians and churchmen who took an active interest in their case. The public appeal of their case was boosted considerably by an RTE investigative documentary programme, broadcast in 1990, which revealed that fingerprint evidence found in the car was more consistent with the presence of three other individuals who actually claimed that they were the culprits. An interview with one of these persons was broadcast, and in it he claimed that neither Meleady nor Grogan was there. The dilemma facing the Irish Government was how to respond to these developments. There was no formal mechanism by which the case could be referred back to the courts for further consideration. The only option was a straight choice between direct executive interference in the administration of justice[7] or doing nothing. Eventually, after much prevarication,[8] the Minister compromised by remitting the remaining months of Meleady's sentence.

The confession cases are much more disturbing, in that the State, through the medium of the police, is a conscious prime mover behind the resulting injustice. Public concern was focused on several cases in the 1970s by allegations that persons suspected of involvement in subversive activity were being arrested and then subjected to ill-treatment in police custody. The objective of the arrests and ill-treatment seemed to be a mixture of procuring confessions, gathering intelligence about subversive organisations and intimidating members and supporters of such organisations. Amnesty International was sufficiently concerned about the volume and content of these allegations to carry out an investigation into them in June 1977.[9] After investigating 28 cases, 26 of which occurred between April 1976 and May 1977, it concluded that a number of persons concerned had been ill-treated while in police custody.[10] The nature of the abuses ranged from food and sleep deprivation over several days to severe physical beatings. Particularly significant was Amnesty's finding that the source of the ill-treatment was a group of plain-clothed detectives from the central detective unit in Dublin, who featured in nearly all of the cases irrespective of their location throughout the

---

7   The Minister has the power, delegated by the Government, to remit or commute sentences imposed by the courts: Criminal Justice Act 1951, s. 23 as amended by the Road Traffic Act 1961, s. 124. The Government can advise the President to exercise the right of pardon and to remit or commute punishment imposed by the courts: Arts 13.6 and 13.9 of the 1937 Constitution.
8   As late as February 1990 the Minister asserted that he could see no grounds for intervening in the case of Meleady who was still serving his sentence. In May 1988 he rejected a petition for Grogan's release.
9   Report of an Amnesty International Mission to the Republic of Ireland in June 1977.
10 *Ibid.* at p. 4.

country. This confirmed a widespread public belief that there was a 'heavy gang' operating within the Garda Siochana with a brief to get results without any questions being asked about their methods.[11] It is hardly surprising, therefore, that the most disturbing example of an apparent miscarriage of justice in the Irish legal system today is a confession case from this period. The case in question is known as the *Nicky Kelly* case.[12]

The facts of the *Nicky Kelly* case and its progress through the legal system reveal an embarrassing parallel with the facts and progress of the *Birmingham Six* case. Nicky Kelly was one of 21 persons arrested in April 1976 on suspicion of involvement in robbing a mail train and being a member of an unlawful organisation. The arrests were effected under s. 30 of the Offences against the State Act 1939, which allows the police to detain a suspect for up to 48 hours without charge. In the event, charges were preferred only against Kelly and five others: Brian McNally, Osgur Breathnach, John Fitzpatrick, Michael Plunkett and Michael Barrett. By the time the case came on for trial in October 1978,[13] the charges against Barrett[14] had been dropped, Fitzpatrick was no longer available to be tried,[15] and Plunkett was discharged in the course of the trial. The sole evidence against Kelly and his remaining two alleged accomplices, McNally and Breathnach, was the confessions they had given during their interrogation in police custody. The Special Criminal Court, which sits without a jury, declared itself satisfied that the confessions were voluntary, and proceeded to convict and impose sentences of 12 years, 9 years and 12 years respectively. The circumstances in which the confessions were obtained, therefore, were of paramount importance.

Kelly's ordeal[16] commenced at 9.55a.m. on 5 April 1976 with his arrest under s. 30. By the time he was charged before a District Court at

---

11 The Amnesty tribunal was satisfied that the primary purpose of the ill-treatment was to secure confessions: *ibid*, at p. 4.
12 [1982] IR 90, [1983] IR 1. For a detailed account of this case, see Joyce, J. and Murtagh, P., *Blind Justice* (Poolbeg Press, Dublin, 1984).
13 The first trial, which commenced on 19 January 1978, had to be aborted owing to the death of one of the presiding judges. Accordingly the trial had to start again in October 1978.
14 The only evidence implicating Barrett was that he was named as an alibi for Fitzpatrick.
15 Owing to the State's failure to present the book of evidence within a reasonable time, the accused were discharged by the District Court in December 1976. Fitzpatrick took this opportunity to go 'underground' and so was unavailable when the State reinstated the case.
16 The facts are set out in European Commission of Human Rights, Decision 1041683 (1984).

10.30p.m. on 8 April, he had dictated a detailed written statement admitting his participation in the robbery and taken the police on a fruitless journey to places where he alleged the guns and money had been hidden. He later claimed, however, that his confession was false and had been forced out of him by a combination of physical beating, exhausting interrogation sessions, threats, and food and sleep deprivation. He was also denied access to a solicitor. It is important to point out at this stage that the interrogation experiences of McNally, Breathnach, Plunkett and Fitzpatrick mirrored that of Kelly. Their allegations of ill-treatment were firmly supported by compelling medical testimony from both their own doctors and the prison doctor.[17] Indeed, Breathnach even had to be transferred from the police station to the hospital on account of his condition after 48 hours in police custody.

When the case finally went to trial, the sole issue was the admissibility of the confessions of Kelly, McNally and Breathnach. The police did not attempt to contest the strong medical evidence in support of the assertion that the confessions had been extracted by ill-treatment and oppression. Instead, they suggested that the accused had colluded to inflict the injuries on each other while remanded in police custody two to a cell. The credibility of this suggestion was undermined by several factors. First, the nature and extent of the injuries were such that they could only have been inflicted over a lengthy period of time accompanied by a considerable degree of noise. There was no evidence, however, that the police on duty in the station where the accused were remanded heard anything unusual from the cells. Secondly, Breathnach was in hospital at the relevant time, so his injuries could not have been inflicted by his co-accused. Thirdly, and most disturbing of all, is the fact that the police would not have been able to raise the suggestion of collusion had they not adopted the most unusual course[18] of requesting that the accused should be remanded into their custody for the night of 7 April, whereupon they irregularly housed them two to a cell. A very credible explanation for these unusual arrangements is that they were engineered by the police intentionally so that they could explain the injuries on the accused by suggesting that they were self-inflicted.

---

17 In Kelly's case the medical evidence revealed bruising on the arms from the shoulder to the elbow, and over the mastoid bone. There was also bruising over the left shoulder blade, over the ribs, over the pubic bone and on his left hip and thigh. All the bruising was very tender and consistent with recent physical ill-treatment.

18 At the trial evidence was given by station house officer Padden that in his lengthy experience he could not remember an adult ever being remanded to a police station and not to a prison.

Despite the strength of the evidence in support of the accuseds'
allegations, coupled with the weak and speculative nature of the police
explanation, the trial court ruled the confessions admissible and proceeded
to convict all three. The fourth, Plunkett, was discharged as the only
evidence against him was an identification which collapsed during the trial.
In the case of the three convicted, however, the court accepted the police
assertion that they were not ill-treated, that the questioning, although
protracted and continuous, was not oppressive, and that even if there was a
breach of the Judges Rules[19] it was not sufficient to warrant exclusion.

Kelly absconded after the confessions were ruled admissible. McNally
and Breathnach, however, appealed to the Court of Criminal Appeal
which overturned their convictions.[20] In McNally's case this was done on
the basis that the Judges Rules had been breached, while in Breathnach's
case the operative factor was oppressive questioning. Heartened by these
developments Kelly returned to the jurisdiction, where he was arrested
and placed in prison to serve the sentence that had been imposed on him
in his absence. Ultimately, he appealed his conviction to the Court of
Criminal Appeal.[21] Remarkably, in view of the outcome of McNally's and
Breathnach's appeals, his conviction was upheld, as the Court could find
no grounds for upsetting the trial court's findings.[22] Furthermore, the
Court of Criminal Appeal did not accept that admitted breaches of the
Judges Rules were sufficient to over-turn the conviction. A final appeal
to the Supreme Court was similarly unsuccessful.[23] Given the very strong
similarity between Kelly's case and those of his co-accused, particularly
McNally's, it is hardly surprising that a strong public perception of a
miscarriage of justice emerged.[24] This perception has been enhanced by
the fact that Kelly had to serve four years of his sentence before release
and had to wait 16 years before being pardoned.

The *Nicky Kelly* case reflects the same fundamental weaknesses in the
Irish criminal process that cases like the *Birmingham Six* have exposed in

---

19 The 1918 English version is still applicable in Ireland. See *People* v *Cummins* [1972]
    IR 312, at pp. 317–18. In *People* v *McNally and Breathnach*, 2 Frewen 43, 16 February
    1981, the trial court accepted that there was evidence of non-compliance with rule IX
    (recording the statement in writing).
20 *People* v *McNally and Breathnach, loc. cit.*
21 Because he was appealing out of time he had to apply to the Court of Criminal Appeal
    for an extension of time. Initially this was refused, but was granted on appeal to the
    Supreme Court: *People* v *Kelly (No. 1)* [1982] IR 90.
22 *People* v *Kelly (No. 2)* [1983] IR 1.
23 *Ibid.*
24 The strong similarity in the cases was specifically cited by the Supreme Court as a
    factor which persuaded it to grant an extension of time to apply for leave to appeal:
    People v *Kelly (No. 1) loc. cit.* at pp. 109 and 115.

the British system. In some respects, indeed, the weaknesses exposed in the Irish system are even more basic than their British counterparts. Broadly speaking they fall into four groups reflecting four stages in the criminal process, namely: pre-trial, trial, appeal, and post-appeal. Aspects of the law and procedure in each of these four stages help to explain how unjust convictions are possible and how difficult it is to secure redress after the event.

Pre-trial

Arrest

Police powers in Ireland mostly have followed the pattern of their counterparts in Britain, though without any fundamental review or codification equivalent to the Police and Criminal Evidence Act 1984. The courts have eschewed any notion of a general power of summary arrest available on suspicion of criminal activity.[25] Instead, at common law and by statute, the police have been conferred with a large number of powers which are defined by reference to specific types of criminal activity. Accordingly, the police may arrest summarily only when confronted with criminal activity in circumstances where there is a specific power of arrest embracing that particular type of criminal activity. A standard precondition for the exercise of these powers of arrest is that the arresting officer should have reasonable cause to suspect that the individual being arrested has committed or is about to commit the offence in question. Furthermore, when effecting the arrest, the arresting officer is normally under an obligation to inform the suspect of the reasons for his or her arrest.[26] It is important, however, not to overestimate the extent to which the powers and procedures of arrest operate as a check on police freedom. The reality is that police officers enjoy a power of arrest in almost every situation in which they reasonably suspect an individual of committing a serious criminal offence.[27] Some of these individual powers embrace a very wide range of criminal activity. Furthermore, the precondition of a reasonable suspicion has been interpreted by the courts to require no more than that there should be some evidence upon which the arresting officer could reasonably form the requisite suspicion; it is not necessary that that evidence should be

---

25 *Dunne* v *Clinton* [1930] IR 366.
26 *People* v *Shaw* [1982] IR 1.
27 Walsh D. P. J., 'The impact of antisubversive laws on police powers and practices in the Republic of Ireland: the silent erosion of individual freedom' (1989) 62 *Temple Law Review* 1105.

sufficient to establish a prima facie case. Lastly, the procedural requirement to inform the suspect on arrest of the reasons for the arrest is no longer enforced rigorously by the courts.[28]

The power of arrest which the police favour most in combating serious crime is found in s. 30 of the Offences against the State Act 1939, an Act introduced to combat the threat of internal subversion posed by the IRA during World War II. The s. 30 power was the one used to arrest all the suspects in the *Nicky Kelly* case. Significantly, of all the arrest powers, it is the one which imposes the least restrictions on the police. It empowers a member of the force to arrest without warrant any person whom he or she suspects of an offence under the Act, or of a scheduled offence, or of having information about any such offence. The flavour of the power is conveyed by the fact that it is not even necessary for the police officer to suspect the individual affected of involvement in any criminal activity; it will be sufficient if the police officer merely suspects him or her of having information about a relevant offence. In this respect the s. 30 power is even broader than those available to a constable in Northern Ireland or Great Britain under the emergency legislation.[29]

The immense scope of the power is also reflected in the range of offences to which it applies. The Act itself creates offences designed to protect the State against subversion. More significant, however, is the power it confers on the Government to extend s. 30 to other existing offences simply by listing them in a statutory order. Such offences are designated 'scheduled offences'.[30] Although the 1939 Act was designed to protect the State against subversion, it is permissible to arrest under s. 30 for a scheduled offence even if there are no subversive overtones.[31] The effect is that ordinary criminal suspects can now be drawn into the much harsher criminal process that has been designed primarily to deal with the challenge and threat posed by subversive suspects.[32] The implications of this for miscarriages of justice is revealed by the extent to which s. 30, and the regime of which it forms an integral part, undermines the traditional safeguards for the suspect in the criminal process.

Not only can s. 30 be used to deal with a wide range of situations, but it can also be used even where there are no reasonable grounds to connect

---

28 *People* v *Walsh* [1980] IR 294.
29 See ch. 9.
30 Currently, these consist of offences under the Malicious Damage Act 1861; the Conspiracy and Protection of Property Act 1875, s. 7; the Explosive Substances Act 1883; the Firearms Act 1925–71; and the Offences against the State Act 1939.
31 *People* v *Quilligan* [1987] ILRM 606 at pp. 617–38.
32 The police have also managed to extend s. 30 to other non-scheduled offences: see Walsh *op. cit.*, at pp. 1109–11.

the individual in question with a relevant criminal offence. Section 30 stipulates that a mere suspicion is sufficient. The courts have interpreted this to mean that a police officer need only have an honestly held suspicion coupled with the existence of at least some evidence upon which this subjective suspicion could reasonably be based.[33] The mere fact that a reasonable person would not have suspected in the same circumstances does not invalidate the arrest. Furthermore, the suspicion need not be personal to the arresting officer. It will be sufficient that he acted on the instructions of a superior officer who had the requisite suspicion.[34] The full significance of this low threshold for suspicion is revealed when arrests are made for membership of an unlawful organisation. The nature of this offence means that the police need not suspect an individual of engaging in any positive criminal act. Membership, by its very nature, is an ongoing state of being. Since all that is needed is a mere honest suspicion based on some evidence, it follows that a large number of people known to the police are constantly vulnerable to arrest under s. 30. Matters such as associating with suspect subversives or selling IRA propaganda will be sufficient to ground a valid arrest.[35] It is not surprising, therefore, that a large number of arrests under s. 30 are for membership. However, they do not usually result in charges. It would appear in practice that many of the arrests are effected primarily for the purpose of gathering intelligence information on subversive organisations.[36]

Detention

The primary legal consequence of an arrest under s. 30 is that the suspect can be held without charge for up to 48 hours. Prior to 1987 an arrested suspect had to be brought before a judicial authority as soon as reasonably possible.[37] The courts did not recognise the possibility of using arrest and detention for the purpose of furthering the investigation into the offence in question. By resorting to s. 30, therefore, not only could a police officer

---

33 Hogan, G. and Walker, C., *Political Violence and the Law in Ireland* (Manchester University Press, Manchester, 1989), at pp. 202–5.
34 *People* v *McCaffrey* [1986] ILRM 687.
35 See, for example, *People* v *O'Leary*, Court of Criminal Appeal, 29 July 1988.
36 Between 1981 and 1986 (inclusive) the rate of charge of persons arrested under s. 30 was as low as 11 per cent and did not exceed 20 per cent: Dail Debs, vol. 369, cols 2559–60; vol. 371, cols 714.
37 *People* v *Shaw* [1982] IR 1. In 1987, s. 4 of the Criminal Justice Act 1984 was brought into force thereby permitting the detention of arrested suspects without charge for a maximum period of 20 hours.

effect an arrest at an earlier stage in the investigation than would otherwise have been the case, but he could also use the 48-hour period of detention to work on the suspect in the hope of procuring a confession. To assist the police in this matter, s. 52 of the Offences against the State Act 1939 imposes an obligation on the suspect, when asked, to account for his or her movements and actions during any specified period and for all information in his or her possession in relation to the commission of any relevant offence by any other person. Failure to cooperate is a criminal offence. In the *Nicky Kelly* case the police made use of this provision to coerce the cooperation of the suspects. When the contents of s. 30 are combined with s. 52, the risk of a false confession being extracted from a suspect is greatly increased. It follows that the law and procedure governing the treatment of persons in police custody are of critical importance in protecting against possible miscarriages of justice.

Up until 1987 the treatment of persons in police custody was governed by the 1918 version of the Judges Rules, the Constitution and general laws such as those on the admissibility of confession evidence. There were no published regulations governing detention in police custody. This was painfully obvious to the suspects in the *Nicky Kelly* case. As well as allegations of physical abuse, their litany of complaints included: being moved around from one police station to another; their where-abouts being concealed from next of kin; no access to medical examin-ation; no access to a solicitor; being deprived of adequate food and rest; being questionned for excessively long periods by an inordinately large number of detectives working in relays; being questioned without caution; notes of interrogation being written after interview; being confronted with co-accused; being left alone with co-accused; being subjected to threats; and being rearrested immediately following on release. Assuming that all of these allegations were true, the most they amounted to was a breach of the Judges Rules and a possible infringement of the constitutional right of access to a solicitor.[38] There were no regulations prohibiting any of these practices, nor, of course, any specifying positively how a suspect should be treated in police custody.

Amnesty International identified the inadequacy of legal safeguards for the rights of the suspect in police custody as a particular cause for concern.[39] This was taken up by the O'Briain Committee, which was set up in 1977 by the Government to recommend safeguards for people in

---

38 In *People* v *Healy* [1990] ILRM 313, the Supreme Court recognised that the right of access to a solicitor while in police custody was a constitutional right.
39 *Op. cit.*, at pp. 4–7.

custody and to safeguard the police from untrue allegations. It reported in 1978[40] with a long list of substantive and procedural recommendations aimed at filling the void. It was not until 1984, however, with the enactment of the Criminal Justice Act, that any of these recommendations were enshrined in law; and it took until 1987 before an actual code for the protection of persons in police custody was put into effect.[41] The Code lays down standards on matters such as access to legal advice and medical examination for the suspect, the structure and conduct of interrogations, and on the protection of the suspect's rights while in police custody. Breach, however, constitutes a disciplinary as opposed to a criminal offence, and it does not result in the automatic exclusion of a confession. It is unlikely, therefore, that the Code can have as much impact as those issued under PACE. Nevertheless, it does represent a radical improvement on the earlier situation. As such it should make some contribution to nipping possible miscarriages of justice in the bud.

Unfortunately, the reforms introduced by the Criminal Justice Act 1984 also curtailed some of the traditional freedoms which the suspect had enjoyed under Irish criminal procedure. Section 4, for example, permits the detention of an individual for questioning in police custody up to a maximum period of 20 hours when that individual has been arrested on reasonable suspicion of having committed an offence which carries a maximum sentence on conviction of five years or more. In other words, the Irish police can now use their powers of arrest to detain a suspect for questioning in an even broader range of situations than was previously the case. The s. 30 approach which had been perceived as the exception is now the norm.[42] Once arrested, the suspect can be compulsorily searched, photographed and fingerprinted; skin swabs and hair samples can also be taken. Restrictions on the right to silence are also a feature.[43] In the case of possession of stolen property or firearms, this is achieved by imposing an obligation on the person to answer questions in certain circumstances. In other defined situations inferences can be drawn from the suspect's refusal to answer certain questions put to him by an investigating officer.

The combination of these provisions will result in a regime where more suspects are held in police custody for longer periods and in

---

40 Prl. 158 (1978).
41 Criminal Justice Act 1984 (Treatment of Persons in Custody in Garda Siochana Stations) Regulations 1987.
42 Walsh, *op. cit.*, at pp. 1112–14.
43 Sections 6, 15, 16, 18, 19. These provisions were precedents for the Criminal Evidence (Northern Ireland) Order 1988, Arts 5 and 6 (see ch. 9).

circumstances where they can be put under more pressure to cooperate with the police investigation. It is unlikely that the accompanying safeguards in the form of the Code will be sufficient to ensure that these measures do not produce false confessions in individual cases. In particular, it is worth pointing out that as yet there is no audio-visual recording of interrogations, nor does the suspect enjoy the right to have a solicitor present during interrogation. These omissions are particularly important for suspects who are so affected by the very fact of police custody that they will confess to anything in the hope that it will secure their release.

Trial — Admissibility of Confessions

In Irish law it is quite permissible to convict solely on the basis of a confession given by the accused while being questioned in police custody. Before such a confession can be admitted in evidence, however, the prosecution will have to establish beyond a reasonable doubt that it is voluntary and that it has not been obtained in circumstances which amount to a conscious and deliberate violation of the suspect's constitutional rights.[44] The standard test for voluntariness is that the confession must not have been obtained from the accused by fear of prejudice or hope of advantage held out by a person in authority,[45] or by oppression.[46] It is not even necessary that any blameworthiness should attach to the police. It will be sufficient if an investigating officer innocently said or did something that excited fear or hope in the mind of the suspect as a result of which he confessed. Furthermore, the constitutional protection afforded the suspect in police custody ensures that if the custody is or becomes unlawful owing to circumstances within the knowledge of the police, any confession given during the period of unlawful detention is automatically inadmissible.[47] Lastly, the trial judge can mop up any cases that fall through the net by exercising his discretion to exclude a confession where, owing to the circumstances in which it was obtained, it would be unfair to the accused to admit it.[48]

In theory these admissibility tests should provide an impregnable barrier against unjust conviction on the basis of confession evidence. In

---

44 Ryan, E. and Magee, P., *The Irish Criminal Process* (Mercier Press, Cork, 1983), pp. 113–15 and 156–76.
45 *People* v *McCabe* [1927] IR 129.
46 *People* v *Lynch* [1982] IR 64.
47 *People* v *Madden* [1977] IR 336; *People* v *McLoughlin* [1979] IR 85.
48 *People* v *O'Brian* [1965] IR 142; *People* v *Cummins*, *loc. cit.*; *People* v *Lynch* [1981] ILRM 389; *People* v *Shaw* [1982] IR 1; *People* v *Healy* [1990] ILRM 313.

practice, however, the law has not always proved an effective filter, particularly where, as in the *Nicky Kelly* case, the trial is in the Special Criminal Court.[49] The distinctive feature of this court is that it sits with an uneven number of judges (not being less than three) and without a jury. Although it is not part of the normal court structure and does not have a permanent existence, it enjoys the same powers as the Central Criminal Court in matters of trial and sentence. Its jurisdiction covers all scheduled offences and can even extend to non-scheduled offences where the DPP has certified in any individual case that the ordinary courts are inadequate to secure the effective administration of justice and the preservation of public peace and order in relation to the trial of that case. In practice, most persons who are tried in the Special Criminal Court will have been arrested and detained under s. 30 of the Offences against the State Act 1939. It follows that if they confessed under the s. 30 interrogation regime, the admissibility and credibility of the confession will be determined by three judges without reference to a jury.

From the case-law it is difficult to avoid the impression that the Special Criminal Court applies a less rigorous admissibility standard than is suggested by the bare words of the admissibility test. The *Nicky Kelly* case itself is a disturbing example. Although the Court accepted (it could hardly do otherwise given the medical evidence) that the accused had suffered serious injuries while in police custody, it concluded that these injuries must have been self-inflicted. In reaching this conclusion, however, the Court did not attempt any explanation as to how the accused persons could have managed to inflict such injuries upon themselves in police custody without the knowledge and intervention of the police. Nor did it see anything sinister about the improper police move to have the accused remanded into their custody and then to house them two to a cell contrary to regulations. It was as if the Court did not want to contemplate the possibility that the police version might not be the truth. The Amnesty International investigation in the late-1970s identified a similar judicial reluctance in the Special Criminal Court to exclude confessions on the ground of involuntariness. It concluded that:

> the onus of proof has in effect been on the defence to establish beyond all reasonable doubt that the maltreatment did occur, rather than on the prosecution to prove that it did not.[50]

---

49 For a detailed analysis of the Special Criminal Court, see Hogan and Walker, *op. cit.*, at pp. 227–44.

50 *Op. cit.*, at p. 8.

Once the Special Criminal Court has ruled a confession admissible, conviction is virtually a foregone conclusion. The same three judges who ruled on its admissibility decide what weight to attach to it. So far there has been no case of an admissible confession being followed by a refusal to convict.

Appeals

The very real possibility of a miscarriage of justice resulting from some of the confession cases emphasises the importance that must be attached to the appellate procedure. In Ireland, an accused who has been convicted in the Central Criminal Court or the Special Criminal Court has no right of appeal to the Court of Criminal Appeal; he or she must apply for leave. In practice this is nothing more than a technicality, as the merits of the appeal are often considered on the application.[51] The appeal, however, is conducted solely on the basis of the transcript of the trial.[52] Fresh evidence may be admitted but only with the leave of the court. Where the fresh evidence was available at the original trial but not used, leave will be granted only in exceptional cases.[53] Further appeal to the Supreme Court is possible, but only if the Court of Criminal Appeal or the DPP certifies that the decision involves a point of law of exceptional public importance and that it is desirable in the public interest that an appeal should be taken to the Supreme Court.[54]

In confession cases the capacity of the appellate procedure to repair miscarriages of justice is heavily dependent on the willingness of an appellate court to upset the trial judge's findings of fact and his application of the admissibility test to those facts. Unfortunately, the current state of the law on this aspect in Ireland does not hold out much hope for appellants. The role of an appeal court in criminal matters was explained as follows by the Court of Criminal Appeal in *People* v *Madden*:

. . . to review as far as may be required any rulings on matters of law, to review as far as may be necessary the application of the rules of evidence as applied in the trial, and to consider whether any inferences of fact drawn by the court of trial can properly be supported by the evidence; but otherwise to adopt all findings of fact.[55]

---

51   Martin Report, *op. cit.*, at p. 6.
52   Ryan and Magee, *op. cit.*, at p. 427.
53   *Ibid.*, at pp. 428–9.
54   Courts of Justice Act 1924, s. 29.
55   [1977] IR 336, at p. 340.

With respect to the trial judge's findings of fact the Court made it clear that they should not be upset unless they were 'so clearly against the weight of testimony as to amount to a defeat of justice'.[56] This can pose a major problem to the accused in a confession case where the trial judge has displayed a tendency to rely on the police version of events and where that version conflicts with the account given by the accused. Unless the accused can expose blatant internal contradictions in the police account, or a straight conflict between the police account and independent evidence, there will inevitably be some grounds upon which the trial judge could have believed the police account. Typically that account will in turn offer some evidence upon which the trial judge could reasonably have concluded that the confession was voluntary and that there was no room for the exercise of discretion.

An appellate court, therefore, will be left with very little room for manoeuvre in upsetting the trial judge's decision on the admissibility of a confession. Indeed, the *Nicky Kelly* case illustrates how an appellate court's attempt to deal at third hand with what happened behind the closed doors of the police interrogation room can actually enhance the appearance of injustice rather than produce the opposite effect. Although all the ingredients which had vitiated the convictions in both McNally's and Breathnach's cases were present in full measure in Kelly's case, the Court of Appeal still managed to uphold Kelly's conviction. It did this by adopting a subtly different approach to the relevant factors in Kelly's case compared to that in the cases of the other two. To make matters worse, the Court did not offer any convincing explanation for the difference in treatment. In supporting the trial judge's finding in Kelly's case that the confession was voluntary, the Court relied solely on the evidence of Kelly's conduct after he had confessed. By contrast, in Breathnach's case it had focused on the length and intensity of the interrogation sessions prior to confession. When dealing with the breach of the Judges Rules in Kelly's case, the Court concentrated solely on whether the breach could have affected the accuracy of the record of the confession. By comparison, in McNally's case the Court focused on the adequacy of the justification proferred for the failure to comply with the Rules. The net result was that Kelly's conviction was upheld, and he was left to serve out a sentence of 12 years' imprisonment while his co-accused were freed. Not only did the Court of Criminal Appeal not explain why it adopted a different approach to the two appeals, but it did not even feel it necessary to address its collective mind to the apparent injustice of the

---

56   *Ibid.*, at p. 339.

conflicting results. It is concerned primarily with the procedural fairness of the trial at first instance and with whether the trial court's findings can be supported by the evidence. It does not regard itself as having a general jurisdiction to act in a positive role to ensure that justice is done.[57]

Post-appeal

When a conviction is upheld on appeal in Ireland, that is effectively the end of the road for the individual concerned. Serious doubts may linger, as in the *Meleady* and *Kelly* cases, about the fairness or reliability of the convictions, but there is no formal procedure whereby the matter can be reopened. Unlike the position in Britain, there is no procedure whereby a case can be referred back to the Court of Criminal Appeal for further consideration even if new evidence emerges. The most that can happen is that a Presidential pardon may be granted on the advice of the Government.[58] Alternatively, the Government has the power to commute or remit, in whole or in part, a sentence imposed on a convicted person so long as the offence in question is not capital.[59] The Government exercised this power in both the *Meleady* and the *Kelly* cases. The Presidential pardon, however, has been exercised on only two previous occasions since the establishment of the State in 1922.[60] The Government's decision to advise a Presidential pardon for Kelly in April 1992 can therefore be described as momentous, even if it was a long time in coming.

The official government statement announcing Kelly's pardon explains that the decision was taken on the advice of the Attorney-General who, in turn, had consulted the DPP. The reasoning in the statement is both interesting and confusing. Almost the first half is devoted to the evidence of two linguistic analysts, who claimed that Kelly was not the author of his alleged inculpatory statement.[61] The opinion of the DPP was that this evidence would probably not have had any effect on the original decision to prosecute. However, the advice of the Attorney-General on this matter was that a court would regard such evidence as admissible and that it could not be said that such evidence would be

---

57 *People* v *Mulligan* 2 Frewen 16. The broader approach adopted by the Court of Appeal in England in *R* v *Cooper* (1969) 53 Cr App R 82 was not approved by the Irish Supreme Court in *People* v *Egan* [1990] ILRM 780.

58 Arts 13.6 and 13.9 of the 1937 Constitution.

59 Criminal Justice Act 1951, s. 23.

60 Thomas Quinn in 1940 and Walter Brady in 1943 (see *The Irish Times*, 30 April 1992).

61 This evidence became public through an RTE documentary in November 1991, which gave a significant impetus to the review which resulted in the pardon.

disregarded. The statement then went on to consider the possible effect on the verdict or appeal and concluded that it could not be definitely asserted that it would not have led the courts to recognise the existence of a reasonable doubt over the voluntariness of Kelly's confession. It is not clear, however, whether this represented the advice of the DPP or the Attorney-General, or simply an awkward attempt by the Government to avoid stating its position on the textual analysis of Kelly's statement.

The second half of the statement would appear to contain the decisive part. It stated that the Attorney-General had advised the Government that it would be unsafe to continue to accept Kelly's guilt as established beyond reasonable doubt. This opinion is based on three considerations, each of which, it is stated, would have been sufficient to have militated against a decision to prosecute. The strange aspect of this assertion is that two of the considerations were operative at the time of the trial[62] and the third was operative at the time of Kelly's appeal.[63] Stranger still is the fact that the textual analysis was not offered as one of the operative considerations. The effect is to give the impression that the miscarriage of justice was entirely excusable, even unavoidable. Perhaps such an over-sensitive approach is to be expected when the executive feels that it has to encroach upon the judicial domain. In the *Kelly* case, however, it is just as likely that the executive was hoping to avoid having to face up to skeletons in its own cupboard. Thus, if the Government and Attorney-General had described the linguistic evidence as instrumental to the decision to pardon, it would have focused the spotlight once more on the veracity of Kelly's claim that he was forced to sign a false confession through police ill-treatment. That the Government, the Attorney-General and the DPP had no stomach for such an eventuality is suggested by the fact that the last two advised that 'any further inquiry into the circumstances of the case would be unlikely to produce any clearer resolution of the issues that arose in it', a view which the first-named was happy to accept.

Another possibility, besides Presidential pardon, for a collateral attack on the soundness of a conviction based on confession evidence alone, is

---

62 The first point was the collapse of the identification evidence against Plunkett. The second was the implausibility of the police attempt to square Fitzpatrick's participation in the robbery with his alibi.

63 The third point was the judgment in *People* v *Shaw* [1982] IR 1, as applied in *People* v *McNally and Breathnach* (2, Frewen 43). The *Shaw* case was interpreted as having laid down a more liberal approach to the admissibility of confessions (to the effect that a confession is admissible only if voluntary and the circumstances in which it was obtained did not fall below the required standards of fairness) than in *People* v *O'Brian* [1965] IR 142 (which demanded a deliberate and conscious violation of rights and the absence of any extraordinary excusing circumstances).

to sue the State for damages for ill-treatment suffered while under interrogation in police custody. In 1983 Kelly was persuaded by the Government to come off his hunger-strike to pursue this course. The implication was that if he was successful, it would be tantamount to establishing that his conviction was unsafe and unsatisfactory. Despite encouraging Kelly to pursue this course, the authorities then sought to have his action struck out on the technical ground that the issues he sought to litigate had already been determined against him at the trial in the Special Criminal Court. Basing himself substantially on the decisions of the English Court of Appeal and the House of Lords in the civil action brought by the *Birmingham Six*,[64] O'Hanlon J, in the Irish High Court, said that to allow Kelly to reopen the findings of the Special Criminal Court on the voluntariness of his confession in the course of his civil action would give rise to an issue estoppel and an abuse of the process of the court.[65] This could be avoided only if fresh evidence was adduced. Again, however, O'Hanlon was guided by the Court of Appeal and the House of Lords in defining the appropriate test to be applied to any fresh evidence adduced. It must be evidence of such a character as to change the whole aspect of the case; it must be evidence which could not, by the exercise of reasonable diligence, have been made available at the previous hearing; and it must be evidence which is well capable of belief in the context of the circumstances as a whole. Clearly the prospects of using the civil action as a means of remedying a possible miscarriage of justice in a criminal case are no more attractive in Ireland now than they were in Britain for the *Birmingham Six*.

Conclusion

The *Meleady* and *Kelly* cases were very much alive as alleged miscarriages of justice throughout the period that the Irish Government was voicing its concerns about the treatment of Irish suspects in Britain. Those campaigning on behalf of Meleady and Kelly took full advantage of the opportunity to contrast the Irish Government's concern at the shortcomings in the British criminal justice system with its refusal to face up to even graver shortcomings at home. The Irish Government's position became even more untenable when justice was finally done in cases such as the *Guildford Four* and the *Birmingham Six*. The question being asked in Ireland was no longer whether the same could happen

---

64   See *Hunter* v *Chief Constable of the West Midlands* [1981] 3 WLR 906.
65   *Kelly* v *Ireland* [1986] ILRM 318.

there, but whether something could be done about it when it did happen. Since the answer, for all intents and purposes, was 'No', the Government was compelled to address the situation, if only to save face. Accordingly, in 1989, it set up a committee of inquiry under the chairmanship of Judge Frank Martin. The Committee's terms of reference required it to address two aspects of the problem and to make recommendations. First, it had to examine whether additional safeguards were needed to ensure that confessions made by suspects to the police were properly obtained and recorded. Secondly, it had to examine whether there was a need for a procedure where cases could be further reviewed even though they had exhausted the normal appeals procedure.

The Committee's report, submitted in March 1990, came in two parts, reflecting the two-fold nature of its terms of reference. With regard to confessions it found that the present methods used to obtain and record confessions from suspects in police custody were less than reliable.[66] The mere fact of being in police custody was, in itself, sufficient to pose a risk to the voluntariness of a suspect's confession, while the procedure for recording the confession ensured that the end result was only a police officer's summary of what actually transpired. Subsequently, if an accused challenged his alleged confession in court, considerable delay, expense and inconvenience for all concerned would have to be expended in establishing what exactly happened behind the closed doors of the interrogation room. At the end of the day the court will be left with the difficult task of weighing up the oath of one person against another. There is no independent factor which can be used to determine the issue with the certainty that justice demands.[67] While the Committee accepted that the current law and regulations governing the treatment of suspects in police custody were sufficient for the most part to ensure that justice was done,[68] it also felt that further, more radical measures were needed, not just to ensure that justice was done in all cases but also to simplify and shorten the lengthy trial procedure associated with the current

---

66 *Op. cit.*, pp. 22–23.
67 *Ibid.*, p. 26.
68 It did make several recommendations for change in the regulations, including the imposition of an obligation on the police to supply a suspect with a list of solicitors willing to attend at police stations (p. 41); wherever possible the number of officers in the interrogation room at any one time should be confined to two (p. 42); and that apart from specified circumstances a suspect should not be interrogated until a reasonable time for the attendance of his solicitor has elapsed (p. 43). It also suggested that some consideration should be given to the introduction of a requirement on trial judges to give a warning to the jury on the dangers of convicting on the basis of confession evidence alone (p. 39).

approach.[69] Accordingly, the Committee recommended the introduction
of audio-visual recording of the interrogation of suspects in police
custody, and the acceptance of the tapes as admissible evidence at trial.[70]
Basing itself on Canadian and Australian experience, the Committee
concluded that the audio-visual recording would present a very accurate
and reliable account of interrogation sessions and would obviate the need
for separate admissibility hearings at the trial in the event of a challenge
to the admissibility of a confession.

On the issue of reviewing cases which had exhausted the normal
appeals procedure, the Committee also produced substantive proposals.
It accepted that there would be rare cases in which substantive doubts as
to the correctness of a conviction would arise.[71] In the interests of justice,
therefore, there was a need for a procedure in which entire cases,
including any new evidence, could fully and publicly be investigated. To
this end the Committee recommended the setting up of a statutory
tribunal of inquiry to deal with any cases in which a substantial doubt had
arisen as to the propriety of the conviction.[72] The Attorney-General
would act as a filter for the referral of cases to this body, which would be
equipped with all the powers of a public inquiry under the Tribunal of
Inquiry (Evidence) Acts 1921–79. Its *modus operandi* would be inquisitorial, and its function would be to inquire into all the available facts
and circumstances surrounding the conviction with a view to expressing
its opinion on the propriety of the conviction. Ultimately it would be a
matter for the Government to decide what action, if any, to take on receipt
of the tribunal's report on any case.

It is now more than two years since the Committee submitted its
report. The Government's official statement announcing Kelly's pardon
intimated that it intended to introduce legislation in the Dail in the
autumn of 1992 to establish a system of reviews for alleged miscarriages
of justice.[73] The statement is silent, however, about the implementation
of the Martin Committee's proposals on interrogation and the admissibility of confessions. This is particularly disappointing given the
progressive nature and urgency of these recommendations. The Committee itself recognised that even if the Government decided today to
implement its recommendations, it would be several years before

---

69   *Op. cit.*, pp. 26–27.
70   *Ibid.*, pp. 32–39.
71   *Ibid.*, p. 9.
72   *Ibid.*, pp. 12–16.
73   It has been suggested that the delay is primarily the result of judicial opposition: *The
     Irish Times*, 30 April 1992.

audio-visual recording was operative in all police stations.[74] Accordingly, it asked for a commitment towards implementation 'with all convenient speed'. The Government's tardiness, therefore, raises questions about its commitment to reform in the whole area of miscarriages of justice in Ireland. Unfortunately, it also provides ammunition to those who interpreted the establishment of the Martin Committee as a cynical exercise in political face-saving. More serious is the prospect that future Irish victims of a miscarriage of justice are more likely to be found in Ireland than in Britain.

EDITORS' COMMENTS

Having seen in chapter 10 how miscarriages of justices arise and are handled in one Irish jurisdiction, the position in the other (and in Scotland) might next be raised. As was mentioned in the Introduction, one of the shortcomings of the Royal Commission is that its purview does not extend to Scotland or Northern Ireland, though, in the light of the *Armagh Four* case, the promise has been made by the Northern Ireland Secretary to take careful account of its findings.[1] No comparable undertaking has been given in respect of Scotland, despite several documented cases involving miscarriages.[2]   In view of the likely impact of the Royal Commission and the fact that the criminal justice system in Scotland exhibits several significant differences in policing, prosecution and court procedures, it is intended in these comments to concentrate wholly upon Northern Ireland.

One of the curious features sometimes remarked upon is that criminal trials in Northern Ireland seem to have produced fewer allegations of miscarriages, notwithstanding the special and difficult circumstances assailing that jurisdiction. The appearance of satisfaction with most outcomes is a fair reflection of reality, in the sense that campaigns against individual convictions of the type seen in England have only recently arisen.

Perhaps the most well-know campaign concerns the *Armagh Four* — *R v Latimer, Allen, Bell and Hegan*,[3] which has already been described in

---

74   *Op. cit.*, p. 36.
1   (1992) *The Times*, 30 July, p. 1.
2   See the case of Meehan in Kennedy, L., *A Presumption of Innocence* (Gollancz, London, 1976); MacLean, J. (1982) 72 SCOLAG 76); the case of Preece in [1981] Crim LR 783; PCA, *Investigation of a complaint about delay in reviewing a conviction for murder in Scotland* (1983–84 HC 191)).
3   [1986] 9 NIJB 1 (trial); [1988] 11 NIJB 1 (appeal); (1992) *The Times*, 30 July, pp. 1, 2. See also (1992) 3 BNIL n. 73.

the Introduction. As explained there, after referral back to the Court of
Appeal in 1992, Allen, Bell and Hegan were all freed on the basis that the
police had tampered with their statements, but Latimer's conviction was
upheld in the light of the identification evidence against him, his
confirmation of his admission at the original trial in 1985 and the finding
that he had lied to the court.

Identification evidence also figures prominently in the '*Casement Park
cases*'[4] arising out of the murder of two Army corporals at a televised
funeral in West Belfast in 1988. The subsequent prosecutions were often
based on film taken from Army helicopters hovvering high above (the
'heli-tele'), which raised issues about the quality of the evidence
presented, the identification and matching processes conducted in
private by the security forces, and whether technicians had processed and
enhanced the images in ways which could be said to be unfair. The
selective disclosure of the tapes to the defence was a further problem,
which meant that evidence which could have placed the accused
elsewhere was not available. The conduct of the trial also caused concern.
Aside from the fact that many of the witnesses were unidentified and gave
evidence behind screens,[5] there arose the inherent problem in non-jury
'Diplock' trials of the dubious effectiveness of judges warning themselves
about the quality of identification evidence. Several of these cases have
also sparked usage of the Criminal Evidence (Northern Ireland) Order
1988 which curtails suspects' rights to silence (discussed in chapter 4).
Lastly, some of the cases were decided on a rather dubious interpretation
of the doctrine of common purpose, which resulted in the accused (whose
role had been exhausted well before a decision was taken to call upon the
services of two IRA assassins and who were not at the scene of the killing)
being convicted of murder.[6]

Although this list is not comprehensive, it is far shorter than the
equally selective list for England and Wales. Given that there are about
600 'terrorists' accused each year passing through the 'Diplock' court
system in Northern Ireland, compared with no more than a dozen in
England, the disparity seems anomalous in the light of the assertion in
the commentary to chapter 9 that this type of case is inherently likely to

---

4 See especially *R* v *Maguire and Murphy*; *R* v *Kelly* (reported in Casement Accused
   Relatives Committee, *The Casement Accused* (1991); Committee on the Administration
   of Justice, Pamphlet No. 19, *The Casement Trials* (1992). Up to April 1992, 41 had been
   charged, 20 convicted and seven were awaiting trial.
5 See Marcus, G., 'Secret witnesses' [1990] P. L. 207.
6 *R* v *Kane and others* (1991, unreported). Compare the developments in South Africa
   reported in Hansson, D. and van Zyl Smit, D., *Towards Justice?* (Oxford University
   Press, Oxford, 1990), ch. 6

produce miscarriages. There may be two explanations. The first is that the quality of justice is higher in Northern Ireland — policemen are more disciplined and effective, the prosecution service is more assiduous, defence lawyers are sharper and Diplock judges are better diviners of the truth than juries. However, there is much evidence against this thesis — especially concerning police abuses of suspects and case-hardening of judges.[7] Therefore, a more likely explanation is that miscarriages are at least as likely in Northern Ireland but are perceived and reacted to in a different light. As far as the Nationalist community is concerned, the response to perceived injustices has been to blame the system as a whole. In their perception, what more can be expected from British justice other than brutal police and biased judges? If convictions are secured, then the system is working well according to its own lights rather than malfunctioning. The remedy to the problem is collective rather than immanent — the nature of the State must be altered fundamentally, and tinkering within the context of a bankrupt political entity will not assist. In this way, the issue of justice is perceived in constitutional rather than individualistic terms.[8] Despite this prevailing view, there is still room for protest in specific cases. In this way, the system may be used instrumentally, even if there is no faith in its morality. Such use has been encouraged by campaigns in Britain, where the success of protest techniques has begun to prompt imitation elsewhere. Lastly, it is consistent with this explanation that there have been campaigns on behalf of Loyalist accused, such as the *Armagh Four*. That community does by and large retain a belief in British norms. At the same time, as the Stormont government fades into history and responsibility for mistakes can be blamed on remote administrators rather than stout-hearted Ulstermen, there is now less pressure on Loyalists to stifle protest which might be construed as anti-British and therefore sympathetic to Republicans. Nevertheless, the reforms they seek are generally within, rather than of, the system — they claim true British justice not its replacement. Whether their fight is worthwhile and whether there are superior models to British adversarial justice is the subject of the next chapter.

---

7   See Hogan, G. and Walker, C., *Political Violence and the Law in Ireland* (Manchester University Press, Manchester, 1989), chs. 2, 4.

8   There have been 'issue' campaigns, especially about police behaviour in interrogation centres and 'supergrasses'.

11

The French Pre-trial System

John Bell

Introduction

There will always be a certain spirit of 'the grass is greener on the other side' in any comparative study of criminal procedure. In recent years, we have had the curious spectacle of the French studying the English adversarial system and separation between judiciary and investigation, while the English were contemplating the advantages of the investigating magistrate system.[1] In the end, both systems will probably remain in their traditional moulds, but they may still be able to draw benefits from comparing each other's approach. In this chapter the principal features of the French pre-trial system are considered which both prevent and help generate miscarriages of justice. They are viewed in the light of the reforms contained in a Law of 4 January 1993 which came mainly into force on 1 March 1993.

The common lawyer's interest in France lies principally in two aspects of its criminal justice system. First, professional judges, either as prosecutors (*procureurs*) or as investigating magistrates (*juge d'instructions*), exert external control over police investigations and are themselves responsible for gathering evidence. Secondly, French criminal procedure

---

1 See, *inter alia*, Monahan, J., 'Sanctioning injustice' (1991) 141 NLJ 629. The French review of the pre-trial system spent some considerable time reviewing the English system, among others: see Commission Justice Pénale et Droits de l'Homme, *Rapport sur la mise en état des affaires pénales* (Paris, 1990).

is essentially written, thus enabling the checking and challenging of materials used to establish guilt which are collected in the file (*dossier*) used by pre-trial, trial and appellate judges alike. Indeed, as Anton put it:

> The comparison between the French and Anglo-American trials is misleading for it is only a slight exaggeration to say that, while in England or in the US a *man* is on trial, in France it is a *dossier*.[2]

The existence and use of the file is both a safeguard for the accused and a permanent record of what is said. It will be about the content of this file that most debate turns in the pre-trial stage.

The role of judges in the preliminary phases of the investigation of the offence, and the importance of the file throughout the proceedings give rise to a radical continuity between the various phases of the criminal process. One can identify three main phases: investigation (*enquête*), decision to prosecute and committal (*instruction*), and hearing and judgment. The continuity between phases lies in the fact that the information from each stage forms part of the *dossier* which will form the ultimate basis of the decision.

Miscarriages of justice can arise for a number of different reasons. In the first place, the evidence presented to a court can be defective. A famous recent example in France was that of the 'Irishmen of Vincennes' in 1982, where policemen almost certainly planted weapons on a number of Irishmen, suspected of involvement with the IRA, staying in a hotel in Vincennes, and then charged them with gun-running. The policemen involved were eventually punished themselves by the French courts.[3] A

---

2 Anton, A., 'L'instruction criminelle' (1960) 9 Am Jo Comp Law 441, at p. 456. For an account of the importance of the file in a trial, see Johnson, C., 'Trial by dossier' (1992) 142 NLJ 249 and Sheehan, A., *Criminal Procedure in Scotland and France* (HMSO, Edinburgh, 1975), ch. 5. For instance, in the appeal of the police officers accused in the 'Irishmen of Vincennes' incident (see *infra*, n. 3), witnesses were not heard despite defence protests on the ground that the court of appeal of Paris considered that it was 'neither useful nor necessary' to go beyond the file. Provided that the parties are heard at some stage, it does not matter that they do not submit all their representations at the formal trial: *Delta v France* (1990) Appl. no. 11444/85, Ser. A, No. 191. For an account of the French criminal justice system generally, see Vogler, R., *A Guide to the French Criminal Justice System* (Prisoners Abroad, London, 1989) and Leigh, L. H. and Zedner, L., *A Report on the Administration of Criminal Justice in the Pre-trial Phase in France and Germany* (Royal Commission on Criminal Justice, Research Study No. 1; HMSO, London, 1992).

3 See *Le Monde*, 25 June 1991 and 26 September 1991. The successful charges were reduced to suborning witnesses, in that the police officers were instructed by the defendant superiors to hide the fact that the searches had been conducted in the absence of the accused Irishmen in breach of procedural requirements.

second problem with evidence occurs in respect of expert evidence. The adversarial approach of the English system makes the expert very much a person appointed by the police who is difficult to contradict. As will be seen, the French situation is that the expert is appointed by the court, and is to that extent independent. On the other hand, the French judges do tend to rely on what the expert has found, and there is less of a culture critical to an expert's findings. A third problem lies in the context of interrogation of a suspect before trial, and the confessions which may be made. The French system leaves interrogation predominantly to a judge but, until recent reforms, has left the suspect with limited legal assistance in preparing for interrogations which may be, in practice, almost conclusive of guilt. For although a trial may involve rehearing of evidence (and there is no formal guilty plea), reliance will obviously be placed on what is said to the investigating magistrate. The role of the various judges in the criminal process may also pose problems for an accused, and the French jury are far less independent than the English one. They sit only in the very serious cases (some 2,000 out of over 8 million criminal cases per year) and with three judges. Perverse verdicts are really out of the question. The only perverse decisions will come from judges themselves.[4] Lastly, the conduct of cases by counsel may be less of a problem in France, in that the day in court is far less important than in England. The preparation of the file is a significant part of the process, and will typically resolve many of the problems of criminal cases.

Preliminary points on the French system

Personnel

The significant actors in the French criminal process discussed here are the judicial police, prosecutors, judges, and lawyers. The judicial police are only one of a number of police forces. This category covers a separate criminal investigation force set up on a national level (National Police) or in small towns (Gendarmerie). Officers of this force have the powers relevant to criminal investigations. In addition, there are administrative, traffic, and frontier police forces, while telephone tapping is conducted by a separate police force (*Renseignements Généraux*). The judicial police

---

4   For example, after members of Parliament granted an amnesty to those guilty of electoral funding irregularities, some judges delivered what can only be described as perverse verdicts. For instance, on 26 April 1990, the *tribunal correctionnel* of Vannes appealed to 'a recent development in the notion of public policy' to justify the imposition of a 30F fine on a woman convicted of fiscal fraud of over 700,000F. Other judges followed suit by releasing from detention a number of persons accused of crimes against property (see *Le Monde*, 4 and 8 May 1990).

conduct the investigation of minor offences on their own. In more serious cases, this will be done under the control of the *procureur* or the investigating magistrate. In practice, their control can be more like a formality until the police produce a suspect, with a delegation of authority (*commission rogatoire*) being given by those superiors to the police in many cases. This is especially true of most ordinary criminal offences, in which only the *procureur* will be involved in the pre-trial process. As Leigh and Zedner remark, 'the reality of many of these cases probably differs little from the reality in England and Wales save that the defence may be less favoured'.[5]

The *procureur* is a member of the judiciary who specialises in criminal prosecution. Equivalent to an English Chief Crown Prosecutor, he or she decides to prosecute and conducts the case in court. In the pre-trial process, the *procureur* has powers to direct and supervise police investigations, and to interview witnesses or the accused. But in some cases it will be necessary to call in the investigating magistrate, another member of the judiciary assigned to this post. His or her main functions are in relation to serious offences and include powers to direct and supervise police investigations, but he or she may also issue search and arrest warrants in both serious and non-serious cases. He or she also directs the *procureur* in serious cases about the decision to prosecute. (The final decision remains formally that of the *procureur*.) The investigating magistrate will take charge either immediately or within a short period (at most 21 days) in the investigation of serious offences. The *Chambre d'accusation*, composed of three judges from the regional court of appeal, takes committal decisions in the most serious cases (*crimes*[6]), but also hears challenges to the validity of pre-trial proceedings.

Trial judges will be a single judge in the lowest criminal court (*tribunal de police*), three judges in the normal serious crimes court (*tribunal correctionnel*), and in very serious criminal cases the *cour d'assises* is composed of three judges and nine jurors in a single panel. In terrorist and military cases, the *cour d'assises* is composed of a panel of seven judges.[7]

---

5   *Op. cit.*, p. 14.
6   The penal code distinguishes between three classes of offence. The most serious (such as murder) are *crimes*, tried by the *cour d'assises*. The next most serious are *délits* (such as theft), tried by the *tribunal correctionnel*. The distinction between these two has much in common with the old common-law distinction between felonies and misdemeanours. The third class is that of *contraventions*, which are typically regulatory offences (failure to carry identity documents, failure to observe many traffic regulations, and so on) and are tried by the *tribunal de police*.
7   A typical case for this procedure would be the prosecution of Basque terrorists: see the *Bidart* case, *Le Monde*, 31 May 1991.

Appeals are heard from the *tribunal de police* and the *tribunal correctionnel* by the regional court of appeal. The appeal takes the form of a rehearing based on the file, though witnesses are not normally heard at this stage. In the case of decisions of the *cour d'assises* there is no appeal, except on a point of law to the *Cour de Cassation*, the highest court in France, which also hears appeals on a point of law from the regional courts of appeal.

Among the many legal professions in France, the principal person involved in criminal cases is an *avocat*, who can advise and make representations on behalf his or her client in pre-trial proceedings, as well as at trial or on appeal.

Content of the file

The French criminal file is made up of four elements which show that the courts judge the person, not the action. The first section contains evidence, i.e. records of police investigation, questioning of witnesses and the accused by police, *procureur* and investigating magistrate, expert reports, and so on. The second section contains detention records, showing when the accused was held and for how long, as well as medical reports which may have been made during this period. The third section is more general. It contains any personal and character details, such as criminal record, family and psychological history, including material that would be in social inquiry reports. Such information is used in pre-trial and trial procedures, even when it is not formally adduced as evidence.[8] There is no sense in France that it should be withheld until sentencing. The fourth section contains formal documents, such as copies of warrants.

The inclusion of reports or matters on a file may be challenged, for example on the ground that they have been obtained irregularly. This avoids the need to challenge admissibility at trial. Irregularity during the *instruction* is more likely to be excluded than at an earlier stage.

Pre-trial procedures

The French system grants different powers to the police and judges, depending on the nature of the offence at stake. In the ordinary procedure (*enquête préliminaire*) the police have limited powers. They can neither arrest nor search without instituting a judicial inquiry (*enquête judiciaire*),

---

8   See the exerpts from a trial in Sheehan, *op. cit.*, pp. 211–14.

i.e. involving the investigating magistrate who has wider powers, but the police are then constrained to act 'on his authority. By contrast, in the flagrant procedure (*enquête flagrante*) there are wide police powers in the early days of the inquiry, albeit under the control of the *procureur*, but the investigating magistrate must be brought in to take over the case as soon as feasible. A flagrant offence is defined as either a *crime* or a *délit* which is being or has just been committed;[9] or where a person is found in possession of objects or there is other evidence that he has been involved in such an offence; or where the head of a household requires the police or *procureur* to investigate such an offence.

There are special terrorist and drugs procedures, under which the police have wider powers of search and detention, even where the offence is not flagrant. Under the Law of 3 September 1986, 'terrorism' is defined as individual or collective acts involving certain offences against persons or property, or with arms or explosives, with the object of causing serious public disorder by intimidation or terror.

L'Instruction

> The investigating magistrate is a figure from the Jacobin State because he is close, in reality and in the imagination, to a functionary bearing the authority of the central State, able himself to investigate and to judge as did the criminal lieutenant and the intendant [of the *Ancien Régime*] in the past . . . The ideal of the investigating magistrate is of the man alone, empowered to manage a judicial situation, a search for the truth and a procedure, as a unity. By contrast, the accusatorial procedure emphasises the search by way of a process, the two-sided debate, the equality, at least in theory, of arms between the prosecution and defence.[10]

This description, given by leading criminal judges, brings out the peculiar position of the investigating magistrate within the French system. The precursor of this office was the criminal lieutenant of Francis I in the 16th century whose role was developed by the criminal ordinance of 1670. That ordinance established a 'secret procedure without debate'. As vividly captured in Kafka's *The Trial*, the suspect would be unaware of the progress of the investigation and the accumulation of material on

---

9   The central requirement is that the case is fresh, hence a rape is still flagrant if reported
     28 hours after the event: Cass crim 26 February 1991, *Bartoli*, D. 1991 IR 115.
10 Bellet, P., Calvet, H. and Soulez-Larivière, D., *Libération*, 10 December 1990.

his or her file until the moment for committal. It is this investigatory character which has gradually been judicialised over subsequent centuries, and turns this judge increasingly into the supervisor of the process, rather than the principal investigator.

The role of the investigating magistrate is diminishing in France. In 1960, such a judge dealt with over 20 per cent of criminal cases. In 1990, the investigating magistrate dealt with only 53,652 of the 703,831 prosecutions (excluding traffic and other regulatory offences), a mere 8 per cent. All the same, his or her role remains significant for serious crimes.

The judicialisation of the office started with the Code of Criminal Investigation (*Code d'instruction criminel*) of 1808, which created the investigating magistrate to perform the tasks of the criminal lieutenant and intendant of the *Ancien Régime*. But it took until 1897 for the rights of the accused to be built into the system, permitting the suspect's lawyer to sit in on the hearing by the investigating magistrate. It is thus necessary to consider both the investigatory powers of the investigating magistrate and the protections afforded to the suspect.

Function of the investigating magistrate

The basic aim of the *instruction* process is to decide whether there is a sufficient case to answer to warrant committal of the suspect to the courts for trial. The tasks of the investigating magistrate are specified in Art. 81 of the Code of Criminal Procedure (CPP) of 1959: 'the investigating magistrate undertakes all investigating acts which he judges necessary to the revelation of the truth'. These acts will include gathering evidence, for example by ordering expert tests or reports, such as about ballistics, by reconstruction of the crime, or by directing further police investigation. Warrants may be issued for arrest or for searches, and this may include telephone tapping.[11] They will also involve formal questioning of witnesses, either by taking formal statements from them one by one, or even staging a confrontation of witnesses to elicit truth. Most

---

11 Powers over telephone tapping have been revised in the light of the decisions of the ECHR of 24 April 1990 in *Kruslin* and *Huvig*, France, Appl. nos 11105, 11801/85, Ser. A. No. 176–B, (1990) 12 EHRR 528, 547. Such tapping has been gradually permitted by the judges in the 1980s, provided that it is not conducted by artifice and its results are open to inspection and comment by the suspect and any other party: see, e.g., Cass crim 17 November 1990, D 1990 IR 221, and Cass crim 6 and 26 November 1990, D 1991 IR 11 and 26. The Law of 10 July 1991 provides further safeguards and sets more detailed limits on the exercise of such a power: see Pettiti, L.E., 'Les écoutes téléphoniques et le droit français', AJDA 1992, 35.

importantly, the investigating magistrate will question the suspect. There will be a first hearing (formal) simply to check details, unless urgent questioning is required. No lawyer will be present. At subsequent hearings a lawyer will be present and the purpose is to get to the truth, which may involve challenging the suspect on statements by witnesses. The investigating magistrate then produces a report which sets out his or her own view on what should be done, and instructs the *procureur* about the next steps to be taken in the case.

The investigating magistrate is seised of a case by the requisition from the *procureur*. This defines the ambit of the investigation *in rem*, and the magistrate will need further instructions from the *procureur* to deal with new offences turned up in the course of the investigation. Unlike the English magistrates at committal, the magistrate is not limited *in personam*, as she or he may investigate both persons named in the requisition or others suspected of the offence. A feature common to most civil law systems is the right of the victim of the crime to initiate the criminal process, both to secure a criminal conviction and to obtain civil redress from the criminal court. A requisition to the investigating magistrate may thus come not only from the *procureur* but also from the civil party.

At present the investigating magistrate is a single individual appointed by the president of the *tribunal de grande instance*. In 1985, there were some 550 judges acting as investigating magistrates, constituting about 10 per cent of the private and criminal law judiciary. All the same, when divided over the country, this provides only some 79 investigating magistrates for Paris and 16 for Marseilles, and an average of 100 cases per judge per year.[12] The nominee may be removed on the ground of the good administration of justice where the *procureur* or one of the parties requests, but reasons must be given for such a decision (Art. 84 CPP). The same power also exists in the *Cour de Cassation*. This was used recently in the case of investigations into electoral irregularities by the Socialist party, and it can have the effect of slowing down the administration of justice. The role of the investigating magistrate may be very political in such circumstances. This was notably the case in July 1992, when an investigating magistrate brought charges against the Speaker of the National Assembly with regard to electoral funding irregularities. The criticism against the judge provoked the President of the *Cour de Cassation* into making an unprecedented intervention to deflect criticism

---

12   See Boyer Chammard, G., *Les Magistrats* (Dalloz, Paris, 1985), p. 75; Perrot, R., *Institutions judiciaires*, 3rd edn (Dalloz, Paris, 1989), para. 168.

of the judicial system.[13] Article 20 of the new Law on criminal procedure involves the possibility of nominating one or more investigating magistrates to act alongside the person in charge.

As under the ordinance of 1670, the three principal characteristics of the *instruction* process are that it is written and secret, but it is now subject to an *inter partes* debate. All the statements of the accused or witnesses are recorded in a *procés verbal* and so the file is built up . In this way, every act of procedure is open to inspection. At any stage the parties, through their lawyers, are permitted to submit written observations which are then put on file (Art. 199, para. 2, CPP). The secrecy of the proceedings is an obligation essentially on the magistrate and the *procureur*. They are not allowed to reveal details of the investigation to third parties. Although conceived as a safeguard of public order, it obviously also serves the function of privacy. In practice, however, the suspect and his lawyer frequently make statements to the press about their version of events. As long as they do not reveal information gleaned from the file, they will not be in breach of the duty of secrecy. (It should be noted that pre-trial publicity which adversely affects the presumption of an accused's innocence is now regulated by Title V of the Law of 4 January 1993. This enables the investigating magistrate to cause a correction to be published in a newspaper or broadcast in which the adverse publicity appeared.) In the section on the accused's rights (below) we will deal with the issue of how far the procedure is open to debate. The additional feature that strikes the English lawyer is the relative informality of the procedure. Questioning takes place in the magistrate's chambers and follows no set form. There are no time limits and the process can take as long as is considered necessary. It is for the magistrate to be satisfied that everything has been covered for a decision on prosecution to be taken.

The most disturbing feature of the French procedure is the use made of the *commission rogatoire*. Under the current Art. 81, para. 3, 'if the investigating magistrate is unable to carry out all the investigatory measures, he may give a *commission rogatoire* to officers of the judicial police so that they may carry out such investigatory acts as are necessary in the circumstances subject to the rules laid down for them'. Certain measures cannot be delegated in this way to the police but only to another judge, especially the issuing of an arrest warrant or questioning the accused (Art. 152, para. 2, CPP). Such powers have been upheld by the *Conseil constitutionnel* in relation to telephone tapping, even where the persons in question were telecommunications officials with the same

---

13   See *Le Monde*, 11 July 1992; *Le Figaro*, 12 August 1992.

status as officers of the judicial police.[14] Since there are so few investigating magistrates in France, it is impossible that they alone could cope even with the small proportion of cases which fall to them. It is necessary in most cases for the work to be undertaken by the police. In that searches, formal questioning of witnesses, requesting expert reports and so on may well be done by police officers, and yet will appear on the file which forms the basis for a judicial decision, a basic weakness in the control exercised by the investigating magistrate emerges, and this was noted by the Delmas-Marty report in 1990.[15] In reality, the police have more power than in England, for they are exercising the powers of a judge, but are subject to less control in that they do not require prior authorisation for searches. It is in this area that the conflict is most apparent between the theory of the system as one directed by the judge and the reality of personnel and resources.

Rights of the accused

The rights of the accused are really the product of the last hundred years. The *loi Constans* of 8 December 1897 gave the suspect's lawyer access to the investigating magistrate's chambers and to the file. In addition, the civil party was given such rights in 1921. As a result, all parties are more or less in an equal formal position, and remaining inequalities will be removed by the Law of 4 January 1993.

The principal safeguard of the suspect is the presence of a lawyer. The function of the first formal interview with the suspect is for the investigating magistrate to ensure that he or she has a lawyer or to provide one.

(a) L'inculpation. *L'inculpation* is a crucial stage in the pre-trial process. From that moment, a person becomes a suspect in the eyes of the law and not merely in the eyes of the police or the civil party. The person is formally under investigation with a view to prosecution, and the investigating magistrate prepares the case for a committal. To be made a suspect, there must be 'serious and concordant indications' of a person's criminal liability. At that stage, the rights of the accused become stronger, notably the right to silence and the right to a lawyer. *Inculpation* does

---

14 See CC decision no. 90–281 DC of 27 December 1990, *Telecommunications Law*, RFDC 1991, 118; Bell, J., *French Constitutional Law* (Oxford University Press, Oxford, 1992), p. 148.
15 Commission Justice Pénale et Droits de l'Homme, *op. cit.*

not automatically lead to prosecution. In 1990, there were 73,649 *inculpations*, of which 11.12 per cent did not give rise to a prosecution.[16]

The normal view is that a person becomes an *inculpé* as a result of the formal first appearance before the investigating magistrate, in which the magistrate sets out the suspicion and informs him or her of the rights to silence and to a lawyer. There is some case-law which suggests that the status is acquired earlier, when the serious and concordant indications are established, but this is treated as too strict.[17]

This formal interview may not be the first time the person has been questioned by the investigating magistrate. Well-established case-law requires that the magistrate should not inculpate a person 'until he has clarified whether the person did take part in the incriminating act in circumstances such as to give rise to his criminal liability'.[18] Nowadays the requisition presented by either the *procureur* or the civil party to the investigating magistrate may well name a suspect directly or indirectly. This is not necessarily sufficient to justify the inculpation of the person named. It may well be necessary for the investigating magistrate to check whether the allegations are substantiated. This will be the case particularly when the requisition is filed by the civil party. But to protect a potential suspect, the Law of 4 January 1993 creates the category of persons 'placed under investigation' (*mises en examen*) applicable to those inculpated and those specifically named in a requisition. Both sets of persons have rights to silence, to a lawyer and to access to the case file before questioning.[19]

In order to avoid the device of interviewing a person as a witness rather than questioning him as a suspect, with the formal constraints which that entails, Arts. 86 and 104 CPP provide that neither the investigating magistrate nor a policeman acting under a *commission rogatoire* may hear as a witness a person who has been 'placed under investigation'. The sanction is not an automatic nullity of the questioning record, but a failure to afford such protection would amount to a breach of a substantial formality affecting the rights of the suspect and would almost always lead to such a nullity under Art. 172 CPP. The failure to warn a person named by the civil party of his right to be treated as a 'person placed under

---

16 *Le Monde*, 27 February 1992.
17 See Pradel, J., *Droit pénal, tome II: Procédure pénal*, 5th edn (Dalloz, Paris, 1990) (hereafter 'Pradel'), para. 429.
18 Cass crim 8 December 1899, D 1903.1.457, note Le Pottevin.
19 An intermediate category of 'assisted witness' was introduced by the Law of 30 December 1987, but was not seen as conferring many advantages on the potential suspect: Pradel, J., 'De la réforme de l'instruction préparatoire', D 1989 Chr. 1.

investigation' does lead to automatic nullity of the proceedings. Such a protection does not apply to police questioning before a person has been referred to the investigating magistrate or *procureur*. Here it is permitted for the police to continue questioning, even after the person has made a confession.[20]

(b)   Rights of the suspect in detention. A suspect may be in pre-trial custody in two ways. First, during the preliminary investigation, he or she may be in police custody *(garde à vue)*. Secondly, after *inculpation*, the suspect may be remanded in custody *(détention provisoire)*, usually in prison. The rights of the suspect are significantly different at these two stages, and it would be fair to say that, until *inculpation*, the suspect lacks many of the rights which would be expected in the common-law world.

(i)   Garde à vue — In 1990, some 347,107 persons were held in police custody, a figure which represents a 26 per cent increase on 1981. There is no power of arrest in the ordinary procedure *(enquête préliminaire)*, but, under Art. 78–2 CPP (imported by the Laws of 10 June 1983 and 3 September 1986), the police may detain a person if it is necessary to verify his or her identity, where he or she was about to commit a crime, or where there is a threat to the safety of persons or property or to public order. In flagrant offences, in addition to a power of arrest, there is a power under Arts. 62 and 63 CPP for the police to detain anyone whom they consider able to provide information, or against whom there are serious signs of guilt.

Such detention in custody may continue for up to 24 hours, though it may be extended for a further 24 hours by the *procureur*. The police must keep a record under Art. 64 CPP of the reasons for the detention, when it began and ended, duration of questioning and rest periods between questioning. Such records then go into the file used by the investigating and trial judges. But it is clear that there is no prohibition on the police questioning a suspect, unless he or she objects. A persistent criticism by the French legal profession and academics is the absence of any right of the person detained to a lawyer, but the 1993 legislative reforms attempted to exclude this,[21] but Arts. 63–4 CPP allows the detainee to

---

20   See Pradel, para. 433, and Cass crim 17 July 1964, JCP 1965 II 14038, note PC. On the exclusion of evidence and the abuse of police powers, see Pakter, W., 'Exclusionary rules in France, Germany, and Italy' (1985) 9 *Hastings International and Comparative Law Review* 1, at pp. 8–14, 28.

21   *Le Monde*, 27 February 1992, notes that the exclusion from the original proposals for reform was the result of a judgment of the Prime Minister as a result of conflict between the Ministry of Justice (favouring access) and the Ministry of the Interior (which was against it); see generally, Pradel, para. 312.

request to see a lawyer and to communicate with him or her. There is a right to request a medical examination after 24 hours.

Put by way of understatement in the explanatory memorandum introducing the 1993 Law, the Ministry of Justice has stated that 'as far as the person kept in custody is concerned, his rights are very rudimentary. Furthermore, the role of the *procureur* in the control over custody is not asserted with adequate force'. Leigh and Zedner note that 'while nothing in French law requires the over-use of detention, a tendency to do so seem deeply ingrained in the legal culture and doubtless derives from a desire not to release a suspect until the truth has been ascertained'.[22] The Law first of all limits the wide power of the police to detain people in the ordinary procedure of police investigation. Until 1 March 1993, the police had a power under Art. 77, para. 1, CPP to detain 'any person' where necessary for the investigation of an offence. Article 77 is now limited to authorising detention of persons against whom there are indications that he has committed or attempted to commit an offence. Only in flagrant offences may any person be detained where it is necessary for the investigation. A new right is given to notify a member of the family that the person is detained by the police, and the right to request a medical examination is immediate on detention. Furthermore, the person detained must be informed of these rights immediately on detention.

Article 1 of the bill emphasises the role of the *procureur* in supervising the whole process of detention, including where it takes place. Despite these reforms, the basic power of the police to question suspects in custody without a lawyer remains a serious threat to their rights of defence. The *procureur* will normally interview a person before making a requisition to the investigating magistrate. This interview is without a lawyer. The *Conseil constitutionnel* upheld this in its *Security and Liberty* decision of 1981 on the ground that, since the *procureur* was a member of the judiciary, this provided adequate safeguards for the suspect.[23]

(ii) *Détention provisoire* — The 1808 Code of Criminal Investigation had a presumption in favour of the detention of a suspect during the inquiries of the investigating magistrate. In its current form (since the Law of 9 July 1984), Art. 137 CPP provides that 'the accused shall remain free unless, for reasons of the necessities of the investigation or as a security measure, he is submitted to *contrôle judiciaire* or, exceptionally, he is remanded in provisional custody.' *Contrôle judiciaire* imposes

---

22   *Op. cit.* n. 2, p. 53.
23   Para. 30 of CC decision no. 80–127 DC of 19 and 20 January 1981, in Bell, J., *op. cit.*, p. 312.

conditions on freedom, such as might be imposed as bail conditions in this country. Provisional custody is very significant in France. On 1 January 1970, there were 10,840 such remand prisoners (as we would call them) in French jails (37.5 per cent of the prison population). On 1 November 1984, this had risen to 21,735 (51.5 per cent). By 1 January 1992, the number had fallen to 19,578 (40.7 per cent). This still left France (after Spain) with the highest remand prisoner population in western Europe (33.4 per 100,000 inhabitants, compared with 20 per 100,000 in England and Wales). The average period of detention also rose from 2.3 months in 1969 to 3.8 months in 1990.[24] In part, the numbers of remand prisoners and the period of their detention is accounted for by appeals and procedural delays outside the control of the investigating magistrate. Nevertheless, delay is also caused by the slowness of the investigatory procedure. It is thus crucial to examine the safeguards for the rights of the prisoner.

Since 1984, the decision to remand a person into provisional custody cannot be taken without hearing both sides (Art. 145 CPP).[25] The decision can only be justified by the need to preserve evidence, to protect public order or the accused or witnesses; reasons must be given. In 1985 and under the Law of 30 December 1987, attempts were made to give the remand decision to a collegial court other than the investigating magistrate, but these never came into operation. All the same, Title VI of the 1993 Law does confer such decisions on a collegial court including the investigating magistrate in charge of the case. Furthermore, there are time limits on the use of custody. In the case of *crimes* the period is a year, though this can be renewed. In the case of *délits* the period is four months. Laws of 16 July 1987 and 6 July 1989 have set a maximum length for custody in the case of first-time offenders accused of *délits* at six months in total, and for other offenders not liable to more than five years' imprisonment at two years. These periods are still long, and France has been found in breach of Art. 5 of the European Convention on Human Rights in a number of recent cases for excessive periods of detention. As the European Court of Human Rights pointed out in *Tomasi v France*, the existence of reasonable supicion that a person has committed an offence is a necessary condition to justify his or her detention, but after a

---

24 Figures drawn from Pradel, pp. 141–2; Ortolland, A., *La Justice: ses moyens financières, ses actions* (La Documentation française, Paris, 1985); *Le Monde*, 27 February 1992, p. 12.

25 Indeed, the presence of the *procureur* with the investigating magistrate after the suspect has gone out may be treated as vitiating the decision to remand the suspect in custody: Cass crim 19 September 1990, D 1991, 91, note Mayer.

period of time it cannot be a sufficient justification without other reasons in support.[26]

(c) *Questioning*. The lawyers of the parties (prosecution, defence and civil party) have the right to attend, or at least to see the results of, any questioning. They are entitled to be present for the questioning of the suspect and the civil party, and may even suggest questions to be asked. Under Art. 102 CPP, witnesses are heard by the investigating magistrate in the absence of the accused or his or her lawyer.[27] The material produced from each question session before the investigating magistrate is reduced to writing and is signed by the person(s) questioned. Comments may then be submitted by any party on what has been said or on questions which have not been asked. These formal records and comments are kept on file and will be used at committal and trial. The defence may also ask for further expert reports to be made (Art. 156, para. 1 CPP).

From the first interview, the suspect has a right to a lawyer. The lawyer has to be informed at least four days before any proposed interview of the suspect by the investigating magistrate, and has a right to see all the file at least two days before each hearing. Thus, there are no surprises, and the lawyer can prepare the case with the accused.

Nullity of L'Instruction

The French law on the consequences of illegalities in the pre-trial process is complex and difficult to operate. In part this is due to the substantive rules which apply, but it is also due to the intricate procedure by which illegalities are challenged. The normal process involves an application to strike out offending items in the file, and this will take place before trial. Until the Law of 4 January 1993, only the *procureur* and the investigating magistrate could apply to the *chambre d'accusation* to strike out such items from the file during the course of investigations. The suspect and the civil

---

26 *Tomasi* v *France*, Appl. no. 12850/87, Ser. A No. 241–1A, (1993) 15 EHRR 1: here a detention of nearly five years and seven months before acquittal was held to be unjustified. For further examples of findings of excessive detention see, for example, *Letellier* v *France*, Appl no. 12369/86, Ser. A, No. 207, (1992) 14 EHRR 83 (2 years and 10 months; *Birou* v *France*, Appl no. 13319/87, Ser. A, No. 232–B, (1992) 14 EHRR 738 (5 years and 3 months); *Kemmache* v *France*, Appl no. 14992/85, Ser. A, No. 218, (1992) 14 EHRR 520 (8 years and 6 months).

27 The presence of the *procureur* does not invalidate such proceedings, provided that he does not intervene in the question and there is no prejudice to the rights of the accused or the civil party: Cass crim 19 June 1990, D 1991, 15, note Coste.

party could make a challenge only after the investigatory process is over. Challenges might also be made at trial to the inclusion of material on file. But the trial court could not raise a procedural irregularity of its own motion unless the ground is one of lack of jurisdiction.[28] This might arise where an investigating magistrate was not territorially competent to authorise a search. Under Title VII of the 1992 bill, all parties will be able to challenge the inclusion of material on the file during the course of the investigation by the investigating magistrate. But after the investigation procedure is closed, all procedural irregularities will be purged and will be unchallengeable. Unless a suspect is competently advised by a lawyer, both the present and future positions could result in a procedural irregularity in the pre-trial period going unchallenged.

When dealing with illegally obtained evidence it is important to identify the way in which it was illegally obtained. Where an irregularity occurs in the preliminary police investigation, this cannot be annulled since it has no formal status.[29] In general, only those acts which are undertaken after the *instruction* has commenced are liable to be annulled. (Though, of course, there are some matters for which the law does prescribe nullity, such as the unlawful detention of a person during the investigation for a flagrant offence.) Evidence gathered as a result of illegal searches, as well as any consequent confessions, may well be annulled.[30] In principle, the evidence gathered at the investigation stage has no binding probative force. The trial judge(s) (and jury) can make of it what they like. An attempt to nullify evidence arising from irregular detention was introduced into the Code of Criminal Procedure in 1981 but removed in 1983. Thus, in the ordinary procedure, the irregularity of acts of investigation arising from abuse of *garde à vue* or illegal searches does not lead to their nullity and to the exclusion of evidence 'unless it is shown that the inquiry into and the determination of the truth have thereby been fundamentally compromised'.[31]

During the *instruction* by the investigating magistrate, irregular decisions may be taken, and the resulting evidence may be included on file. Some specific legal provisions (especially Art. 171 CPP) do prescribe nullity as a sanction for breach, such as those dealing with searches and

---

28   Cass crim 25 February 1991, *Dometz*, D. 1991 IR 158.
29   Cass crim 12 March 1898, D. 1898.1.208.
30   Pakter, *op. cit.*, pp. 34–7, e.g., Cass crim 21 July 1982, JCP 1982 IV 346. A much criticised example is the decision of the *Cour de Cassation* to quash an alcohol test conducted by the police when they were 'invited' to enter a man's house after the legal hour for searches (i.e. after 9 p.m.): *Le Monde*, 21–22 July 1991.
31   Cass crim 17 March 1960, *Kissari*, JCP 1960 II 11641; Pakter, *op. cit.*, p. 13; Pradel, para. 317.

seizures, as well as bodily searches and unlawful detention (Arts 56, 56–1, 57, 59, 63, 63–1, 76 and 77 CPP). But there is also Art. 172 CPP which provides that there shall also be nullity in the case of substantial breaches of other provisions concerning the *instruction*, especially where there are breaches of the rights of the defence. This creates the potential for a wide category of nullities, which has been restricted by the Law of 6 August 1975. By virtue of the Law of 4 January 1993 Art. 802 CPP now provides:

> Except for the situations provided for in Art. 171, a nullity may only be ordered where the breach of the procedures prescribed by law or the failure to observe substantial formalities has the effect of infringing the interests of the party in question.

As Pradel points out, this significantly reduces the scope of nullity.[32] Only where there is a public interest (for example in judges keeping within their own jurisdictional area) or a private interest (such as prejudice to the accused) will a nullity be ordered.

The overall position is, thus, that illegally obtained evidence may well not be excluded from the file, and the real sanctions, if they operate, are frequently only disciplinary.

Appeals

The pre-trial procedure is of the greatest sophistication in serious offences (*crimes*) because they are tried by the *cour d'assises* from which there is no appeal, unlike in other criminal cases. Only the civil party may contest an acquittal by the *cour d'assises*, and this is because of the consequences for the person's civil action for damages. In the case of other courts, there is a right of appeal given to all parties (Art. 497 CPP). The hearing is based on the file and is, in principle, a rehearing. If the court finds a defect, it can not only quash the decision, but also decide itself on the merits by *évocation* of the case to itself (Art. 520 CPP). In all cases a decision may be sent to the *Cour de Cassation* for a point of law.

Since 1808, *révision* of a decision may be invoked in relation to *crimes* or *délits* for the rare cases where, for instance, the victim of a murder is found alive, there has been perjury of witnesses, or a subsequent trial produces a contradictory finding (Art. 622 CPP).

This scope for appeal is very limited, and so a Law of 8 June 1895 (amended in 1989) provides that where after conviction, 'a fact occurs or

---

32 *Op. cit.*, para. 467.

a new fact is discovered or a new element unknown to the court at the date of trial arises such as to give rise to a doubt on the guilt of the accused' (Art. 622 CPP), then the case can be submitted to the *Cour de Cassation*. Until 1989, it was necessary to show that this new feature was such as to show that the innocence of the convicted person was probable. Again, until 1989, the case could be submitted only by the Minister of Justice (*Garde des sceaux*), but now it may be submitted also by the convicted person, or his family or heirs (Art. 623 CPP). A number of famous cases, such as *Dreyfus* and *Danval*, have ended in acquittals under this provision.[33] In the latter case, a person was convicted of arsenical poisoning, only for it later to be discovered that a peculiar kidney complaint had caused the death. The availability of the criminal file makes it all the easier to reopen a case.

On such a reference, the *Cour de Cassation* sits as a court of five judges who will investigate the case. This *instruction* process allows the court to give a *commission rogatoire* to the police to conduct investigations, much as in the procedure under the control of the investigating magistrate. As in that process, the convicted person is able to make representations, and the *ministère public* at the *Cour de Cassation* gives his observations. The usual outcome of a successful investigation is that the decision of the trial court is quashed and a retrial ordered by a court of coordinate jurisdiction. If this is no longer possible or useful, e.g. if the innocence of the convicted person is now certain, then the conviction is simply quashed (Art. 625, para. 5, CPP).

Conclusion

> The best in the inquisitorial system is the recognition of the importance of the phase preparatory to trial and the affirmation of strict rules governing the search for and preservation of evidence during this period . . . The best in the accusatorial system is to promote the judges as a genuinely neutral umpire by separating the judicial and investigative functions, which permits a new balance of power between the prosecution and defence . . ..[34]

The benefits of the inquisitorial system have to be viewed in the context in which it operates. The most important feature is the checkability of the

---

33 Cass ch. réun. 12 July 1906, *Dreyfus*, D. 1908.1.553; Cass crim 28 Dec. 1923, *Danval*, D.P. 1924.1.66. See generally, Pradel, paras 643–52.
34 Mme M. Delmas-Marty, *Le Monde*, 21 November 1991.

written file and the access which the suspect's lawyers have to it. There is a way of ensuring that no improperly obtained evidence is on file before the case comes to trial, and this streamlines the system significantly. The open access to the file also minimises the dangers of non-disclosure of exculpatory evidence such as occurred in the Judith Ward case.[35] The file also makes an appeal easier, and the willingness of the French to allow appeals on new evidence is one of the good features of their system. The other important feature is the limit imposed on the powers of the police to act on their own initiative. But it is here that the problems arise.

The 1993 reforms are expected to require another 65 investigating magistrates, more than a 10 per cent increase in personnel. Even then, little will be done to reduce the effective power of the police granted through the procedure of the *commission rogatoire*. It was intended essentially for the delegation of specific tasks, but has become a significant departure from judicial control over the pre-trial process. Furthermore, the inquisitorial system works to the benefit of the accused only if adequate rights are given to the defence during the pre-trial process and to challenge any illegalities which may occur. At present, this is far from the case in France. The other disadvantage is delay. Remand in custody is a serious problem and will not be eased by the 1993 reforms, since there is every chance that interlocutory applications by the civil party or the suspect will slow down the conduct of the *instruction* by the investigating magistrate. Thus, while there may be advantages in theory of an inquisitorial system, it needs to be well structured and resourced, problems which have already led the Italians to move towards a more adversarial system,[36] and which strongly tempted the French.

Leigh and Zedner conclude their recent study into inquisitorial systems on behalf of the Runciman Commission with the following remark:

We do not believe that the examining magistrate is a real protection against overbearing police practices save in rare cases where physical brutality is involved. Furthermore, despite the fact that only 10 per cent of cases go before the *juge d'instruction*, the system is overburdened and works slowly.'[37]

---

35   (1992) 96 Cr App R 1.
36   See M. Zander, 'From inquisitorial to adversarial — the Italian experiment' (1991) 141 NLJ 678.
37   *Op. cit.*, p. 68. A good example of police brutality being detected is the *Tomasi* case, n. 26. But in this case, the police brutality was not prevented by the later supervisory control of the investigating magistrate.

There is much truth in this comment. Even if it were working better, the investigating magistrate system forms only one part of a complex structure which is not directly comparable with anything which exists in England and Wales. What we can learn is that supervision over the police by independent persons and the continuity and availability of evidence in a file can be safeguards against miscarriages of justice. But we have to examine how well these would fit into our existing structures and how easily they could be adapted to the English system. This author's own view would be that the system of the single pre-trial case-file, cumbersome thought this can be, has merits which are worth exploring more than the system of the investigating magistrate.

EDITORS' COMMENTS

In the light of the successive scandals arising out of miscarriages of justice in recent years, some maintain that the English system of criminal justice has totally failed and can be salvaged only by fundamental change rather than revision.[1] Amongst the faults inevitably associated with adversarial systems[2] are slanted and self-serving investigative processes, unequal resources as between prosecution and defence, and a commitment to oral evidence which generates strict and apparently artificial rules as to relevance as well as a limited use of experts.[3] The Philips Commission endorsed without argument the view that an adversarial form of justice should be maintained.[4] However, curiosity in inquisitorial systems has again been revived at the invitation of the present Runciman Commission.[5]

---

1   For example Mansfield, M., 'Presumed innocent', *Inside Story* (BBC TV) 9 October 1991; Lawton, Sir F., 'What follows the Judith Ward case?' (1992) 136 Sol Jo 616.

2   It follows that the problems are not unique to England. Infamous miscarriages elsewhere include the cases of Sacco and Vanzetti in the USA (see Ehrmann, H.B., *The Case That Will Not Die* (W. H. Allen, London, 1970)) and Lindy Chamberlain in Australia (see Royal Commission into the Chamberlain conviction, 1987). Several other Australian cases are covered in Carrington, K., et al., *Travesty!* (Pluto Press, NSW, 1991).

3   See Frankel, M. E., 'The search for the truth' (1975) 123 U Pa L Rev 1031; Golding, M.P., 'On the adversary system and justice' in Bronaugh, R., (ed.), *Philosophical Law* (Greenwood, Westport, 1978); Sargant, T. and Hill, P., *Criminal Trials* (Fabian Society, London, 1986), ch. 4; McEwan, J., *Evidence and the Adversarial Process* (Basil Blackwell, Oxford, 1992).

4   Cmnd 8091, 1981, paras 1.6–1.8.

5   Indeed, research has been expressly commissioned on the subject: Leigh, L. H. and Zedner, L., *A Report on the Administration of Criminal Justice in the Pre-trial Phase in France and Germany* (HMSO, London, 1992).

The resultant submissions to the Commission suggest that any initial enthusiasm for such a fundamental reform has in fact waned in the light of further reflection upon shortcomings in the Continental alternatives.[6] Thus, the Bar Council, CPS, Law Society and Liberty, for example, all accept that an adversarial system is at least as likely as the alternative to avoid confusion and injustice.[7] It is also claimed that the adversarial system is fairer; the police would be just as coercive under an inquisitorial system, and it is more likely that an independent solicitor will serve the accused's interests.[8] Though there is little enthusiasm for any agency to take over, direct or supervise police investigations,[9] it could be argued consistently with an adversarial system and the principle of an independent prosecution agency,[10] that the CPS should be empowered to clear up inconsistencies in the papers forwarded to them by asking the police for further investigations to be carried out.[11] Advantages might include the closer examination of contested evidence and of the fullness of disclosure of evidence by the police to the CPS. A power of this kind is already granted to the Scottish procurator fiscals under s. 17 of the Police (Scotland) Act 1967.

The prime champion of inquisitorial features is the Police Service, which calls for elements of an inquisitorial pre-trial system, with a 'formal interview' similar to a Scottish judicial examination, except that it would be held for every suspect to be prosecuted rather than intermittently as in Scotland.[12] A variant of this concept also appeals to the CPS.[13] However, experience of judicial examinations in Scotland suggests that such an injection of inquisitorial hearings into a fundamentally adversarial system does not work well. The main problems in Scotland have been the patchy invocation of the procedure[14] and the

---

6   Academic support has likewise become muted. See Zander, M., 'From inquisitorial to adversarial — the Italian system' (1991) 141 NLJ 678; Monahan, J., 'Sanctioning injustice' (1991) 141 NLJ 678; Gow, N., 'The revival of examinations' (1991) 141 NLJ 680; Zuckerman, A. S., 'Miscarriages of justice' [1992] Crim LR 323; McEwan, J., *op. cit.*

7   CPS, *Submission* (1991), para. 7.2.11; General Council of the Bar, *Submission* (1992), para. 33; Liberty, *Submission* (1991), p. 4.

8   Law Society, *Submission* (1991), para. 2.4.

9   But see General Council of the Bar, *Submission* (1992), para. 124.

10 Some entertain doubts on these grounds. See Police Service, *Submission* (1991), p. 51; Home Office, *Memoranda* (1991), paras 2.21, 2.70.

11 JUSTICE, *Submission* (1991), para. 11; CPS, *Submission* (1991), para. 5.5.5.

12 *Op. cit.* para. 2.2.1. The *Submission* also recommends that trial judges should be able to call witnesses (p. 181).

13 *Op. cit.* pp. 6, 7.

14 See Gow, N., *op. cit.*; Grosskurth, A., 'Scotland's pitfalls' October 1991 *LAG Bulletin* 7; Macphail, I. D., 'Safeguards in the Scottish criminal justice system' [1992] Crim LR 144.

reasonableness or otherwise of the exercise of silence, especially if advised by a solicitor.[15]

If an inquisitorial system is not acceptable, would it be possible to cross-check in other ways that the conclusions reached by the police pursuant to their investigations are correct? A power for prosecutors to demand further inquiries might be of modest assistance, though the invocation of the powers would be limited by the background and experience of prosecutors and by whether over-enthusiatic or dishonest police officers remember to cover their tracks with appropriate papers. A more far-reaching suggestion has been made that cases based on evidence which inherently gives rise to doubts, such as confessions or identification, should be reinvestigated by another detective from the same force.[16] On reflection, this is not an attractive idea. Aside from fears about police solidarity and the closing of ranks, it is difficult to see how these cases could be 'reinvestigated' by police techniques. Is it intended to hold the suspect for questioning all over again, and will not the prior identification or testimony taint any later confirmation by a witness? The reconstruction of the facts without evaluative overlays is a valuable technique of verification. However, such reconstruction should be left to those who are completely independent of the police. The defence would seem fitting candidates for this task, and, rather than spend money on police white-wash, it would be better to give more legal aid so that the defence could carry out wider interviews and testing than possible at present. Similar considerations cast doubt on the efficacy of imposing a statutory duty on the police to investigate in an impartial manner,[17] though perhaps it could be concretised by a detailed code of practice backed by documentation of the kind recommended by the Working Group on Pre-trial Issues.[18]

---

15 See *Gilmour* v *HM Advocate* 1982 SCCR 590; *Alexander* v *HM Advocate* 1990 SCCR 590; *McEwan* v *HM Advocate* 1990 SCCR 401; *McGhee* v *HM Advocate* (1991) *The Scotsman* 11 May. The editors thank Chris O'Gorman, Wolverhapton University, for these Scottish sources.
16 *Ibid.*
17 See 'Note: towards a constitutional right to an adequate police investigation' (1978) 53 NYUL Rev 835.
18 Report of the Working Party on Pre-trial Issues (Home Office, 1991).

General Bibliography

(Note that references to individual cases or specific issues are not reproduced here but may be found in the notes to the relevant chapter.)

Books

Brandon, R. and Davies, C., *Wrongful Imprisonment: Mistaken Convictions and their Consequences* (Allen, London, 1973)

Carrington, K., et al., *Travesty!* (Pluto Press, NSW, 1991)

Du Cann, C., *Miscarriages of Justice* (Muller, London, 1960)

Hill, P. and Young, M., *Rough Justice* (BBC, London, 1983), *More Rough Justice* (Penguin, London, 1986)

JUSTICE, *Home Office Review of Criminal Convictions* (London, 1968), *Miscarriages of Justice* (London, 1989)

Lewis, D. and Hughman, P., *Just How Just?* (Secker & Warburg, London, 1975)

Sargant, T. and Hill, P., *Criminal Trials* (Fabian Research Series No. 348, London, 1986)

Woffinden, B., *Miscarriages of Justice*, 2nd ed. (Avon, 1989)

UK Official Reports (HMSO, London)

Home Affairs Committee, *Miscarriages of Justice* (1981-82 HC 421) and Government Reply (Cmnd 8856, 1982)

Home Office Working Group, *The Right to Silence* (1989)

May, Sir John, *Interim Report on the Maguire Case* (1989-90 HC 556), *Second Report on the Maguire Case* (1992-93 HC 296)

Report of the Departmental Committee on evidence of identification in criminal cases (1975-76 HC 338) (Lord Devlin)

Report of the Inter-departmental Committee on the Court of Criminal Appeal (Cmnd 2755, 1965) (Lord Donovon)

Royal Commission on Criminal Procedure (Cmnd 8092, 1981) (Sir C. Philips)

Standing Advisory Commission on Human Rights in Northern Ireland, *17th Report for 1991–92* (1992–93 HC 54)

Submissions to the Runciman Committee

(There are, of course, many other submissions not listed below. We have included only the more wide-ranging reports from groups or organisations.)

Amnesty International, *Submission* (1991)

Attorney-General, *Evidence* (1991)

Commission for Racial Equality, *Evidence* (1991)

Committee on the Administration of Justice, *Submission* (1991)

Criminal Bar Association, *Submission* (1991)

Crown Prosecution Service, *Submission* (1991)

General Council of the Bar, *Response* (1992)

Home Office, *Memoranda* (1991)

JUSTICE, *Evidence* (1991)

Law Society, *Evidence* (1991)

Legal Action Group, *Submission* (1991)

Liberty, *Let Justice be Done* (1991)

NACRO, *Submission* (1991)

Police Service, *Evidence* (1991, not including a separate confidential paper)

Index